Off and Running

ASPEN COURSEBOOK SERIES

Off and Running

A Practical Guide to Legal Research, Analysis, and Writing

Angela C. Arey

Legal Writing Professor

University of Maine School of Law

Nancy A. Wanderer

Legal Writing Professor

Director, Legal Research and Writing Program

University of Maine School of Law

Wolters Kluwer

Law & Business

Wolters Kluwer Law & Business serves customers worldwide with CCH, Aspen Publishers, and Kluwer Law International products. (www.wolterskluwerlb.com)

To contact Customer Service, e-mail customer.service@wolterskluwer.com, call 1-800-234-1660, fax 1-800-901-9075, or mail correspondence to:

Wolters Kluwer Law & Business
Attn: Order Department
PO Box 990
Frederick, MD 21705

Printed in the United States of America.

1 2 3 4 5 6 7 8 9 0

ISBN 978-1-4548-3615-5

Arey, Angela Crossman, author.
    Off and running / Angela C. Arey, Legal Writing Professor, University of Maine School of Law; Nancy A. Wanderer, Legal Writing Professor, Director, Legal Research and Writing Program, University of Maine School of Law.
        pages cm. — (Aspen coursebook series)
    Includes bibliographical references and index.
    ISBN 978-1-4548-3615-5 (alk. paper)
    1. Legal composition. 2. Legal research—United States. I. Wanderer, Nancy A., author. II. Title.
KF250.A74 2014
808.06′634—dc23
                                                                            2014003047

Certified Chain of Custody
Product Line Contains At Least
20% Certified Forest Content
www.sfiprogram.org
SFI-00756

About Wolters Kluwer Law & Business

Wolters Kluwer Law & Business is a leading global provider of intelligent information and digital solutions for legal and business professionals in key specialty areas, and respected educational resources for professors and law students. Wolters Kluwer Law & Business connects legal and business professionals as well as those in the education market with timely, specialized authoritative content and information-enabled solutions to support success through productivity, accuracy and mobility.

Serving customers worldwide, Wolters Kluwer Law & Business products include those under the Aspen Publishers, CCH, Kluwer Law International, Loislaw, ftwilliam.com and MediRegs family of products.

CCH products have been a trusted resource since 1913, and are highly regarded resources for legal, securities, antitrust and trade regulation, government contracting, banking, pension, payroll, employment and labor, and healthcare reimbursement and compliance professionals.

Aspen Publishers products provide essential information to attorneys, business professionals and law students. Written by preeminent authorities, the product line offers analytical and practical information in a range of specialty practice areas from securities law and intellectual property to mergers and acquisitions and pension/benefits. Aspen's trusted legal education resources provide professors and students with high-quality, up-to-date and effective resources for successful instruction and study in all areas of the law.

Kluwer Law International products provide the global business community with reliable international legal information in English. Legal practitioners, corporate counsel and business executives around the world rely on Kluwer Law journals, looseleafs, books, and electronic products for comprehensive information in many areas of international legal practice.

Loislaw is a comprehensive online legal research product providing legal content to law firm practitioners of various specializations. Loislaw provides attorneys with the ability to quickly and efficiently find the necessary legal information they need, when and where they need it, by facilitating access to primary law as well as state-specific law, records, forms and treatises.

ftwilliam.com offers employee benefits professionals the highest quality plan documents (retirement, welfare and non-qualified) and government forms (5500/PBGC, 1099 and IRS) software at highly competitive prices.

MediRegs products provide integrated health care compliance content and software solutions for professionals in healthcare, higher education and life sciences, including professionals in accounting, law and consulting.

Wolters Kluwer Law & Business, a division of Wolters Kluwer, is headquartered in New York. Wolters Kluwer is a market-leading global information services company focused on professionals.

To my children, Hannah, Ellie, and Isaac, small in
stature, but mighty in imagination.
—*A.C.A.*

To my mother, Marjorie Miller Wanderer, master
teacher, grammarian, and storyteller.
—*N.A.W.*

Summary of Contents

Contents

Acknowledgments

We offer our heartfelt thanks to everyone who has helped us make this book possible, especially our knowledgeable reference librarians Christine Hepler, Maureen Quinlan, and Julie Welch; our hard-working research assistant Juliana O'Brien; our ever-helpful administrative assistants Heidi Gage and Frances Smith; administrative assistant for Career Services Tara Wheeler and library assistant Victoria Durant, who helped to produce our charts and illustrations; our gifted former colleague, Angela Caputo Griswold, who came up with so many of our best teaching ideas; all of our wonderful students and former students who keep us on our toes, especially Lisanne Leasure, who wrote the original Jonah assignment, and Regina Stabile, who developed enjoyable games and exercises to help students master citation; the pioneering legal research and writing teachers, like Anne Enquist, Laurel Currie Oates, Ruth McKinney, Mary Barnard Ray, Terri LeClercq, and Christina Kunz, who wrote the textbooks we used and who mentored us over the years; Dean Peter Pitegoff and the University of Maine School of Law for many summers of research support; and, of course, our wonderful spouses, Jason Arey and Susan Sanders, who listened to our ideas, both good and bad, and supported us in every way possible as we labored over this book.

Thanks also to our wise and diligent editors at Wolters Kluwer Christine Hannan, Dana Wilson, and Richard Mixter—who believed in us and guided us every step of the way.

The following materials were reprinted with permission of Thomson Reuters:

American Law Reports, Sixth Series, vol. 23, pp. 697, 709

Atlantic Reporter, Second Series, vol. 733, p. 347

Atlantic Reporter, Second Series, vol. 675, pp. 968-973

Federal Supplement Second Series, vol. 324, no. 1, p. 240

Maine Key Number Digest State & Federal Authorities, vol. 10, pp. vii, x, 689; 2013 pocket part p. 58(1)

Maine Key Number Digest, vol. 20, Descriptive Word Index LI-PN, p. 62

Maine Revised Statues Annotated tit. 24, § 2902, p. 25, and pocket part § 2902, p. 24

Maine Revised Statutes Annotated (1964), vol. 7, tit. 14, § § 1 to 4650; pocket part § 853, p. 39

Maine Revised Statutes Annotated (2012), General Index, M to Z Popular Name table, p. 8

Off and Running

Introduction

At the most basic level, a lawyer's job is to identify a legal issue, find the law that relates to that issue, and determine how that law would be applied in a particular set of circumstances. As a lawyer, you will probably learn about the circumstances first, either from a client who seeks your counsel about a legal problem or from a supervisor who asks you to research the law on his or her behalf. The process you will use is circular: It begins with a set of facts, which lead you to the relevant law, which you must apply to the original set of facts to reach a legal conclusion. The process looks like this:

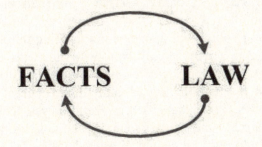

FACTS   LAW

This book is intended to provide you with the background and skills you need to get started in this most essential legal process. In the first chapter, "Foundations of Legal Research, Analysis, and Writing," you will learn about the United States legal system, the different levels of court in both the state and federal court systems, and how the federal and state systems relate. You will learn about the sources of legal authority and the difference between primary and secondary sources, and how the court uses statutes and cases to reach decisions. You will find out what is meant by concepts like "common law" and the role of precedent in deciding cases. You will learn where cases and statutes are published and how to cite to them in your writing. You will also learn how to go about reading cases and statutes and how to interpret the words of a statute, even when those words are ambiguous. Finally, you will come to understand the basics of legal analysis: how a lawyer takes a set of facts, identifies an issue, finds the relevant law, explains that law, applies it to the facts at hand, and reaches a legal conclusion.

Once you have digested this foundational material, you will be ready to move on to the rest of the book, in which you will assume the role of a new associate in a law firm who has been given an assignment to research and write an objective memorandum regarding a legal question presented by a potential client. Throughout the book, you will be led through the process an associate would follow to learn the facts from the client, research the law, and write an objective memorandum predicting how a court would likely apply the law to your client's facts.

We have set the story in Maine, but it could have taken place anywhere. The process of legal research, analysis, and writing would still be the same. As the book leads you through all the different steps in that process, we expect your professor to be assigning you a similar project, involving a story taking place somewhere other than in Maine. You will be asked to research and analyze how the law applies to that fact pattern, using the tools you are learning to use in the book, possibly completing exercises your professor will assign as you go along. The process described in the book will serve as a model for you as you undertake your own assignment, involving a different fact pattern, set in a different place, involving different law.

After learning about your assignment and being introduced to your clients, James and Jonah Malloy, you will move on to Chapter 2, "Researching Your Problem," where you will learn how to assess the situation and find the relevant law in many different legal sources. This chapter discusses both secondary sources—legal encyclopedias, law review articles, and treatises—and primary sources—statutes and cases. The book teaches you how to research the law in printed materials—case reporters, statute books, and other materials found in hard copy in libraries—and also through electronic resources like Westlaw and LexisNexis. Although electronic research is becoming more popular all the time, to be a truly competent legal researcher, you must understand the relationship between what can be found in print and how it has been translated to resources on the Internet. Furthermore, electronic research can be expensive, and not every legal employer encourages its use if print sources are readily available. Some legal research tasks can be performed more economically using electronic sources, like checking to see if the cases you have found still contain good law. Others, however, like conducting massive searches, can be costly and often do not uncover the best results. Relying exclusively on electronic research is dangerous because its effectiveness depends so heavily on the search terms you use. If those search terms are not on target, you can falsely believe you have found the correct law, a result that could get you in a lot of trouble with your employer or the court. Also, flipping through the pages of a book—something that cannot really be done electronically—often leads to unexpected and valuable discoveries.

Finally, because electronic research is in such a rapid stage of development, you will need to seek continual training from the Westlaw and LexisNexis representatives who make themselves available to law schools and legal work settings. The fundamentals of legal research presented in this book will remain constant. Specific instruction and future developments in electronic research, however, are beyond the scope of this and any other book explaining how to conduct effective legal research.

In Chapter 3, "Legal Analysis," you will learn how to analyze the statutes and cases you found in Chapter 2. You will see how your legal analysis becomes the basis of an objective memo in Chapter 3. Once you understand the process used to research and analyze the law in the model fact pattern in the book, you will be able to use that process as a model when researching and analyzing the law for your own objective memorandum.

In the next three chapters, you will see how you can translate your legal conclusions from legal language to plain English in a letter to your clients. You will also learn how to use your legal analysis in other documents, like memoranda and briefs to a court, and to write effective, professional e-mails.

Finally, Chapter 7, "Effective Legal Writing," is intended to be a resource for you to consult when deciding how to avoid plagiarism by quoting, how to paraphrase, and how to cite legal authority correctly. It also contains a basic review of grammar, punctuation, and style and provides tips on how to use transitional words and phrases effectively.

We hope that you will feel confident to undertake any legal research and writing assignment after you have immersed yourself in this book. We have used plain English and presented the material in an order that makes sense in the real world. Obviously, there is much more that could be said, and many other examples we could have provided, but we believe this book will give you the grounding you need to get "off and running" as a successful legal researcher and writer.

Chapter 1

Foundations of Legal Research, Analysis, and Writing

As a lawyer getting ready to research a question presented by a client, your first step is to determine the jurisdiction in which the case would be tried, should you end up taking it to court. The word "jurisdiction" refers to a court's authority to decide a case or to the geographic area within which that authority may be exercised, like the State of Maine or the United States District Court for the District of Maine. To make that determination, you need to understand how the legal system in the United States is organized, where different kinds of cases are litigated, and what sources of legal authority exist.

1.1. Understanding the United States Legal System

1.1.1. Structure of the Court System: Trial and Appellate Courts

A. Trial Courts: Fact Finding

The United States court system is made up of trial and appellate courts. Cases are tried in the trial courts, where witnesses testify and evidence is admitted. This process is known as "fact finding." Such cases are decided by either judges or juries, who consider the evidence and render decisions based on the applicable law. Cases can also originate in state and federal agencies and commissions as well as the Court of Federal Claims, where claims against the United States government are brought, and the Court of International Trade, which addresses cases involving international trade and customs issues. In all of these instances, the "fact finder" decides the outcome of the case, based on an assessment of the credibility of the witnesses and how the law should be applied to the evidence presented at trial. As fact finders, judges enter "judgments" or "orders" while juries reach "verdicts."

B. Intermediate Appellate Courts: Standard of Review

A final judgment or order reached at trial can be appealed, either to an intermediate court of appeals or, if a state does not have an intermediate court of appeals, to the highest court in the jurisdiction. Generally, these courts do not have the power to pick and choose which appeals to hear. They are obligated to consider any appeal that is brought before them. Their job is to decide whether the trial court applied the correct law and whether the evidence at trial was sufficient to support the jury's verdict or the trial court's findings of fact and conclusions of law. They make their decisions based solely on the written "record" of everything that transpired at trial and the arguments made by the attorneys in their briefs and oral arguments. They do not hear any testimony from witnesses and, thus, have no way to assess their credibility from their demeanor. All they can do is read the written transcripts, examine other written material, and question the attorneys appearing before them. They do not even hear directly from the parties in the case, only from their attorneys.

Thus, the intermediate court of appeals is highly deferential to evidentiary determinations of the fact finder in the trial court. The court will only overturn, or "vacate," a judgment of the trial court on the basis of insufficient evidence if it is "clearly erroneous" or "obvious error." The intermediate court of appeals is not at all deferential to the trial court when deciding whether the trial court applied the correct law, however. If the appeal involves a question of law, the intermediate court of appeals may undertake a brand new analysis of which law applies in the case and how that law applies to the facts established in the trial court.

The degree of deference an appellate court must pay to a trial court is called the "standard of review." When determining the "sufficiency of the evidence"—that is, whether the evidence presented was sufficient to warrant a fact finder's judgment, an appellate court must use a highly deferential standard of review requiring "clear error" or "obvious error." If a question of law is on appeal, however, the appellate court may decide the legal question "de novo," meaning that it can begin all over again and make its determination anew. Other intermediate standards of review exist as well for mixed questions of fact and law. For example, the "abuse of discretion" standard of review is often used by appellate courts reviewing trial judges' decisions on matters that come up during trial, like whether evidence should be admitted or someone should be certified as an expert witness. In such matters, the appellate court must show some deference to the trial court, but not as much as when the question of sufficiency of the evidence is raised.

C. Highest Appellate Court

After an intermediate court of appeals renders its decision, a case may be appealed to the highest court in a jurisdiction. Such courts are primarily concerned with making law and resolving conflicts between different lower court divisions or circuits that have adopted or applied conflicting rules of law. If a state does not have an intermediate court of appeals, however, the state's highest court does not have the luxury of choosing only the legally significant cases to decide. The high court is obligated to hear and decide all cases that come before it from the trial courts.

Like the intermediate courts of appeals, the highest courts do not hear witnesses or examine evidence. They base their decisions on the written record of the case and the oral arguments of the attorneys representing the parties. Not every case is granted an oral argument; it is only granted in those cases in which the court determines that something would be gained

Table 1-1: The Levels and Functions of the Courts

Level of Court	Function of the Court
Trial court	• Serves "fact finding" role by admitting evidence and hearing witnesses testify • Bench or jury trial
Intermediate appellate court (Some states do not have this level of court)	• Decides appeals from the trial courts • Reviews only the written record of what happened in the trial court • Defers to the trial court on questions of fact unless clearly erroneous • Decides questions of law on its own
Highest appellate court	• Decides appeals from the intermediate appellate courts or from the trial courts in states with no intermediate appellate court • Reviews only the written record from what happened in the trial court • Defers to the trial court on questions of fact unless clearly erroneous • Decides questions of law on its own • In states with an intermediate appellate court, the highest appellate court mostly decides questions of law and can resolve conflicts among the intermediate courts

by questioning the attorneys about the arguments made in their briefs. If a case is decided without oral argument, it is said to be decided "on the briefs."

In a jurisdiction having an intermediate appellate court, the highest appellate court will likely be hearing only appeals involving questions of law. All the cases involving sufficiency of the evidence or abuse of discretion are likely to be resolved in the intermediate appellate court and are considered insufficiently important to warrant review by the jurisdiction's highest court. The standard of review in cases involving questions of law is de novo; thus, the standard of review in the highest court in jurisdictions having an intermediate appellate court, like the United States Supreme Court, is virtually always de novo.

1.1.2. Two Parallel Court Systems: Federal and State

The judicial branch of our government was established in Article III, Section 1, of the United States Constitution, which provides that the judicial power of the United States shall consist of one Supreme Court and such "inferior courts" that Congress may establish. State constitutions have established the courts in their respective states, using much the same language. For example, Article VI, Section 1, of the Maine Constitution provides that the "judicial power of this State shall be vested in a Supreme Judicial Court, and such other courts as the Legislature shall from time to time establish." Thus, the United States legal system consists of two parallel court systems: the federal courts and the state courts. Most of the time, these two systems operate in complete isolation from each other. Before you can begin to research the issues in a client's case, you need to determine whether those issues should be litigated in state or federal court. In other words, you need to determine which court has jurisdiction, or the power to decide the case.

A. Federal Courts: Federal Questions and Diversity of Citizenship

Federal courts handle two different kinds of cases: (1) cases that raise "federal questions" such as whether a state or federal law is constitutional under the United States Constitution and (2) cases based on the "diversity of citizenship" of the litigants, such as disputes between citizens of two or more states or between citizens of the United States and citizens of a different country. Federal questions also include controversies between states or between the United States and foreign governments, admiralty and bankruptcy cases, and disputes involving ambassadors and public ministers. Federal courts will only hear diversity of citizenship cases involving more than $75,000 in potential damages. Claims involving potential monetary damages less than $75,000 must be heard in state court. Furthermore, diversity of citizenship cases may be brought in state court, even if they do involve more than $75,000 in damages.

1. Federal Trial Courts: United States District Courts

In the federal court system, the trial courts are called United States (or federal) district courts. At least one federal district court is located in every state. For example, a less populous state like Maine has only one federal district court: the United States District Court for the District of Maine. California, on the other hand, has four federal district courts: the United States District Court for the Northern, Southern, Central, and Eastern Districts. Select opinions of the United States district courts are published in the *Federal Supplement* or *Federal Rules Decisions*, two case law "reporters" published by West Publishing. A "reporter" is a set of numbered volumes, organized chronologically, that contains the published decisions of a particular court. Legal researchers can locate decisions though legal citations that identify the volume number, the reporter, and the first page of the decision. Decisions from specialized trial courts like the United States Tax Court, the Court of Federal Claims, and the United States Court of International Trade are published in specialized reporters.

2. Intermediate Federal Appellate Courts: United States Circuit Courts of Appeals

The intermediate court of appeals for the federal system is the United States court of appeals, which includes thirteen circuits: eleven numbered circuits organized geographically throughout the United States, the District of Columbia Circuit, and the Federal Circuit, which reviews decisions of the Court of Federal Claims and the United States Court of International Trade, as well as some United States district court and administrative decisions. Most opinions of the United States circuit courts of appeals are published in the *Federal Reporter*, a West Publishing case law reporter. Illustration 1-1 provides a map of the federal circuit courts.

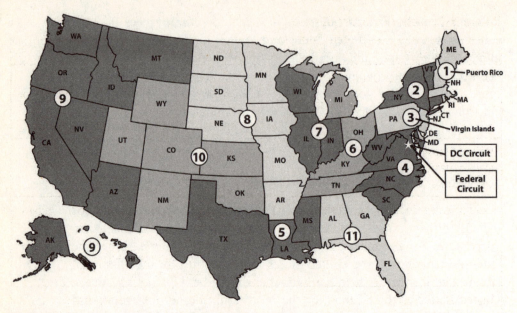

Illustration 1-1: Federal Circuit Court Structure

3. Highest Federal Appellate Court: United States Supreme Court

Opinions of the United States courts of appeals and the highest state courts may be appealed to the United States Supreme Court. People seeking review of an opinion in the United States Supreme Court must file a "petition for writ of *certiorari*" with the Court, arguing why the case should be heard. Each year, the Court receives thousands of these requests for review but grants only about 160 of them. Most of these requests involve cases decided by the United States courts of appeals.

The United States Supreme Court plays two major roles. First, it is the court of last resort for cases originating in the federal court system. Second, it interprets the United States Constitution and determines whether a state or the federal government has violated rights granted under the Constitution. Official opinions of the United States Supreme Court are published in the *United States Reports*, a publication of the United States government.

Table 1-2: Federal Court System

Name of Court	Level of Court
United States District Court	• Trial court in the federal system • 94 districts in 50 states and territories of the United States • No appellate jurisdiction
United States Tax Court United States Court of Federal Claims Unites States Court of International Trade	• Specialized trial courts in federal system
United States Court of Appeals	• Intermediate appellate court in the federal system • 13 judicial "circuit" courts (including the D.C. Circuit and the Federal Circuit) • Appellate jurisdiction
United States Supreme Court	• Highest court in the federal system • Appellate jurisdiction through the *certiorari* process • Last court of appeals for federal cases • Interprets the United States Constitution to determine whether state or federal laws have violated the rights granted under the Constitution • Nine justices, sitting in Washington, D.C.

B. State Courts

1. Trials Involving State and Federal Law: State Trial Courts

State courts handle the majority of legal disputes in the United States. For example, state courts hear personal injury cases, property disputes, divorce and child custody matters, probate and inheritance cases, contract disputes, traffic violations, and most criminal cases. States often have special courts to handle particular legal matters, such as probate court for disputes involving wills, estates, and adoptions; family court for divorces and child custody questions; small claims court for minor matters; and juvenile court for cases involving young people. Many state trial court decisions are not published; the ones that are published can usually be found in state law libraries or on the state judicial system's website. Matters of state and federal law may be litigated in state court. Cases involving federal law or the United States Constitution may be removed from state court and litigated in federal court. Matters involving solely state law or constitutions can only be litigated in state court, however.

2. Appeals: State Intermediate and Highest Appellate Courts

Most states have intermediate courts of appeals that are obligated to hear appeals from state trial courts. Although these courts may choose not to publish every opinion, when opinions are published, they may be found in official reporters published by the state, in regional reporters published by West Publishing, or on the state's judicial website.

All states have highest courts, although not all of those courts are called the "Supreme Court." In New York, for example, the highest court in the state is called the "Court of Appeals" while the trial court is named the "Supreme Court." In most cases, opinions of the state's highest court are published in official state reporters, in regional reporters published by West Publishing, and on the state's judicial website. Like the intermediate appellate court, the highest court can decide not to publish an opinion in a reporter. Such an opinion will resolve the issue in that case, but the court may not wish to have it form a part of the evolving law in that state. Such an opinion is sometimes called a "Memorandum of Decision" and can usually be found only on the judicial website.

C. The Relationship Between State and Federal Courts

Although most cases brought in state court involve state law, cases that involve federal law or a provision of the United States Constitution may also be brought in state court. Cases involving state law, however, can only be brought in federal court when the cases involve diversity of citizenship—that is, when the parties are from two or more different states. Deciding which state's law will be applied in such cases is a complex matter in which the court must determine which state has the most significant contacts with the circumstances of the dispute.

Sometimes, in a diversity case, a federal court will "certify" a question of state law to that state's highest court, asking the court to clarify a point of state law the federal court must apply. The question of law is presented to the state's highest court in the same manner as an appeal from a state trial or intermediate appeals court, with both sides filing briefs and presenting oral arguments. Federal courts are obligated to interpret and apply state law in diversity cases but cannot establish new state law. That is why the certification mechanism is essential to ensuring that the federal court understands and applies the law in the same way the law would be applied in state court.

Contrary to what some people think, the United States Supreme Court can only hear cases originating in the federal system or cases that involve a federal question, implicating federal statutory or constitutional law. Although people often say they will take their case all the way to the United States Supreme Court, they cannot do that if the case did not originate in the federal system or if it involves only state statutory or constitutional law.

Table 1-3: Where Cases Originate

State Courts	Federal Courts
Cases involving state law	Cases involving state law when diversity of citizenship and more than $75,000 in potential damages exist
Cases involving federal law or the United States Constitution	Cases involving federal law or the United States Constitution

1.2. Legal Authority

To answer a legal question posed by a client, you must be able to locate relevant law in the proper jurisdiction and determine how it applies to your client's situation. Before you can do that, you need to know how to determine the proper jurisdiction, what sources of law exist, and how various kinds of legal authority are used by lawyers when preparing cases and courts in making decisions.

1.2.1. Primary and Secondary Sources

After meeting for the first time with a client who has a legal problem, you need to begin by attempting to identify the legal questions involved and doing some preliminary research in both primary and secondary sources. Primary sources include constitutions, statutes, regulations, and opinions in previous court cases. Primary sources are recognized as the law itself and, if relevant and from the proper jurisdiction, must be considered by the court in making a decision. For this reason, relevant primary sources are considered "mandatory" authority; the court is mandated to base its opinion on relevant primary sources.

Not all primary sources are mandatory authority, however. Only primary sources in the jurisdiction where a case will be tried are mandatory authority. For example, if you are trying a case in a California state court, under California law, the court will only be required to consider primary sources from California. Although the holdings or reasoning in cases from other courts might be persuasive, the court is mandated to base its decision on primary legal authority, like statutes or prior cases, only from California. Even a case decided by a federal district court in California or the Ninth Circuit, which covers the state of California, would not be mandatory authority for a California state court; only prior cases decided by the supreme court in California would be mandatory authority.

Furthermore, in jurisdictions like Florida that have intermediate appellate courts, a trial court is bound only by decisions of the appellate court in its district. Decisions of other appellate courts would be highly persuasive but are not mandatory authority.

Similarly, in the federal system, which is divided into many different jurisdictions, each has its own mandatory authority and is not obligated to base decisions on primary authority from other federal jurisdictions. For example, the United States Court of Appeals for the First Circuit does not need to base its decisions on cases from the Eighth Circuit, and the United States District Court for the District of Maine does not need to consider the holdings of a federal district court from another state. It does, however, need to base its decisions on holdings of the First Circuit because the First Circuit is the intermediate appellate court for the United States District Court for the District of Maine.

All jurisdictions, however, are bound to follow decisions made by the United States Supreme Court, which is the ultimate court of appeals for the entire United States judicial system. Those decisions, interpreting federal statutes and the United States Constitution, are mandatory authority in all state and federal jurisdictions. However, the United States Supreme Court cannot determine state law and merely applies the law established by state supreme courts in diversity cases. Thus, states' highest courts are the ultimate arbiters of their state's constitutional, statutory, and common law, over which the United States Supreme Court has no jurisdiction. Although state courts can interpret the United States Constitution and federal laws, their decisions may be reversed by the United States Supreme Court. The United States Supreme Court, however, cannot tell states' highest courts how to interpret matters of state law. Preserving that power for the states is a primary tenet of federalism.

Although mandatory primary sources must eventually form the basis for your reasoning when reaching a conclusion about a legal question, you will also want to consult secondary sources when conducting your research. Secondary sources include legal dictionaries and encyclopedias, law review articles, and scholarly commentary on legal opinions and the evolution of the law. Secondary sources are not the law itself, but merely people's opinions or commentary about the law. Although they cannot be presented as legal rules upon which your conclusion rests, they can be persuasive and may be used to support your reasoning in an objective memorandum for a supervisor or an argument for a court.

Ultimately, you will need to find the primary sources related to your client's legal question before offering any legal advice. To do that, you will use secondary sources, first to help you understand the issue in general, and then to help you find the statutes and cases that relate to your client's situation in particular.

Table 1-4: Primary Versus Secondary Sources

Primary Sources—*Are* the Law	Secondary Sources—*Explain* the Law
Constitutions	Legal encyclopedias
Cases	*American Law Reports* (ALR)
Statutes	Restatements
Regulations	Law review or journal articles
Agency decisions	Treatises
	Legal forms
	Uniform Laws Annotated

A. Sources of Primary Authority

Primary authority includes written statements of the law created by the three branches of government: legislative, executive, and judicial. Constitutions—both state and federal—are also primary authority. The legislative branch creates law by enacting statutes, which are published initially as individual laws ("slip laws"), then in chronological order with all the laws of a session ("session laws"), and finally in volumes with other statutes, organized by subject matter ("codes"). To find statutes that relate to your client's situation, you may use an index to the statutes, searching for key words that relate to the legal question you are researching. The executive branch creates law by promulgating agency rules and regulations that explain how statutes are to be implemented. The judicial branch creates law by publishing opinions in which courts reach decisions in particular cases and explain the legal bases for those decisions.

Table 1-5: Primary Authority from the Branches of Government

Branch of Government	Documents Produced
Executive branch	Agency decisions, agency orders, regulations
Legislative branch	Laws, statutes, legislative documents (bill drafts, committee reports, legislative studies)
Judicial branch	Court decisions

B. Reading and Interpreting Statutes

When statutory language is unambiguous, courts interpret it using the "plain meaning rule," which requires the words of a statute to be given their ordinary meaning. When the meaning of a statute is not plain on its face, however, courts must interpret, or "construe," the statute to fulfill its underlying purpose. The process of construing statutes is called "statutory construction." Sometimes, courts will look to legislative history to discover what the legislature was trying to achieve when enacting a statute. Over time, courts will determine the meaning of a statute by construing its language in cases coming before them. The court's responsibility when construing statutory language is simply to determine what the legislature intended from the text of the statute and legislative history, regardless of whether or not the court approves of that legislative intent.

As a legal researcher, you need to read statutes carefully to understand exactly what they provide. First, you must locate the statute that applies to your client's situation and read it from beginning to end, noting which provisions are particularly applicable. Once you identify a specific provision, break it down, identifying the elements that must be shown or the factors to be considered along with any exceptions or special circumstances. In addition to focusing on a particular provision, you should consider the statute as a whole and how your specific provision fits into the statutory scheme and contributes to the legislature's purpose in enacting the statute. Finally, as you study the specific provision, note any special words that determine its meaning, such as "or" and "and," and the use of punctuation, such as colons and semicolons.

For example, Maine's Criminal Code provides that a person is guilty of burglary if he or she "enters or surreptitiously remains in a structure knowing that [he or she] is not licensed to do so, with the intent to commit a crime therein."[1] When construing this statute, you would begin by noting that a person can be guilty of burglary in two different ways: either (1) by entering or (2) by surreptitiously remaining "in a structure knowing that [he or she] is not licensed to do so, with the intent to commit a crime therein." If you had not noticed the word "or," you might have thought the person had to enter the structure *and* surreptitiously remain there, which would be an incorrect interpretation of the statute. Similarly, you must take note of the punctuation used in a statutory provision. A semicolon means the same thing as the word "and" and should be read as "and" when construing a statute. A colon, however, usually comes before a list or an explanation. The two punctuation marks are not interchangeable. To understand the meaning of statutes, then, you must keep your eye out for words and punctuation marks that affect the meaning of the statute.

Unfortunately, legislatures sometimes do not use sufficient care in drafting statutory provisions. When that happens, lawyers are given the opportunity to argue for different and sometimes even contradictory meanings of the statutes. In such cases, it is up to the courts to settle the disputes by construing the statutes themselves, establishing what they mean by examining the language, punctuation, and legislative history. The meaning of a statute established by the highest court in a jurisdiction will have precedential value in that jurisdiction and serve as mandatory authority in future cases involving that statute.

C. Court Opinions and Citation

Court opinions, or cases, are published in reporters, which contain cases organized in chronological order. Some reporters contain only cases from one jurisdiction or level of court. For example, cases decided by the Massachusetts Supreme Judicial Court are published in Massachusetts Reports, which has been the official reporter for Massachusetts highest court since 1804. Cases from the intermediate appellate and trial courts are published in separate reporters. Similarly, cases from each level of federal court are published in separate official reporters: Cases from the United States Supreme Court are published in United States Reports, cases from the United States Circuit Courts of Appeals are published in the Federal Reporter, and cases from the United States District Courts and Bankruptcy Courts are published in the Federal Supplement. Some sets of reporters are divided into different series, representing different time periods. For example, the Federal Reporter includes cases from 1880-1924; the Federal

---

1. 17-A Me. Rev. Stat. § 401 (2013).

Reporter, Second Series, includes cases from 1924-1993; and the Federal
Reporter, Third Series, covers cases from 1993 to the present.

Some reporters are published by the government and others are
published by commercial publishers like Thomson Reuters/West
(formerly West Publishing Company). Ordinarily, only reporters published by the government are considered "official" reporters, although
in some cases, jurisdictions have adopted as official reporters that are
published commercially. Sometimes, cases are published in both an
official and a commercial reporter. Because every reporter has its own
citation for a case, cases published in two or more reporters have "parallel
citations" including one citation to each reporter in which the case is
published.

West is the largest commercial publisher of court opinions. This is
because, many years ago, West developed the National Reporting System,
which pulls together state court opinions from all over the country and
organizes them into seven regions, as indicated in Illustration 1-2 and
Table 1-6.

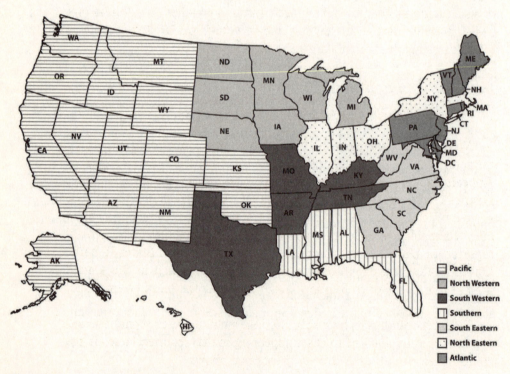

Illustration 1-2: Regional Reporters (State Cases)

Table 1-6: Regional Reporters

Regional Reporters	States Included
Atlantic Reporter (A., A.2d, A.3d)	Connecticut, Delaware, District of Columbia, Maine, Maryland, New Hampshire, New Jersey, Pennsylvania, Rhode Island, Vermont
North Eastern Reporter (N.E., N.E.2d)	Illinois, Indiana, Massachusetts, New York, Ohio
Southern Reporter (So., So. 2d)	Alabama, Florida, Louisiana, Mississippi
South Eastern Reporter (S.E., S.E.2d)	Georgia, North Carolina, South Carolina, Virginia, West Virginia
South Western Reporter (S.W., S.W.2d, S.W.3d)	Arkansas, Kentucky, Missouri, Tennessee, Texas
North Western Reporter (N.W, N.W.2d)	Iowa, Michigan, Minnesota, Nebraska, North Dakota, South Dakota, Wisconsin
Pacific Reporter (P., P.2d, P.3d)	Alaska, Arizona, California, Colorado, Hawaii, Idaho, Kansas, Montana, Nevada, New Mexico, Oklahoma, Oregon, Utah, Washington, Wyoming

West also publishes United States Supreme Court opinions in the Supreme Court Reporter, decisions of the United States Courts of Appeals in the Federal Reporter, and those from the United States District Courts in the Federal Supplement. Although these are not considered official, citations to the Federal Reporter and Federal Supplement are acceptable because the government only publishes an official reporter for United States Supreme Court cases, United States Reports. United States Supreme Court cases are also published in the United States Supreme Court Reports, Lawyers' Edition, another unofficial reporter.

Each reporter has its own abbreviation, including each separate series, which is used in citations to cases appearing in that reporter. Here are the abbreviations for all the reporters mentioned above:

Table 1-7: Reporter Abbreviations

Reporter	Reporter Abbreviation
Atlantic Reporter	A., A.2d, A.3d
North Eastern Reporter	N.E., N.E.2d
Southern Reporter	So., So. 2d
South Eastern Reporter	S.E., S.E.2d
South Western Reporter	S.W., S.W.2d, S.W.3d
North Western Reporter	N.W., N.W.2d
Pacific Reporter	P., P.2d, P.3d
United States Reports	U.S.
Supreme Court Reporter	S. Ct.
United States Supreme Court Reports, Lawyers' Edition	L. Ed., L. Ed. 2d
Federal Reporter	F., F.2d, F.3d
Federal Supplement	F. Supp., F. Supp. 2d, F. Supp. 3d

Most states also have their own official reporters. You should cite to both the state and regional reporter if required to do so by local rule or if that would be particularly helpful to the reader. When using parallel citations, you should cite to the official reporters before unofficial reporters and include a "pin cite" or "pinpoint cite"—a citation to the specific page on which the proposition you are citing is found—for each separate citation unless local rules do not require multiple pin cites. A pin cite appears in a citation after the citation to the first page of the opinion and a comma—for example, *Weaver v. Edwin Shaw Hospital*, 819 N.E.2d 1079, 1083 (Ohio 2004). In this example, the writer is citing to a proposition on page 1083 of an opinion that is found in Volume 819 of the North East Reporter, Second Series, which begins on page 1079.

West also publishes 31 state reporters that include cases that are pulled from the regional reporters and bound together with the state's name on the cover rather than the name of the regional reporter. The page numbering is the same as in the regional reporter. Citations to cases contain all the information someone needs to find them. Every citation contains the following components: case name, reporter volume, reporter abbreviation, first page, and, in parentheses, the court abbreviation and year decided. A citation should also generally include a pin cite following the first page and may include subsequent history after the court/date parenthetical—for example, *Abbott v. Bragdon*, 107 F.3d 934 (1st Cir. 1997), *vacated*, 524 U.S. 624 (1998).

Some states[2] require "neutral citations" in addition to citations to a regional reporter. Neutral citations are sometimes called "public domain citations" because they do not refer to regional reporters or online databases, such as Lexis or Westlaw. Neutral citations generally include the following components: case name, year of decision, court abbreviation, opinion number, pin cite (paragraph number), followed by a citation to a regional reporter. The Maine Supreme Judicial Court began requiring neutral citations in 1997 when it started posting opinions with numbered paragraphs on its website. An example of a neutral citation is *Merrill v. Sugarloaf Mountain Corp.*, 1997 ME 180, ¶ 3, 698 A.2d 1042. Always use neutral citations when they are required by local court rule.

The *ALWD Guide to Legal Citation*[3] and *The Bluebook*[4] contain all the citation rules you will ever need to know. You should consult one or both of those manuals frequently when writing a memo for a law partner or any sort of filing for a court. Providing accurate and complete citations is essential. Whether your reader is a law partner, judge, or law clerk, your credibility hangs on your ability to apply precedent to the facts in your case. Your reader will want to look at the sources you are citing to see whether you have described them accurately and interpreted the law correctly. If your citation is incorrect or it does not include a pin cite, your reader will become frustrated trying to find what you have referred to and will ultimately lose faith in the persuasiveness of your position. Never underestimate the power of a missing or incomplete citation to sink your legal argument. Providing accurate citations and pin cites is a tedious job but is a vitally important one that should never be shortchanged.

D. Reading and Briefing Cases

1. How to Read an Opinion

Courts declare and explain the law in opinions, which are published as cases in reporters. Those reporters include not only the opinion, as written by the court, but also additional materials intended to aid the legal researcher. After locating a case in a reporter, you need to recognize the difference between the opinion written by the court and the research aids provided by the publishing company.

Reporters often preface opinions with introductory material that helps orient the reader. Following the caption providing the name of the case, the

---

2. Courts in Arkansas, Colorado, Louisiana, Maine, Mississippi, Montana, New Mexico, North Dakota, Oklahoma, Puerto Rico, Utah, Vermont, Wisconsin, and Wyoming require neutral citations.

3. *ALWD Guide to Legal Citation* (5th ed., Wolters Kluwer Law & Business 2014).

4. *The Bluebook: A Uniform System of Citation* (19th ed., Columbia Law Review Ass'n et al., eds., 2010).

court, and the date the case was argued and the opinion issued, you may find a syllabus or overview of the opinion that gives you a quick sense of the basic facts, issues, and holdings discussed in the case. Next, "headnotes" may be provided, which allow you to see what legal principles were used to support the court's opinion. Finally, after all this preliminary material, you will come to the opinion itself. When citing to the opinion, you need to be careful to cite only to the pages containing the opinion itself, not any of the preliminary material in the syllabus or headnotes.

After reading the preliminary material and noting any headnotes that relate to the issue you are researching, you may wish to skim through the opinion to see if anything looks useful to your issue. You may quickly be able to dispense with some cases based upon what you read in the preliminary sections and found when skimming the opinion. You may decide that the issues are not really on point with yours, or the court's explanation of the principles is too brief and does not further your understanding of the law, or the case may not be useful for a variety of other reasons.

Once you have decided which cases look relevant to the analysis of your issues, you must carefully read each of those cases. First, take careful note of the level of the court issuing the opinion. Is it an opinion from a trial court, an intermediate appellate court, or the highest court? Is it from a court in your jurisdiction or another jurisdiction? Taking note of the court will let you know whether the opinion is binding authority for your issue.

Most opinions will contain similar elements that you will want to understand in each case: the underlying facts, procedural history, issues, holdings, rationale, and judgment (or remedy). The underlying facts explain the factual basis for the parties' dispute. Read the facts carefully; just because you see a fact written down does not mean that the court accepted that fact as true. You must read the context around the fact to make sure that the court is explaining what happened (or its findings about what happened) rather than summarizing what each side presented for evidence of what happened. Similarly, the procedural history explains the facts regarding what has happened procedurally in the dispute. Take note of which party started the lawsuit and what has happened in the lawsuit to get the parties to the point they are at in the opinion you are reading. What type of order is being decided or appealed?

Next, you must figure out the particular issues discussed in the opinion. Understanding the issues addressed by the court is a critical step in your analysis of the case. You cannot determine the court's holdings in an opinion if you have not properly identified the issues.

If the opinion you are reading contains multiple issues, many of which are unrelated to your issue, you do not necessarily need to read the entire opinion carefully. The analysis in an opinion is often divided into discrete issues (usually, helpfully, with their own subheadings). You can carefully read the facts, procedural history and any analysis relating to your issue, and then skim the rest of the opinion to make sure you do not miss anything that you should look at more closely.

Once you have identified an issue, its holding can be readily determined. The holding is simply the answer to the issue raised. If you have properly and precisely identified the issue, the holding can be summarized in a "yes" or "no" answer. The holding may, however, be a broader statement taken from the language of the opinion.

After you find the holding for an issue, read the opinion carefully to understand the rationale that supports the holding. The rationale may be explicitly stated in the opinion, or it may be implicit in the opinion. Either way, you will only be able to discern the rationale by closely studying the opinion. The rationale may include legal principles relied upon by the court, specific facts in the dispute, or policy considerations. The portion of the opinion addressing a court's rationale may be quite lengthy as a court may walk the reader through a considerable amount of precedent in explaining how it reached its decision. Finally, take note of the judgment or remedy in the opinion: What does the court order? Is it granting or denying a particular order? Reversing, vacating, or affirming a lower court opinion? Most often, the judgment can be found at the end of the opinion.

As you read each case, be aware of any "dicta" in the opinion. Oftentimes, language in an opinion may look promising, but when read closely, it turns out to be a "dictum." A dictum is a statement in an opinion that is not necessary for the court's decision but is nevertheless said in passing in the court's opinion. (The plural of dictum is dicta.) A dictum is not considered to have precedential value, though it may be persuasive and can provide insight into how a court views a particular issue. You will not necessarily recognize dicta, however, unless you read the opinion carefully.

Finally, read through any "concurring" or "dissenting" opinions. In a concurring opinion, sometimes called a "concurrence," one or more judges agree with the holding, but for different reasons than stated in the majority opinion. In a dissenting opinion, or "dissent," one or more judges disagree with the holding of the majority decision. Both types of opinions will typically outline the reasoning for the disagreement. If you are trying to argue a position opposite the one taken by the majority, you can sometimes find useful reasoning in concurring and dissenting opinions.

2. How to Write a Case Brief

After you have read your cases carefully, you may want to write case briefs for the ones that appear promising. A case brief is a summary of the important components of an opinion: the essential facts of the case, the prior proceedings, the issues before the court, and what the court decided and why.[5] Writing case briefs helps you to focus on the important aspects of the case and helps you to identify the most useful cases. Later, you can use the case briefs to refresh your memory about the cases as you decide whether or where to use them in your memo. A case brief is most helpful when it is true to its name: *brief*. Be concise. Case briefs should usually be only one or two pages long.

Before briefing a case, read it at least two or three times. Then, at the top of the page, put the name of the case and its formal citation. Then discuss each of the following aspects of the opinion in the order given.

PROCEDURAL HISTORY:

Tell who is suing whom for what or, in a criminal case, what crime the defendant was accused of committing.

Tell how the lower court ruled in the case.

Identify the parties, stating which party appealed to which court and what relief was requested.

FACTS:

Summarize the historical facts, focusing on the facts that were important to the court in deciding the case.

ISSUES:

Specify the issues or questions in controversy in the case on appeal.

Each issue should be written in the form of a separate question.

HOLDING:

Each holding is the answer to each issue, or question, before the court.

The holding is a rephrasing of the question to a declarative sentence.

---

5. A case brief is not the kind of brief lawyers write for appellate courts. Although both types of brief should be as short as possible, appellate briefs tend to be lengthy, persuasive documents, submitted to courts in cases on appeal. Case briefs, in contrast, are simply used as study and research aids by the people who write them.

RATIONALE:

Explain the court's reasoning in reaching its decision.

Identify any public policy considerations.

Note any significant dicta.

DISSENT/CONCURRENCE:

Describe important points made in dissenting and concurring opinions.

3. Example of a Case Brief

Here is an example of a case brief for the opinion reprinted below: *Fournier v. Rochambeau Club*, 611 A.2d 578 (Me. 1992).

OPINION OF CASE TO BE BRIEFED

Fournier v. Rochambeau Club, 611 A.2d 578 (Me. 1992)

ROBERTS, Justice.

Defendant Rochambeau Club appeals from a judgment entered in the Superior Court (York County, *Cole, J.*) after a jury-waived trial. On appeal the Club argues that the court misconstrued the nature of its relationship with plaintiff Donald A. Fournier and applied the wrong standard of duty owed to Fournier. Finding no error, we affirm the judgment.

Fournier has been a member of the Rochambeau Club since approximately 1963. One of the Club's regular activities is to host beano games two or three nights a week. From 1986 until 1988 Fournier helped to prepare the Club's kitchen on those nights. The preparations included getting pre-formed hamburger patties ready for cooking. Normally the patties would already be thawed, but one night in February 1988 they were still frozen. Roger Lajeunesse, the president and manager of the Rochambeau Club, instructed Fournier to separate some of the frozen patties so the cooks could start on them, and to get others out to thaw. Lajeunesse provided no specific instructions on how to accomplish the task. When Fournier attempted to separate the patties with a knife, he sliced his thumb, inflicting substantial damage.

Fournier brought this action against the Club, alleging that the Club had been negligent in failing to instruct him on a safe method of separating the patties. The court found that, although Fournier was negligent in ignoring the obvious danger of using the knife, the Club was also negligent in failing to instruct him on how to separate the patties. The court then found that Fournier was less than equally at fault, under our comparative negligence statute, 14 M.R.S.A. § 156 (1980), and awarded damages. This appeal followed.

Contrary to the contention of the Rochambeau Club, its duty to Fournier was that owed to a gratuitous employee and not that owed to a mere volunteer. That Fournier was not paid for his services does not preclude the existence of an employment relationship, *Lunt v. Fidelity & Casualty Co. of New York*, 139 Me. 218, 224, 28 A.2d 736 (1942), although a contrary rule applies for purposes of workers' compensation, *Cook v. Bangor Hydro-Elec. Co.*, 402 A.2d 64, 66 (Me.1979). Fournier submitted to the direction and control of Lajeunesse for the primary purpose of serving the Club, an activity in which Fournier had an interest. *See Bond v. Cartwright Little League, Inc.*, 112 Ariz. 9, 536 P.2d 697, 702 (1975).

The Club next argues that, even assuming it breached a duty of care owed Fournier, such breach was not the proximate cause of his injury. That argument is bottomed on the unstated premise that there can be only one proximate cause of an injury. Contrary to that assertion, however, there may be more than one proximate cause of a particular injury. *Cf. Allen v. Hunter*, 505 A.2d 486, 488 (Me.1986) (analysis under 14 M.R.S.A. § 156 presupposes that each party was a proximate cause of the injury).

In this case, the finder of fact determined that the Club's direction that Fournier separate the frozen patties, coupled with its failure to instruct him on the proper method of achieving that end, were both an inadequate protection from a reasonably foreseeable harm and a substantial factor in bringing about that harm. We cannot say as a matter of law that the court erred in so determining. *See Jackson v. Frederick's Motor Inn, 418 A.2d 168, 173 (Me.1980).*

Finally, the Club argues that the court erred in failing to hold, again as a matter of law, that Fournier's negligence was equal to or greater than the Club's negligence, thus precluding any recovery under section 156. We disagree. As in *Jackson*, the assessment of the relative causative fault of the parties regarding liability is in the instant case a determination properly left to the court in its role as trier of fact. *See id.*

The entry is:
Judgment affirmed.
WATHEN, C.J., and GLASSMAN, J., concurring.

CLIFFORD, Justice, with whom COLLINS, Justice, joins, dissenting.

I respectfully dissent. I do not disagree with the legal principles as stated by the Court. In my view, however, the court applies those principles improperly to the facts in this case, facts that are largely undisputed. This case does not involve the use of a complex piece of machinery or an injury to a child. Fournier, an intelligent adult, who had worked in the Rochambeau Club's kitchen for two years, was given the task of separating frozen hamburger patties. He chose to use a common kitchen knife. He was familiar with the techniques for using such a knife safely and knew of the risks involved. He cut his own hand. When compared to what was found to be the negligent conduct of Roger Lajeunesse, vicariously attributed to the Rochambeau Club, the negligent conduct of Fournier is, as a matter of law, and of common sense, clearly equal to or greater than that of Lajeunesse. I would vacate the judgment.

CASE BRIEF

Fournier v. Rochambeau Club, 611 A.2d 578 (Me. 1992)

PROCEDURAL HISTORY:

Plaintiff Fournier sued Defendant Rochambeau Club (the Club) for negligence. The Superior Court ruled for Fournier after a jury-waived trial. The Club appealed to the Law Court.

FACTS:

Fournier worked in the Club's kitchen for two years getting hamburger patties ready for cooking. One night when the patties were still frozen, the Club's president told Fournier to separate the patties without providing any instructions on how to do so. Using a knife to perform the task, Fournier seriously injured his thumb.

ISSUES:

1. Did the Superior Court erroneously apply the wrong standard of care by finding that Fournier was a gratuitous employee of the Club, not a mere volunteer?
2. Did the Superior Court erroneously find that the Club's breach of due care was the proximate cause of Fournier's injury?
3. Did the Superior Court err in finding that the Club's negligence was greater than Fournier's?

HOLDINGS:

1. No. The court correctly found that the Club's duty to Fournier was that owed to a gratuitous employee and not that owed to a mere volunteer.

The fact that Fournier was not paid for his services does not preclude the existence of an employment relationship.

2. No. The court did not err in determining that the Club's breach of due care was a proximate cause of Fournier's injury. The Club's direction to separate the patties and failure to provide instruction on the proper method to do so were inadequate protection from a reasonably foreseeable harm and a substantial factor in bringing about that harm.

3. No. The assessment of the relative causative fault of the parties under 14 M.R.S.A. § 156 is a question of fact that is properly left to the trier of fact.

REASONING:

1. Fournier "submitted" to "the direction and control" of the Club for "the primary purpose of serving" the Club, an activity in which Fournier "had an interest." Underlying public policy consideration: The world and legal process work better if defendants like the Club owe a duty to instruct plaintiffs like Fournier.

2. There can be more than one proximate cause of an injury.

3. Assessment of relative causative fault of parties is best left to the trier of fact who sees parties and witnesses and can judge credibility. Also, appellate courts pay great deference to facts found by triers of fact.

DISSENT:

The trial court did not assess the relative causative fault of the parties correctly.

1.2.2. Common Law: Role of *Stare Decisis* and Precedent

Cases fall into two categories: (1) cases that interpret and apply "enacted law" and (2) cases that set out, interpret, and apply "common law." (See Illustration 1-3.) Enacted law includes statutes and regulations created by the legislative and executive branches of government and also includes constitutions. Common law is a system of law that has evolved strictly through judicial opinions reflecting common practices for resolving disputes. Common law principles apply to areas of law that are not governed by codes or regulations, although statutes and regulations may, at times, come into play in such cases. Sometimes, a legislature will decide to pass a law embodying, modifying, or even abandoning common law principles. When that happens, the statute becomes the controlling law. Any cases decided before the statute took effect would still be good law only if their holdings remain consistent with the subsequent statutory law.

Enacted Law			Common Law
⇧	⇧	⇧	⇧
Legislative	Executive	Judicial	Judicial
Branch	Branch	Branch	Branch
Creates	Creates	Interprets	Creates

Illustration 1-3: Sources of Law

The United States judicial system is a common law system, which means that courts look to previous cases, called "precedent," when deciding cases. Other countries, like France, have "civil law" systems, which rely more on codes in resolving disputes and not so much on how similar cases were decided previously. Courts in France look to the letter of the law as laid out in statutes and codes in resolving disputes and are not bound by earlier court decisions. French courts also are not expected to provide in-depth reasoning for their decisions, whereas American courts, particularly appellate courts, generally produce "reasoned decisions," opinions in which the court's rationale is spelled out, including the names of the cases the court relied on in reaching its decision.

In the United States, even opinions interpreting enacted law are based on precedent. In such cases, American courts are bound by precedent under the doctrine of "*stare decisis*," a Latin term meaning "to stand by things decided." Rarely will a court reject *stare decisis*, but when it does, it must be because the old way of resolving a legal issue no longer serves society, and a new direction must be taken. An example of such a departure from *stare decisis* occurred when, in *Brown v. Board of Education*, 347 U.S. 483 (1953), the United States Supreme Court held that racial segregation, as embodied in the "separate but equal" principle adopted in *Plessy v. Ferguson*, 163 U.S. 537 (1896), was no longer acceptable in American society. In doing so, the Court adopted a new legal rule that children of all races should be educated in the same classrooms, rejecting the legal precedent established in *Plessy v. Ferguson* and recognizing that American society could no longer tolerate such discrimination.

Under *stare decisis*, the court must consider what a prior court in its jurisdiction at the same or a higher level held previously with respect to the issue currently under consideration. That means that the court will need to determine the prior court's holding in the previous decision by analyzing both how the case came out and also the prior court's reasoning, or rationale, for its decision. Without a thorough understanding of the prior court's reasoning, it is difficult for the court to know how a previous holding should apply to the current case.

Applying Precedent to a New Case: The Importance of Rationale

For example, consider the case of Henry Miller, who granted the use of a driveway over his property to his neighbor, Susan Brown, in a deed that states that the driveway is to be used by "Susan and her guests to access her residence." After a few years, Susan began holding yard sales at her home every Saturday from June until September. After asking Susan, to no avail, to stop holding yard sales, Henry finally put his foot down. He placed a locked gate at the end of the driveway and informed Susan that she may continue to drive to her home over the driveway, but she cannot allow the public to come to weekly summer yard sales any longer.

After being asked to help out with the case, you learn that the driveway is an "easement," and that the highest court in your jurisdiction has issued several opinions explaining how people may and may not use their easements. One of the opinions involves a right of way that was originally granted for the purpose of logging and hauling crops to market. *Guild v. Hinman*, 1997 ME 120, ¶ 3, 695 A.2d 1190. Many years later, when a subsequent landowner sought to build a home and install utility lines along the right of way, the Maine Supreme Judicial Court, sitting as the Law Court,[6] refused to allow the landowner to install the utility lines. *Id.* ¶ 1.

You immediately notice some similarities between Henry's situation and the situation in the *Guild* case, but the facts are not exactly the same. You wonder whether this precedent applies to Henry's case, but you cannot really tell without knowing more about how the court reached its decision. You decide to read the case again, hoping to discover why the Court held as it did.

This time, reading the case more carefully, you notice that the Court focused on the fact that "the parties to the original conveyance creating the right of way did not contemplate that the property would be used for residential purposes." *Id.* After thinking it over, you decide that the case is definitely helpful to Henry because his situation is analogous to that of the landowner in *Guild*, whose predecessor granted an easement for a commercial purpose and, later, was confronted with someone wanting

---

6. The Maine Supreme Judicial Court is "sitting as the Law Court" when deciding cases and controversies. The court is "sitting as the Maine Supreme Judicial Court" when making other sorts of rulings. Thus, it is proper to refer to the "Law Court" or the "Maine Law Court" when discussing cases that court has decided.

to use that easement for a different purpose—a residential purpose. Although Henry's situation is the opposite of that—he granted the easement for residential purposes, but Susan wants to use it for commercial purposes—you can see that the same principle should apply. The court ought to find that Susan cannot use the easement for a purpose that was not originally intended by the parties to the original conveyance.

Once you figured out why the Court held that the utility lines could not be run along the easement in *Guild*, you could see how the Court's holding would probably apply to Henry's situation. Without deciphering the Court's rationale, however, you might have thought that the Court reached its decision in some other way that might not apply to Henry's situation. Perhaps the court did not want houses being built on rural land or was sympathetic to the property owner for some other reason. Once you realized that the court was focusing on whether running utility lines would result in an unintended use of the easement, you could see that the case would serve as useful precedent in Henry's case. The court hearing Henry's case, however, would still need to be convinced that holding weekly summer yard sales is a commercial purpose that is beyond the residential purpose of the easement. Nevertheless, you have accomplished your first goal: finding precedent that supports your client's contention that holding weekly summer yard sales must stop. Without reading the *Guild* case carefully and identifying the court's rationale for its decision, however, you would not have been able to recognize its value as precedent or use it effectively in arguing your client's case in court.

Furthermore, the *Guild* case would be mandatory authority because it was decided by the Maine Supreme Judicial Court, the highest appellate court in your jurisdiction. If it had been decided by the Maine Superior Court, a Maine trial court, it would have been merely persuasive authority, not mandatory. Only precedent from the Maine Supreme Judicial Court—a higher court than the Maine Superior Court—would be mandatory authority in the trial court, where your firm would be taking Henry's case. Under the doctrine of *stare decisis*, therefore, your firm should be able to convince the court that using the driveway to allow customers access to frequent weekly summer yard sales is beyond the scope of the easement and needs to stop.

1.3. The Basic Components of Legal Analysis

Analyzing a legal problem is a process. It takes time, attention, and careful reading and thinking. Fortunately, most legal analysis involves the same essential components; thus, each time you go through the process, you should follow these basic steps:

1. Identify the issue(s)
2. find and understand the relevant legal rules;
3. identify previous cases that further explain the legal rules or illustrate how those rules have been applied to specific facts in the past;
4. apply the legal framework to the facts of your problem; and
5. reach a conclusion about the likely outcome of the issue.

Although these are set forth in the order in which you are likely to consider the components, be aware that the process of legal analysis is not linear and most often requires you to go back and forth between these components. What you learn in a later step may require you to go back and refine your understanding in an earlier step. Regardless of whether you are analyzing a simple problem or a complex one, you will need to consider each of these components in your analysis. The complexity of the problem may change, but the underlying process remains the same.

1.3.1. Identifying the Legal Issue

Before you can research and analyze a problem, you need to know what the issues are. You may identify many initial issues in your problem; however, some of them may have clear answers, while others may be irrelevant to the outcome of the problem. Your job is to identify the issues that are in need of analysis so that you make the most efficient use of not only your time, but your reader's time as well. You do not want to waste time analyzing irrelevant issues or those with clear answers.

For example, consider the situation where an adult woman filed a complaint in 2012 alleging that from 1970-1973, when she was 8 to 12 years old, her parish priest sexually assaulted and abused her. Her complaint details the facts of what she alleges happened and sets forth eight causes of action against the priest and the church: sexual assault and battery, invasion of privacy, intentional infliction of emotional distress, negligent infliction of emotional distress, negligent supervision of employee, clergy malpractice, fraudulent concealment, and breach of fiduciary duty. Assume you represent the church. You may be tempted to jump into the analysis of each of these individual torts to determine whether the priest or church is liable. Although those are the issues you have identified, your assigning partner tells you that she wants to know whether the state's statute of limitations for tort claims prevents the lawsuit from proceeding.

Each state has a statute of limitations that sets forth the time limit within which certain types of claims must be filed. If the time limit has expired for the woman's claims, the court will have to dismiss her lawsuit. Thus, whether any of the claims in the woman's complaint have merit is irrelevant until you determine whether or not the complaint is timely. The only issue to focus on, then, is whether the statute of limitations prevents her from suing the priest and the church. You would waste your time and your client's money if you spent time researching the other issues at this point.

Often you will not be able to identify all the issues until you conduct some research and understand the basics of the applicable law. Then, you will need to go back and refine your understanding of the issues that need to be analyzed. You might also find that you want to divide the issues you have identified into sub-issues in order to analyze discrete parts of a larger issue. For example, your issue might be whether your client committed burglary under the state's burglary statute. The burglary statute has several requirements that the state must prove: "A person is guilty of burglary if . . . [t]he person enters or surreptitiously remains in a structure knowing that that person is not licensed to do so, with the intent to commit a crime therein."[7] Once you study the language of the statute, you might identify several sub-issues that need to be analyzed in order to answer the larger question of whether your client committed burglary. You might need to analyze whether she "surreptitiously remained" in the structure and had the "intent to commit a crime." Those would be two sub-issues of the initial issue you identified.

When researching and analyzing a problem, it is easy to get off track and begin researching tangential, irrelevant issues. Before you begin, and as you go along, make sure you understand the specific issue you are examining. If you ever find yourself uncertain about whether you are still focused on the right issue, go back and seek clarification.

1.3.2. Identifying and Working with Legal Rules

Once you have identified your initial issue, you need to find and understand the applicable legal rules. Legal rules are statements of the governing law that are relevant to your problem. Think of them as the guiding principles that would apply in any situation. Like the rules of a game, they remain constant, regardless of how many different ways that game is played. You cannot analyze the facts of your problem until you know what the governing rules are. Thus, you need to know where to find the

---

7. 17-A Me. Rev. Stat. § 401.

rules and be familiar with some of the common types of legal rules you may encounter.

A. Sources of Legal Rules

The legal rules come from primary authority, such as constitutions, statutes, cases, and agency rules and regulations. Secondary sources explain the legal rules and point to primary authority where they can be found. You may find a statement of a rule in a single source, such as a statute, or you may need to consult several sources to understand what the legal rule is. For example, a statute may set forth a rule, but then judicial opinions interpreting that statute provide additional requirements or limits for that rule. Likewise, understanding a common law rule may require you to read many cases and synthesize what you learn in each in order to correctly identify the legal principle.

B. Types of Legal Rules

Sometimes a legal rule sets forth a series of elements that must be satisfied in order for the rule to apply. Consider again Maine's Criminal Code, which sets forth the requirements the State must prove in order to successfully prosecute someone for burglary. Under the statute, "A person is guilty of burglary if . . . [t]he person enters or surreptitiously remains in a structure knowing that that person is not licensed to do so, with the intent to commit a crime therein."[8] This rule can be broken down into individual elements the State must prove:

1. the person must enter or surreptitiously remain in a structure;
2. the person must know that [s]he is not licensed to enter or remain at the time [s]he does so; and
3. the person must have had the intent to commit a crime
4. when [s]he entered or remained in the structure.

The State must prove that all four elements are satisfied in order for a person to be guilty of burglary. If any one of these elements is missing, a person cannot be guilty of burglary.

Other legal rules present a list of factors that must be taken into account when deciding an issue. For example, in many states, when dealing with issues of child custody, a court must consider the best interest of a child to determine how the parental rights and responsibilities will be allocated. To determine the best interest of the child, a court must consider the following factors:

---

8. *Id.*

1. The age of the child;
2. the relationship of the child with the child's parents and any other person who may significantly affect the child's welfare;
3. the preference of the child, if old enough to express a meaningful preference;
4. the duration and adequacy of the child's current living arrangements and the desirability of maintaining continuity;
5. the stability of any proposed living arrangements for the child;
6. the motivation of the parties involved and their capacities to give the child love, affection and guidance;
7. the child's adjustment to the child's present home, school and community;
8. the capacity of each parent to allow and encourage frequent and continuing contact between the child and the other parent, including physical access. . . .

The list of factors continues until nineteen factors are enumerated.

Unlike the burglary statute, where every element had to be satisfied in order for a person to be guilty, the determination of the best interest of a child does not require that all nineteen factors be satisfied; it simply requires the court to give consideration to each of the factors in making its decision. Judicial opinions considering the factors may give you additional insights about how the court weighs each factor, including whether some factors carry more weight than others. You would need to read the opinions and synthesize the material to determine the weight of the factors and how they apply.

A legal rule may also set forth a "balancing test," where a court must balance competing interests in resolving an issue. For example, the text of the Fourth Amendment requires that a search of a person must be reasonable. In interpreting this requirement, the United States Supreme Court explained that whether a warrantless search is reasonable is determined "by assessing, on the one hand, the degree to which it intrudes upon an individual's privacy and, on the other, the degree to which it is needed for the promotion of legitimate governmental interests." *U.S. v. Knights*, 534 U.S. 112, 118-19 (2001). This legal rule tells you that a court must balance the individual's expectation of privacy against the State's[9] interest in conducting the warrantless search. Under this rule, the warrantless search is

---

9. You should always capitalize the *S* in "State" when referring to the government. For example, "The State is generally not permitted to conduct warrantless searches." Do not capitalize it when referring to a particular state, such as Florida, unless you are using the word as part of the proper name: State of Florida or Sunshine State. example, "We love vacationing in the State of Florida. That state is known as the Sunshine State."

reasonable only if the State's interest in the search is greater than the individual's expectation of privacy.

C. Rule Synthesis

Many times, you will need to read multiple cases and synthesize what you are learning in order to understand how the legal rule works and what it requires. Rule synthesis is the process of reconciling and combining what you learn in each case about the legal rule and integrating it into a single statement of the legal principle. The result is a single legal rule derived from several cases. For example, consider the following hypothetical cases related to landlord/tenant disputes:

First case: The court held that a landlord had to pay for repairs to fix a leaking basement in a house that a tenant was renting. The foundation of the house had multiple cracks through which the water was seeping into the basement. The court reasoned that the foundation was a structural component of the building, the maintenance of which was the responsibility of the landlord.

Second case: The court held that a landlord did not have to pay to repair a hole in the wall in a tenant's apartment. The tenant had been intoxicated and had punched the hole in the wall while fighting with his girlfriend. The court reasoned that the landlord should not have to pay for damage caused by the tenant.

Third case: The court held that a landlord was responsible for fixing a broken railing in the main stairwell in a multi-level apartment building. The court reasoned that the stairwell was in a common area of the apartment building and no evidence had been presented as to who had caused the damage to the stairwell.

Fourth case: The court held that a landlord was not responsible for paying for water damage to a bathroom floor resulting from a toilet that overflowed in a tenant's apartment. The tenant's two-year old child had filled the toilet with various objects in the bathroom, such as rolls of toilet paper, bottles of shampoo, conditioner and lotion, and bath toys, and then attempted to flush the toilet multiple times. The court noted that the landlord had no control over the use of the bathroom by the child.

You could likely identify a single principle in each one of these individual cases. To synthesize a rule, however, requires that you look at all of these cases together and state what you have learned from all of them in a clear and concise statement that explains the guiding principle that can be gleaned from these cases. Sometimes, creating a chart of the cases can be useful in synthesizing the cases. A simple chart for this example could look like this:

Landlord Responsible	Landlord Not Responsible
Leaking basement; rationale: structural component of building	Hole in the wall caused by tenant
Broken railing on common stairwell in building when unknown cause of damage	Water damage from overflowed toilet caused by tenant's child

By studying the cases and the chart, you can look for the commonalities in the types of things for which the landlord was responsible. You can see that landlords have been responsible for repairs that seem to be part of the structure or common area of the building. On the other hand, landlords have not been responsible for damage in the tenant's apartment caused by the tenant. Therefore, after synthesizing the cases, you would probably come to the following rule:

A landlord will be liable for structural damage to a building and damage in common areas of a building, but will not be liable for damage caused by a tenant or someone within the tenant's control.

Synthesizing cases takes time. It requires reading the cases carefully to determine how they can be reconciled. Sometimes the process is relatively straightforward, but often you encounter language and holdings that, at first glance, appear different or inconsistent from case to case. When you study the cases closely, however, you may find that the court is just using different terms to explain the same concepts or that the different outcomes in the cases are the result of the differences in the underlying facts in each case. Once you have an understanding of how the cases can be reconciled with each other, you should have a good understanding of the rule and how it works.

1.3.3. Rule Explanation, Illustration, or Proof (Analogous Cases)

Sometimes a rule needs no further explanation. Its meaning is clear, and it can easily be applied to the facts of your problem in a simple, straightforward analysis. Much of the time, however, for a variety of reasons, you need to consider previous cases that have applied the rule. First, you can use the cases to show how the courts have further interpreted, explained, or defined a rule. Second, you can use the cases to provide the basis for analogical reasoning in your analysis by explaining how the courts have applied the rule to similar facts in cases before yours. Finally, you can use the cases to explain any policy considerations that underpin the rule.

In the burglary statute, the first element can be satisfied when one enters a structure. The meaning of this appears to be straightforward and may need no further explanation.[10] The other way the first element can be satisfied, though, is when one surreptitiously remains in a structure. The meaning of this part of the rule is less clear, and cases applying the burglary statute may provide further explanation of what it means to surreptitiously remain in a place. Thus, you would need to look at the cases in which courts have applied the rule to better understand the meaning of the rule and how it works

Next, cases can be used to provide the basis for analogical reasoning, which is an important part of legal analysis. Analogical reasoning involves looking at the facts of the precedent cases to find factual similarities and distinctions between those cases and your own factual problem. Because courts follow the doctrine of *stare decisis*, the outcome of your case is likely to be the same as the outcome of previous cases in your jurisdiction with facts that are similar to yours. Thus, by studying the facts of the cases previously decided, you can craft arguments by making comparisons to and distinctions from those previous cases. Then, you can make predictions about the likely outcome of your case. When you are looking at the facts of the previous cases, the similarities and differences between those facts and your facts need to be meaningful; otherwise, the comparisons and distinctions will not be useful to you or your reader. The similarities and distinctions are meaningful if they affect the outcome of the case.

In addition to the facts, study the rationale underlying the court's decision. Does the court explain why it decided the case a certain way? Is the reasoning implicit in the decision even if the court does not expressly explain it? Like the facts, the court's reasoning is important for you to note because the court is likely to apply similar reasoning in future cases. Thus, the reasoning can help you craft arguments and predict outcomes. When studying the precedent cases, think about how the facts and rationale support, and also how they undermine, your client's arguments.

When you are looking for analogous cases, try to find cases that show both sides of the issue you are researching. For example, John King was

---

10. One caveat here: Just because the language of a rule seems straightforward to you, do not assume that it means the same thing in the legal world as it does in lay terms. Reading cases applying the rule may reveal that a court has broadened or narrowed the meaning of the word from the meaning with which you are familiar.

discharged by his employer. After he filed for unemployment benefits, a deputy from the Unemployment Insurance Commission disqualified John from unemployment benefits, finding that John had been discharged for misconduct. Under the state's unemployment statute, individuals discharged for misconduct are disqualified from receiving unemployment benefits. John wants to challenge the deputy's decision and comes to you for an opinion on the likelihood that he will succeed.

The statute defines misconduct as "a culpable breach of the employee's duties . . . or a pattern of irresponsible behavior, which in either case manifests a disregard for a material interest of the employer," 26 M.R.S.A. § 1043(23) (Supp. 2002); however, you will likely want to find some specific examples of the types of actions that constitute misconduct by looking at previously decided cases. In one case, the actions of a waitress did not constitute misconduct when she was discharged for violating a company rule by talking too much with customers. *Moore v. Me. Empl. Sec. Commn.*, 388 A.2d 516, 519 (Me. 1978). The court reasoned that denying a discharged employee benefits on the basis of the "employer's subjective assessment" that the employee talked too much would be inconsistent with the statute, especially when her job called for interaction with customers. *Id.* In another case, a truck driver's single act of negligence did rise to the level of misconduct when the driver made an unsafe lane change, passing two vehicles without making sure they were visible in her rearview mirror before pulling back into their lane where she struck one of the vehicles. *Forbes-Lilly v. Me. Unempl. Ins. Commn.*, 643 A.2d 377, 379 (Me. 1994). The court reasoned that the driver's act, which caused significant personal injury and property damage and exposed her employer to liability, could have been avoided by following the company's reasonable driving policy and was the equivalent of an intentional violation of that policy. *Id.*

These analogous cases go both ways: In one, the court found misconduct; in the other, to did not. To prove that your client's actions did not constitute misconduct under the statute, you will have to show how his actions were more like those of the waitress who talked too much and not at all like those of the reckless truck driver.

Finally, explaining the policy behind the rule can provide the basis for a policy argument. Courts will often discuss the policy considerations behind a statutory rule by examining the legislative history of the rule. This provides the reader with an explanation of what the court thinks the legislative body intended when it drafted the statutory provision. Courts will also explain their own policy considerations when creating common law rules. Take note of the policy considerations when you read cases. Think about whether a favorable outcome in your client's case furthers or undermines the policy behind the rule.

For example, many states allow plaintiffs to seek punitive damage awards in their tort lawsuits. Punitive damage awards are monetary awards that go beyond compensating the plaintiff for his or her injury. States justify the use of punitive damage awards in torts cases because the awards further the policy of punishing wrongdoers while deterring future wrong-doing by others. *State Farm Mut. Automobile Ins. Co. v. Campbell*, 538 U.S. 408, 416 (2003). However, the United States Supreme Court has placed federal constitutional limits on punitive damage awards by holding that the amount of punitive damages that a jury awards cannot be arbitrary; the jury's discretion must be limited. *Id.* The policy underlying the Court's[11] holding was to provide defendants with adequate notice of potential sanctions (which they would not have if the awards were arbitrary), and to recognize that large punitive damage awards could force one state's policy choices onto other states. *Id.* Knowing the policy goals and concerns underlying punitive damage awards could be useful if you were arguing to reduce a punitive damage award for your client.

1.3.4. Application of the Rule to the Facts

As you learn about the rules and how those rules have been interpreted and applied in previous cases, you will need to be thinking about how what you are learning applies to the facts of your problem. When you apply the legal framework to the facts of your case, you need to consider how the rule applies to your case, how the facts of your case are similar to or different from previous cases, and how the underlying policy will be affected in your case.

For example, recall that your client John King was discharged for misconduct. You know that under the state's unemployment statute, individuals are disqualified from receiving unemployment benefits when they are discharged for misconduct, which the statute defines as "a culpable breach of the employee's duties . . . or a pattern of irresponsible behavior, which in either case manifests a disregard for a material interest of the employer." 26 M.R.S.A. § 1043(23). You also read two cases in which the court applied the statute, providing you with an understanding of what has and has not constituted misconduct in the past. Nevertheless, your understanding of the legal framework alone cannot answer the question of whether the Commission erred in concluding that John was discharged for misconduct.

---

11. You should always capitalize the "C" in Court when referring to the United States Supreme Court and when referring to the court for which you are writing in a court filing. You may also capitalize the "C" when referring to the highest court in your jurisdiction. Otherwise, you should not capitalize the "c" in "court" when simply referring to something a court has said or done unless you are using the full name of the Court—for example, "Kansas Court of Appeals."

To answer that question, you need to know what John did and apply your understanding of the legal framework to John's actions.

Assume that John tells you that he was a bus driver for a transportation company for two years. During his last five months of employment, he was involved in four accidents with stationary objects. The first two accidents occurred when he was on practice runs without passengers: In one, he hit a fire hydrant; in another, he hit a telephone pole. The third accident occurred when he was driving a small van while transporting elderly passengers. He backed out a driveway and hit and damaged a parked car. His supervisor warned him that because this accident was preventable, it was unacceptable to the company. Two months later, John was involved in his fourth accident when he was driving a medium-sized bus equipped with a wheelchair lift on the side. When he stopped to pick up some handicapped passengers, some of whom were in wheelchairs, he helped the wheel-chair-bound passengers onto the bus. John then returned to the driver's seat without closing the side door or retracting the wheelchair lift, which protruded more than three feet from the bus. When backing out of the driveway, he failed to use his side mirrors and, thus, did not see the lift sticking out from the side of the bus. He also did not notice the red warning light on the dashboard that would have informed him that a door was open. As John drove down the street, the lift hit the trunk and rear window of a car that was parked on the side of the street. The company concluded that this, too, was a preventable accident and discharged him, explaining that the two preventable accidents established that John had violated the company's driving policies.

Now that you know the facts, you need to consider whether John's actions fit the statutory definition of misconduct and think about whether the facts are similar to and different from the facts in the misconduct cases you read. Are his actions similar to the waitress, who was discharged for talking too much? Or are they more like the truck driver, who failed to look in her rearview mirror before pulling back into the lane after she passed two cars? Your job is to find a way, if possible, to argue that John's actions were more like the actions of the waitress. Sometimes, as in this case, that may not be possible, but it is your job to explore the possibilities, even if they seem remote.

1.3.5. Conclusion

The final component of legal analysis is the conclusion. What do you think the likely outcome will be, and why do you think so? Your conclusion should make sense based upon your analysis and your objective assessment of the strengths and weaknesses of your case. In reaching a conclusion, you must exercise your judgment. How certain you feel about your conclusion will differ from case to case. In cases where the facts of your case are very similar to facts analyzed under the same law in precedent cases, you can have a high degree of certainty that the outcome will fall in line with the precedent cases. If you have different facts, but an outcome in your favor advances the rationale underlying the legal rules, then you will still have confidence that the outcome will be in your client's favor. The conclusions become less certain the more you are asking a court to stray from its precedents or extend the law.

In the case of John King, you might conclude that the facts of his case are very similar to the facts of the case where the truck driver's failure to drive safely was an intentional violation of the company's driving policy. Thus, you could be confident in your prediction that a court would agree with the Commission that John was discharged for misconduct.

1.4. Presenting Your Analysis in Writing

1.4.1. Using Charts to Aid in Analysis

As you gather and read legal authorities through your research process, you may need a way to help you keep track of and synthesize the material you are finding. One useful method is to create a chart. If you have a rule with elements or factors, you can create a chart by element or by factor, and then keep track of the cases in which those elements or factors were explained further, or were or were not satisfied. For example, using the burglary statute discussed earlier, you could create a chart around the elements in the statute. Then, you could fill in the rule explanation and analogous cases as you find them in your research.

Statutory Elements	Rule Explanation from Cases or Statute	Facts of Analogous Cases
A person must enter or surreptitiously remain in a structure.		
The person must know that [s]he is not licensed to enter or remain at the time [s]he does so.		
The person must have an intent to commit a crime when [s]he entered or remained in the structure.		

Case Name	Misconduct	No Misconduct
Moore v. Me. Empl. Sec. Commn., 388 A.2d 516, 519 (Me. 1978)		Actions did not constitute misconduct when waitress was discharged for talking too much with customers. *Reasoning*: Discharge based on employer's subjective assessment that employee was talking too much was inconsistent with the statute, especially when her job called for interaction with customers.
Forbes-Lilley v. Me. Unempl. Ins. Commn., 643 A.2d 377, 379 (Me. 1994)	Truck driver's actions constituted misconduct when she made an unsafe lane change by passing two vehicles and failing to make sure they were visible in her rearview mirror before pulling back into their lane. *Reasoning*: The driver's act amounted to an intentional violation of the company's reasonable driving policy and exposed the company to liability.	

You can also chart the cases around specific issues. For example, when you were trying to determine what constituted misconduct in the unemployment statute, you could create a chart to keep track of the facts that did and did not constitute misconduct in previous cases.

A chart like this would help you keep track of the cases, particularly if you find many cases dealing with your issue. When you chart the cases like this, you can visualize any patterns or trends in the reasoning throughout the cases, and you can more easily see which cases will be most useful to you in your analysis of your issue.

1.4.2. Prewriting: The Outline

Before you start writing, you may find it useful to develop an annotated outline of your analysis so far. While charting can help you keep track of your research and your analysis, outlining is useful to get the large-scale organization of your document in place before you begin to write. You will likely find that it is much easier to move content around in an outline than in a complete draft of your analysis. Outlining will also help you see what you have found and learned so far and aid you in identifying any remaining gaps in your research or analysis. This can then help direct your future research efforts regarding the issues, or it may tell you that you need to spend more time reading and understanding the material you have already found in order to better understand the legal principles.

The outline does not need to be fancy. Because it is for your use only, you can make it as detailed and polished as you need it to be. The simplest way to create a useful outline is to number and identify each separate issue you have to address. Below each number, write "Rules" and then, below that, "Analogous Cases." As you go through the material you have found in your research and conduct your analysis of the material, dump what you are finding in the appropriate place in your outline. You need not even spend much time processing the information at this point or worrying about rewriting it. You might just quote the rules you are finding in the cases verbatim into your outline. Just remember to include quotation marks and full citations in your outline so that when you go to write the memo, you do not inadvertently think these are your own words.

1.4.3. How to Organize Your Legal Analysis

Most legal readers are accustomed to seeing the following organizational structure for presenting the components of a legal analysis in a logical way, although they will allow for a certain amount of variation in format: First, the reader expects to see a statement of the issue, or a conclusion about the issue, up front. Next, he or she will want to read about the relevant law, followed by an explanation of how that law has been interpreted and applied in previous cases in your jurisdiction or in other jurisdictions if there is a lack of precedent in your jurisdiction. The reader then expects to see an explanation of how the law and precedent apply to the facts in your case. Finally, he or she will want to read a prediction of how the issue will be resolved.

There are a variety of acronyms used to describe this system for organizing and presenting legal analysis. Some examples are IRAAC, CREAC, IRAC, and TREAC. Each letter in these acronyms stands for a component of legal analysis; the letters are then presented in the order in which the legal analysis should be organized. For example, IRAAC stands for **I**ssue, **R**ules, **A**nalogous **C**ases, **A**pplication of the Rules, **C**onclusion; CREAC stands for **C**onclusion, **R**ules, **R**ule **E**xplanation, **A**pplication of the Rules, **C**onclusion; IRAC is similar to IRAAC, except the law and the explanation of the law get collapsed into section R (**R**ules and Rule Support); and TREAC stands for **T**hesis, **R**ules, Rule **E**xplanation, **A**pplication of the Rules, **C**onclusion. Regardless of which acronym you are accustomed to, they all require essentially the same thing: an explanation of the law, followed by further explanation of how that law has been previously interpreted and applied, and an application of the law and precedent to the facts of your case. Once you understand the components of legal analysis, you will be able to adapt how you arrange those components to fit any of these organizational systems. The biggest difference among these systems is that some start by stating the issue as a question, while others start by stating a conclusion about the issue. This is not usually a big adjustment to make; it simply requires restating your issue as a conclusion or assertion about your issue.

To illustrate, the components of the IRAAC system are identified in the example below. The example demonstrates the written presentation of the legal analysis for one issue. That issue is whether police officers had a right to enter a home without a warrant when, while responding to a noise complaint at the home, police officers saw teenagers rushing around, clearing bottles off a table, and a young woman dropping to the floor, and the teenager who answered the door told them that underage drinking was occurring in the home.

I (Issue): The issue is whether police officers had probable cause and exigent circumstances to enter a home without a warrant.

R (Rules): The Fourth Amendment provides that the "right of the people to be secure in their . . . houses . . . against unreasonable searches . . . shall not be violated," U.S. Const. amend. IV, and imposes a warrant requirement "on agents of the government who seek to enter the home for the purposes of search or arrest," *Welsh v. Wisc.*, 466 U.S. 740, 748 (1984). Searches conducted inside a home without a warrant are presumptively unreasonable. *Id.* at 749. Nevertheless, a warrant is not required when law enforcement needs are so compelling that a warrantless search becomes objectively reasonable under the Fourth Amendment. *Brigham City v. Stuart*, 547 U.S. 398, 403 (2006). Such a warrantless search is objectively reasonable only if "(1) it is supported by probable cause; and (2) exigent circumstances exist requiring a prompt search, without the delay occasioned by the need for a warrant." *State v. Bilynsky*, 2007 ME 107, ¶ 17, 932 A.2d 1169. The State bears the burden of establishing an exception to the warrant requirement by proving probable cause and exigent circumstances. *Welsh*, 466 U.S. at 749-50.

A search is supported by probable cause when police officers' personal knowledge of facts and circumstances, combined with any other reasonably trustworthy information they acquire, would lead a reasonably prudent person to conclude that a crime had taken place. *Bilynsky*, 2007 ME 107, ¶ 18, 932 A.2d 1169. "Exigent circumstances exist when there is a compelling need to conduct a search and insufficient time in which to secure a warrant." *Id.* ¶ 26. Examples of exigent circumstances include the risk of imminent serious bodily injury to a person, *id.* ¶ 2, or the risk of imminent destruction of evidence, *Stuart*, 547 U.S. at 403. The exigent circumstances exception, however, rarely applies when there was "probable cause to believe that only a minor offense . . . had been committed." *Welsh*, 466 U.S. at 753.

A (Analogous Cases): Applying these principles, the Supreme Court held that a warrantless entry into a home did not violate the Fourth Amendment when police officers, responding to a noise complaint, saw juveniles drinking beer in the yard, and, through a window, a juvenile punch an adult in the face, causing him to spit blood in the sink. *Stuart*, 547 U.S. at 406-407. The Court reasoned that the police had an objectively reasonable basis for believing that an occupant was seriously injured or imminently threatened with such injury. *Id.* at 406. Distinguishing *Welsh*, 466 U.S. at 753, in which the only exigency was the need to preserve evidence of a misdemeanor crime, the Court concluded that the officers in *Stuart*, 547 U.S. at 405, "were confronted with ongoing violence occurring within the home," and, thus, their warrantless entry was reasonable.

In *Welsh*, the Supreme Court came to the opposite conclusion, based on the lack of gravity of the crime that had been committed, a civil traffic offense. 466 U.S. at 754. Similarly, the Illinois Appellate Court did not recognize an exception justifying officers' warrantless entry into a home, when they observed minors drinking alcohol inside and running around. *Ill. v. Eden*, 615 N.E. 2d 1224, 1225 (Ill. App. 4th Dist. 1993). Although probable cause existed that a misdemeanor crime was taking place, *id.* at 1228-29, and evidence might be destroyed, *id.*, the court concluded that one officer could have easily obtained a warrant while other officers secured the premises, *id.* at 1230. *See also Pa. v. Roland*, 637 A.2d 269, 271 (Pa. 1994) (holding that underage drinking was not a grave or dangerous enough offense to justify a warrantless search and that the risk of evidence being destroyed was negligible where evidence consisted of beer cans).

A (Application): The defendant, Tyler Blackburn, can argue that the officers did not have probable cause to enter his home because they merely saw bottles being cleared and offered no evidence that alcohol was consumed by minors. Furthermore, Blackburn can assert that, as in *Welsh*, *Eden*, and *Roland*, even if probable existed, no one was in imminent harm from a violent crime, and the risk of evidence being destroyed was negligible; as in *Eden*, the home could have easily been secured while one of the officers obtained a search warrant.

The State, however, can argue that probable cause did exist and exigent circumstances did justify the search because evidence was potentially being destroyed and public safety appeared threatened. The State can point to evidence of teenagers clearing bottles from a table and a young woman dropping to the floor to support its claims, indicating the potential for further injury, as in *Stuart*. Furthermore, Blackburn admitted that underage drinking was occurring in the home. The State can distinguish *Welch*, which, unlike the present case, involved an already completed traffic offense that Wisconsin classified as non-criminal, with no potential destruction of evidence. Citing legislative history, the State can contend that the crime of furnishing alcohol to minors, which the Maine Legislature considers serious, was on-going, and the potential for destruction of evidence was great.

C (Conclusion): A court would likely conclude that the police officers had probable cause that underage drinking was occurring in the home because Blackburn admitted as much to them. Further, a court would likely conclude that exigent circumstances justified the warrantless search because of the potential for the destruction of the evidence of the underage drinking.

1.4.4. Writing Tips for Certain Sections of the IRAAC

A. Writing About the Rules

When you are writing about the legal rules, you need to do the analytical work for your reader; do not make the reader do the heavy lifting of figuring out what the rules mean, how they fit together, and how they work. Therefore, do not just plop down on the paper a bunch of rules in quotation marks that fail to show the relationship between the rules to your reader. Try to focus your reader on the key language in a rule by quoting only that language verbatim. It is important for the reader to know when you are using a court's own words. When a writer quotes judiciously, the reader is drawn to the key language and its significance becomes more apparent. Do not just copy and paste blocks of text. Your job is to process the information and focus the reader on the key to understanding the issue and the relevant law. When you copy and paste blocks of text, you put the burden on your reader to process the information and figure out what is important, which makes reading the document more work for your reader. Refer to Chapter 7 on quotations before you sit down to write your document.

For example, consider the following explanations of the statute of limitations for bringing a claim under Maine's Workers' Compensation Act. In the first explanation, the writer has copied and pasted sections of the statute and plopped them into the memo in no particular order and without helping the reader to see the relationship among the sections of the statute.

In the second, the writer has thought about the statute and what it means and has explained how the sections all work together.

Explanation of the Law Where Writer Has Simply Copied and Pasted Sections of the Statute:

Section 306 of the Maine Workers' Compensation Act provides: "Except as provided in this section, a petition brought under this Act is barred unless filed within 2 years after the date of injury or the date the employee's employer files a required first report of injury if required in section 303, whichever is later." 39-A M.R.S. § 306(1) (Supp. 2013). "If an employer or insurer pays benefits under this Act, with or without prejudice, within the period provided in subsection 1, the period during which an employee or other interested party must file a petition is 6 years from the date of the most recent payment." *Id.* § 306(2). Section 303 explains when an employer has to file a report of injury:

> When any employee has reported to an employer under this Act any injury arising out of and in the course of the employee's employment that has caused the employee to lose a day's work, or when the employer has knowledge of any such injury, the employer shall report the injury to the board within 7 days after the employer receives notice or has knowledge of the injury. The employer shall also report the average weekly wages or earnings of the employee, as defined in section 102, subsection 4, together with any other information required by the board, within 30 days after the employer receives notice or has knowledge of a claim for compensation under section 212, 213 or 215, unless a wage statement has previously been filed with the board. A copy of the wage information must be mailed to the employee. The employer shall report when the injured employee resumes the employee's employment and the amount of the employee's wages or earnings at that time. The employer shall complete a first report of injury form for any injury that has required the services of a health care provider within 7 days after the employer receives notice or has knowledge of the injury. The employer shall provide a copy of the form to the injured employee and retain a copy for the employer's records but is not obligated to submit the form to the board unless the injury later causes the employee to lose a day's work. The employer is also required to submit the form to the board if the board has finally adopted a major substantive rule pursuant to Title 5, chapter 375, subchapter 2-A to require the form to be filed electronically.

Id. § 303. Section 304 talks about when the Workers' Compensation Board must give notice. It says: "Immediately upon receipt of the employer's report of injury required by section 303, the board shall contact the employee and provide information explaining the compensation system and the employee's rights. The board shall advise the employee how to contact the board for further assistance and shall provide that assistance."

Explanation of the Law Where Writer Has Processed the Information for the Reader, Uses Quotes Appropriately, and Shows the Relationship Among the Rules:

The Workers' Compensation Act sets forth two limitations periods for workers' compensation claims: First, a claim is "barred unless filed within 2 years after the date of injury or the date the . . . employer files a first report of injury as required in section 303, whichever is later." 39-A M.R.S.A. § 306(1) (Supp. 2013). According to section 303, an employer must file a first report of injury with the Board only when an employee misses one or more days of work because of the injury. 39-A M.R.S.A. § 303 (Supp. 2013). Once an employer files the first report, the Board is required to inform the employee of his rights under the compensation system. 39-A M.R.S.A. § 304(1) (2001). If an employee does not miss any days of work, but needs medical treatment, the employer must complete a first report and give a copy to the employee, but need not file the report with the Board until the employee misses work. *Id.* at § 303. Second, when an employer "pays benefits under this Act," which include an employee's medical payments for an injury, "within the period provided in subsection 1," the limitations period is extended to "6 years from the date of the most recent payment." *Id.* at § 306(2).

Notice how difficult it is to get through the first explanation. Notice that in the second explanation, the writer has considered how the rules relate to each other and has taken the time to explain those relationships to the reader. One technique for showing the relationship among the rules is to use the dovetailing technique. Dovetailing is when you repeat a term or phrase that you just used in the previous sentence. To use it to connect the rules, use a term or phrase from the previous rule as you are explaining the next rule. In addition, use transitional words or phrases to connect the rules when you are explaining them. If you use transitions and dovetailing techniques effectively, you will avoid having a disjointed, choppy explanation of the law. Refer to Chapter 7 for more detail on using dovetailing and transitions in your document.

B. *Writing About Analogous Cases*

When using analogous cases to make specific factual comparisons and distinctions, you need to explain the relevant facts of those cases in order to make your comparisons and distinctions meaningful. You also need to explain what the court held and why. When writing about the cases, then, you need to convey three things to your audience:

1. What did the court hold regarding your particular issue?
2. What were the legally significant facts of the case?
3. What was the court's reasoning?

You may find it helpful to use the following structure when describing analogous cases:

[Explain the relevant holding] when . . . [explain the legally significant facts in as many sentences as you need]. The court reasoned that . . . [explain the court's rationale in as many sentences as you need].

Additionally, as you write about analogous cases, use transitional words, phrases, or sentences to introduce each case. Try to avoid using the case name as a transition. The case name will be in the citation clause after the sentence and is not necessary as part of the text.

To demonstrate these concepts, consider the following examples. In a bench memo to the Maine Law Court, the issue was whether a defendant consented to a warrantless search of his computer. The analogous cases were used to show examples of the types of words or actions that constituted consent to a warrantless search.

In the first example, the case names are included in the text of the sentences as a way of providing transitions to the explanation of the analogous cases. The explanations also include unnecessary language, such as "this Court held." Finally, the explanations in the first example are not presented in a way that makes it easy for the reader to follow the three things that should be highlighted: the relevant holding regarding consent, the legally significant facts, and the court's rationale.

In the second example, stronger transitional phrases are used in place of the case names, and the unnecessary introductions are omitted, making the sentences less cluttered and more focused on the important concepts. In this example, the writer has also presented each case using a similar structure for each explanation:

A defendant consented to a warrantless search when . . . [explain what happened]. The [name of court] reasoned that . . . [explain any relevant reasoning].

Example 1

In *State v. Seamen's Club*, 1997 ME 70, ¶ 8, 691 A.2d 1248, this Court explained that a woman who was a cook at the defendant restaurant company told a police officer that she guessed she was in charge, and without protest, directed him to a lobster tank, turned on the lights and provided the officer with a container. This Court reasoned that from the woman's action's, the trial court could properly have inferred that she consented to the search, and so it held that the defendant restaurant consented to the warrantless search. *Id.* In *State v. Cress*, 576 A.2d 1366, 1367 (Me. 1999), this Court held that a defendant taxidermist who accompanied game wardens into his shop, and unlocked, opened, and emptied the freezers, consented to the warrantless search, even though he did not expressly consent to the search.

In *State v. Barlow*, 320 A.2d 895, 888-90 (Me. 1974), this Court reasoned that when an officer makes affirmative representations about his right to search without a warrant, "the defendant's consent to the search given in response to such false assertions must be regarded as the mere submission of a law-abiding citizen to an officer of the law and cannot be construed as a valid waiver of his constitutional rights against an unreasonable search and seizure." In that case, the police erroneously told the defendant that they had the right to search his vehicle without a warrant if they saw anything suspicious in the car. *Id.* The defendant believed that the officers had a right to search the vehicle when they told him they saw a bullet clip under the seat, and the defendant responded, "Well, okay, if that is the way it is." *Id.* This Court held that the defendant did not consent to the warrantless search. *Id.*

Example 2

For example, a defendant restaurant company consented to warrantless search when a woman who appeared to be a cook at the restaurant told the officer that she guessed she was in charge, and without protest, directed him to a lobster tank, turned on the lights and provided the officer with a container. *State v. Seamen's Club*, 1997 ME 70, ¶ 8, 691 A.2d 1248. This Court reasoned that from the woman's actions, the trial court could properly have inferred that she consented to the search. *Id.* Likewise, a defendant taxidermist consented to a warrantless search even though he did not expressly consent to the search, when he accompanied game wardens into his shop, and unlocked, opened, and emptied the freezers. *State v. Cress*, 576 A.2d 1366, 1367 (Me. 1990).

In contrast, a defendant did not consent to the warrantless search of his car when the police erroneously told the defendant that they had the right to search his vehicle without a warrant if they saw anything suspicious in the car, the defendant believed that the officers had a right to search the vehicle when they told him they saw a bullet clip under the seat, and the defendant responded, "Well, okay, if that is the way it is." *State v. Barlow*, 320 A.2d 895, 888-90 (Me. 1974). This Court reasoned that when an officer makes affirmative representations about his right to search without a warrant, "the defendant's consent to the search given in response to such false assertions must be regarded as the mere submission of a law-abiding citizen to an officer of the law and cannot be construed as a valid waiver of his constitutional rights against an unreasonable search and seizure." *Id.* at 900.

Always remember to include a citation, including pin cite, after each sentence in your analogous cases. Also, your explanations will generally be clearer to the reader if you explain what happened in the cases using generic terms, such as "defendant," instead of the parties' names from the cases because your reader will not be familiar with (nor does your reader need to be familiar with) the parties in the previous cases.

1.5. Reviewing Your Work

The first draft is never the last draft. As Justice Louis D. Brandeis once said, "There is no such thing as good writing. There is only good rewriting."[12] Always leave yourself plenty of time for editing and rewriting. The most effective editing will often require multiple drafts.

Your first review should focus on the organizational aspects of your legal analysis. One useful tool is to color-code the various components of your legal analysis to make sure you have included them all and presented them in a logical order using one of the organization systems, such as IRAAC and CREAC. First, print out a hard copy of your document. Then, highlight the components of each IRAAC (or CREAC) using the following code (or something similar).

Issue	Pink
Rules	Orange
Analogous Cases	Yellow
Application	Green
Conclusion	Blue

While coloring the draft may seem like a silly idea to you at first, many people find the visual aspect of color-coding their drafts extremely helpful. It should help you to immediately see whether you have left out any components or failed to organize them logically. Additionally, many lawyers who used color-coding in law school continue to use it when they are reading cases in practice.[13]

Once you are satisfied with the overall organization, spend some time reviewing paragraph and sentence structure. Refer to Chapter 7 on Effective Writing; in particular, review the concepts of transitions, sign

---

12. The exact source of this quote is unknown, but it has been widely used in books on writing.

13. To use this system of color-coding while reading cases, highlight any rules in the case in orange, analogous facts or reasoning in yellow, arguments in green, and the court's conclusion in blue. This creates a visual reminder (and visual case brief) of the case when you look at it again.

posts, and roadmaps. Those techniques are all useful in improving the paragraph structure in a document.

Finally, proofread your writing carefully. Proofreading is different from the editing and revising that you should have already done at the organizational, paragraph, and sentence level. Proofreading involves carefully checking your memo for errors. First, go through your memo checking for punctuation, grammar, and spelling mistakes. Keep track of any common grammar mistakes so you can consult a grammar guide to get clarity on the grammatical rule. You might try one of the following techniques for proofreading, each of which forces you to slow down and focus on each word you are reading: Read your memo aloud to yourself or someone else while following along with a pencil; use a ruler underneath each line you are reading; or read your memo backwards, sentence by sentence, focusing on the mechanics of each individual sentence, not the flow of ideas from one sentence to the next.

Next, proofread your citations. Do this separately from proofreading your memo because you are looking for different types of errors here. It might help to highlight all the citations before you begin to proofread them, forcing you to focus on the citations and not be distracted by the text.

Ethics Alert: Proofreading Errors

A United States District Court in Pennsylvania blasted a lawyer for making so many typographical errors in a fee petition, including these misspellings: "plaintf," "judgemnt," "shouold," "Philadehia," "attoreys," "reasonbale," "plainitff," "withint," "Ubited States," and "Bargining Agreemnt." He noted that the opening sentence of the fee petition featured "eleven errors, nine misspelled words, and two citation errors. After reducing attorney fees by $154,000, based on the lawyer's "slip-shod submissions," the court added this "Postscript": "A long time ago in a galaxy far, far away, each lawyer knew he and she could not nail any old slap-dash parchment to the church door and expect someone else to pay for it. Most lawyers who practice in this court also know that. They all should."

McKenna v. City of Philadelphia, 2008 WL 4435939 **1-2, 17 (E.D. Pa. Sept. 30, 2008).

Chapter 2

Researching Your Problem

2.1. Your First Assignment

You have landed your dream job, working as an associate at a small law firm in Portland, Maine. After lining up all your books on the shelves and hanging your law school diploma on the wall behind your desk, Ellen Walker, one of the partners at the firm, comes into your office to discuss your first assignment.

Ms. Walker tells you about a potential client, James Malloy, who has come to the firm to see whether he might be able to file a lawsuit against Maine General Hospital on behalf of his brother Jonah for a bad outcome following Jonah's knee surgery. James revealed that he was appointed Jonah's legal guardian following the surgery and that Jonah has been mentally disabled since birth. Before learning anything more about the case, however, Ms. Walker has asked you to perform a conflict check to determine whether the firm would be able to represent James and Jonah Malloy. If your conflict check reveals no conflicts of interest in representing James and Jonah, Ms. Walker wants you to interview them to learn more about what happened before, during, and after the surgery.

Then, following the interview, Ms. Walker would like you to write an objective memorandum of law analyzing the relevant law and how it applies to the facts you uncover in the interview to be used by the firm's partners to make strategic decisions about the case. The memo will also form the basis for the firm's communications with James and Jonah about the strengths and weaknesses of their case. It will include the arguments both your clients and the hospital may make, based on existing law, and predict an outcome.

A thoroughly researched and well-written memo provides an invaluable basis for decision-making about a case. A memo that is truly objective will lay out the strengths and weaknesses of a case, giving attorneys the necessary background for advising clients about whether to pursue a case in court or attempt to settle out of court. It can also be used to draft a multitude of other documents as the case unfolds, including letters to clients and opposing attorneys, motions to the trial court, and even briefs to an appellate court.

Lawyers use objective memos to report on their research regarding legal questions in many different employment settings, not only in law firms considering a client's chances of prevailing in a lawsuit. Lawyers must be able to explain the law accurately and clearly to other people, including senior partners, supervisors in an administrative agency, and clients. They must be able to predict how a court would likely rule on a particular legal question, based on the relevant law in their jurisdiction. Often, that law will be applied to a particular fact pattern in the memo, but sometimes a supervisor just wants an explanation of the law as it exists in a jurisdiction. In that case, the memo will merely provide an overview of the law with an explanation of how it has been applied in the past and would likely be applied in various factual situations in the future. It is important to know what your senior partner or supervisor needs before writing an objective memo.

Memos vary in length and format. You will need to discuss with Ms. Walker her preferences for format and length of the memo she has asked you to write before you begin. Before anything more happens, however, you must perform a conflict check to determine whether the firm can go any further with the case.

2.2. The Conflict Check

Before agreeing to represent a prospective client, lawyers must perform a conflict check to make certain no conflicts of interest exist regarding the representation. Eliminating the possibility of such conflicts is an important ethical obligation. Rule 1.7 of the American Bar Association Model Rules of Professional Responsibility states that a conflict of interest exists if representing one client will be adverse to another client. Thus, before accepting a new client, lawyers must check carefully to determine whether agreeing to represent a prospective client would be adverse to any other clients the firm is currently representing or may have represented in the past.

In this case, because James may be filing a lawsuit against Maine General Hospital on Jonah's behalf, you will need to research whether the hospital has ever been a client of your firm. If it has, it is unlikely that the firm will be able to represent Jonah in a lawsuit opposing the hospital as that would surely be a situation in which representing one client—Jonah—would be adverse to another client—Maine General Hospital. After thoroughly researching the law firm's records and learning that the firm has never represented Maine General Hospital, you are now ready to find out more about what happened to Jonah and determine the prospects of his prevailing in a suit against the hospital.

2.3. The Client Interview

In an interview with James and Jonah, you learn that Jonah, who is 30 years old, was born with an intellectual disability that has prevented him from learning to read beyond a third-grade level. He is able to shower, shave, dress himself, and prepare simple meals, but cannot perform any complex intellectual tasks, like balancing a checkbook. Nevertheless, before his knee surgery, Jonah was an outstanding athlete who regularly competed in Special Olympics competitions, often coming home with numerous gold and silver medals. He was able to live in a group home with other men like him, and he was happy with his life, especially his job as a janitor at a nearby daycare center, where he enjoyed interacting with the children while performing his maintenance and cleaning responsibilities.

During the fall of 2008, Jonah injured his knee when he tripped on a tree root while running along a rustic, cross-country trail. His doctor referred him to an orthopedic specialist when Jonah did not experience any relief from prescription medication or physical therapy. After examining Jonah and performing an MRI and CT scan, the orthopedist recommended that Jonah undergo surgery to repair a small tear in his meniscus. On February 4, 2009, Jonah underwent the surgery under local anesthesia in the outpatient surgical unit of Maine General Hospital. Although the doctor thought the surgery was successful, a few days later, Jonah's knee began to swell, and he experienced excruciating pain. After Jonah was admitted to the hospital the next day, the doctors discovered that he had contracted a virulent bacterial infection, presumably during the surgery, requiring his leg to be amputated above the knee in order to save his life.

Following the amputation, Jonah went into a deep depression and could no longer live in the group home or work at the daycare center even though he was fitted with a prosthetic leg, which allowed him to walk and, eventually, it is hoped, to run. Jonah moved in with his brother, James, who was declared Jonah's legal guardian on March 15, 2009.

James has come to us, asking whether Jonah can sue the hospital for inadequate care, leading to his bacterial infection and subsequent problems. He and Jonah are upset about the way the surgery turned out and want to take their case to court. James would like to sue the hospital for enough money to ensure that Jonah will be financially secure throughout his lifetime. He and Jonah also said they wanted to "punish" the hospital for the bad care Jonah received, hoping their lawsuit would force the hospital to be more careful in the future. They do not want anything like this to ever happen again.

2.4. Assessing the Situation

After your interview with James and Jonah, you need to assess the situation they described and determine whether legal representation is appropriate and likely to be helpful. Some situations are more conducive to informal resolution rather than legal intervention. In such situations, getting lawyers involved might even create more problems, especially if emotions are running high. Furthermore, some kinds of problems exist for which there are no legal solutions—just human ones that involve communication, understanding, and compassion.

After thinking it over and perhaps conducting some preliminary research, you have concluded that the damage done to Jonah's leg probably does lend itself to a legal resolution. James has come to the firm asking whether the hospital can be sued, so it is clear that he is interested in litigating the matter, at least at the present time. Before answering James's question, however, you will need to conduct further research, both to determine whether it is possible for Jonah to sue the hospital and also, if that is possible, whether filing a lawsuit would be the best course of action to take, based on the strengths and weaknesses of the case. Once you have a clearer understanding of the strength of the case, you can discuss various options with James and Jonah, including the possibility of negotiating a financial settlement with the hospital.

Your first step would be to determine the jurisdiction in which the case would be tried, should you end up taking it to court. You need to consider whether the facts of the case implicate state or federal law, and whether a constitution, statute, or common law would determine the outcome. Because the case involves medical malpractice, an area governed by state law, you begin your research by turning to Maine statutes and cases.

2.5. Finding Relevant Legal Authority

Your first job will be to refine the legal issue to ensure that you are focusing on the proper question. One important consideration will be whether any preliminary procedural questions exist that must be answered before addressing the merits of the actual medical malpractice claim.

2.5.1. Preliminary Procedural Question: Statute of Limitations

Before researching the merits of any claim, it is essential to determine what the "statute of limitations" is for such a claim. A statute of limitations is a law placing a time limit on bringing a claim for wrongful conduct. Statutes of limitations serve the purpose of promoting justice by avoiding unnecessary delay, preventing the litigation of stale claims, and providing finality so people and institutions can move on without potential law suits hanging over their heads. Under statutes of limitations, injured parties have the responsibility to bring claims within a reasonable length of time.

Various statutes of limitations exist for different claims. In Maine, for example, the statute of limitations for fraud is six years while it is only two years for defamation. If a claim is brought after the statute of limitations period expires, or has "run," the court will reject the claim as "untimely." Thus, as eager as you are to get into the specifics of the medical malpractice claim, which sounds much more interesting than a dry procedural question, you must find out what the statute of limitations is for medical malpractice claims in Maine and determine whether the time limit has already expired for Jonah's claim.

2.5.2. Statutory Research

In addition to finding out what the statute of limitations is for any claims your client may be considering, you should also begin your legal research by locating any other statutes that are relevant to those claims. If you are unfamiliar with an area of law, you might decide to do some background reading in secondary sources to refine understanding of the issues before looking for statutes, but you should always make it a practice to check for relevant statutes early in your research process.

The best way to find the statute of limitations for medical malpractice claims is to look first to see whether there is a statute governing medical malpractice claims in general. You will need to consult that statute, if it exists, when researching the merits of the malpractice claim anyway, so it makes sense to look for that statute first.

Maine statutes are published in two places, Maine Revised Statutes Annotated and Maine Revised Statutes. Both of these statutory compilations can be found electronically and in hard copy. An annotated code, like Maine Revised Statutes Annotated, not only includes the text of the statute, which is primary authority, but also provides citations to other primary authority such as relevant cases and references to secondary resources that explain the law: historical notes, law review and journal articles, and commentaries in legal encyclopedias and treatises. These secondary sources often prove to be efficient and effective research tools. An annotated code is frequently updated with statutory changes. In hard copy volumes, these updates are contained in a pamphlet, called a "pocket part" or supplement, slipped into the back of the volume.

To find the right statute, you must look in the index, which is organized alphabetically by subject. You may also look in the Popular Name Table if the statute you need is most commonly known by the name of the act of which it is a part, like the Workers' Compensation Act.

You begin by identifying some search terms to look for in the index, shown in Illustration 2-1. "Medical malpractice," "physicians and surgeons," and "statute of limitations" seem promising, so you begin by consulting the index for those search terms. Under "M" in the index, you find a reference to "Malpractice," which directs you to "Physicians and Surgeons" and the "Health Security Act," also to be found in the Index. Looking under "H," you find a reference to the Health Security Act, which can be found in Title 24 of the Maine Revised Statutes Annotated, beginning with section 2501. Looking under the sub-heading "Medical malpractice," you find a reference to "Limitation of actions," to be found in section 2902.

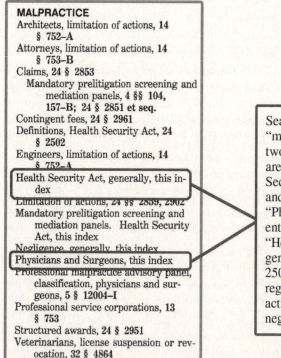

MALPRACTICE
Architects, limitation of actions, 14
§ 752–A
Attorneys, limitation of actions, 14
§ 753–B
Claims, 24 § 2853
Mandatory prelitigation screening and mediation panels, 4 §§ 104, 157–B; 24 § 2851 et seq.
Contingent fees, 24 § 2961
Definitions, Health Security Act, 24 § 2502
Engineers, limitation of actions, 14 § 752–A
Health Security Act, generally, this index
Limitation of actions, 24 §§ 2859, 2902
Mandatory prelitigation screening and mediation panels.   Health Security Act, this index
Negligence, generally, this index
Physicians and Surgeons, this index
Professional malpractice advisory panel, classification, physicians and surgeons, 5 § 12004–I
Professional service corporations, 13 § 753
Structured awards, 24 § 2951
Veterinarians, license suspension or revocation, 32 § 4864

Searching for the term "malpractice" in the index, two relevant cross-references are found: "The Health Security Act" and "Physicians and Surgeons." Going to the "Physicians and Surgeons" entry directs the researcher to "Health Security Act," generally found at 24 MRSA 2501, and to 24 MRSA 2902 regarding the limitations of actions for professional negligence.

Illustration 2-1: Index for Maine Revised Statutes Annotated

Next, you locate the Health Security Act in the main volume of the Maine Revised Statutes Annotated containing Title 24. Turning to section 2902 (shown in Illustration 2-2), you find that the statute of limitations for "actions for professional negligence" against health care providers and practitioners is three years "after the cause of action accrues. For the purposes of this section, a cause of action accrues on the date of the act or omission giving rise to the injury." After consulting the pocket part and determining that the legislature has not amended this statute, you now know that the statute of limitations for Jonah's claim is three years.

Immediately, you go back to the notes of your meeting with James and Jonah and, to your dismay, you realize that Jonah's injury occurred on February 4, 2009, more than three years ago. You are about to phone James to tell him the bad news when you begin thinking about Jonah and his limited mental capacity, wondering if his disability might create some sort of exception to the rule, perhaps waiving the three-year statute of limitations or giving him some additional time to file a lawsuit.

You go back to the statute book and begin looking to see whether the legislature has recognized the unfairness of expecting someone with limited intellectual ability to file a lawsuit within the same time period as other individuals. Rather than looking in the index for statutes about medical malpractice claims, however, this time you look for anything related to statutes of limitations in general. After some digging, you discover Chapter 205, which deals with "Limitation of Actions," another way to

---

§ 2902. Statute of limitations for health care providers and health care practitioners

Actions for professional negligence shall be commenced within 3 years after the cause of action accrues. For the purposes of this section, a cause of action accrues on the date of the act or omission giving rise to the injury. Notwithstanding the provisions of Title 14, section 853, relating to minority, actions for professional negligence by a minor shall be commenced within 6 years after the cause of action accrues or within 3 years after the minor reaches the age of majority, whichever first occurs. This section does not apply where the cause of action is based upon the leaving of a foreign object in the body, in which case the cause of action shall accrue when the plaintiff discovers or reasonably should have discovered the harm. For the purposes of this section, the term "foreign object" does not include a chemical compound, prosthetic aid or object intentionally implanted or permitted to remain in the patient's body as a part of the health care or professional services.

If the provision in this section reducing the time allowed for a minor to bring a claim is found to be void or otherwise invalidated by a court of proper jurisdiction, then the statute of limitations for professional negligence shall be 2 years after the cause of action accrues, except that no claim brought under the 3-year statute may be extinguished by the operation of this paragraph.

1977, c. 492, § 3; 1985, c. 804, § 13, eff. Aug. 1, 1988.

Illustration 2-2: 24 Me. Rev. Stat. Ann. § 2902

> **§ 853.   Persons under disability may bring action when disability removed**
>
> If a person entitled to bring any of the actions under sections 752 to 754, including section 752–C, and under sections 851, 852 and Title 24, section 2902 is a minor, mentally ill, imprisoned or without the limits of the United States when the cause of action accrues, the action may be brought within the times limited herein after the disability is removed.
>
> R.S.1954, c. 112, § 97; 1959, c. 242, § 8; 1959, c. 317, § 148; 1977, c. 492, § 2; 1985, c. 343, § 2.

Illustration 2-3: 14 Me. Rev. Stat. Ann. § 853

phrase "statutes of limitations." Within that chapter, you find section 853 of Title 14 of Maine Revised Statutes Annotated (see Illustration 2-3), which states that people who are "mentally ill" when "the cause of action accrues" may wait until "the disability is removed" before filing a claim. Such a statute, called a "tolling provision," essentially stops the clock from running on the limitations period for a person who is "mentally ill" until he no longer has that disabling condition, as long as he was "mentally ill" at the time the alleged injury occurred.

2.5.3. Refining the Issues

Although you are encouraged to discover that the door may not yet have closed on Jonah's claim, you do not know yet whether Jonah's limited intellectual ability actually qualifies him as "mentally ill." You must also be certain that Jonah was mentally ill, whatever that means, at the time of his surgery, when the cause of action accrued. Finally, you are wondering whether it makes any difference that James became Jonah's guardian within the three-year period after the surgery. Perhaps the tolling provision does not apply if someone is being cared for by a guardian who could presumably have filed a suit on his behalf within the limitations period. You will need to address all these issues before telling James and Jonah whether Jonah's lawsuit may proceed.

The issues are beginning to come into focus now. The statute of limitations will be tolled if you can show that Jonah was mentally ill at the time of his surgery and that it does not matter that James became his guardian shortly thereafter. Thus, you will need to address two issues.

Under the tolling provision, (1) was Jonah mentally ill at the time the cause of action accrued and (2) does the tolling provision still apply if Jonah was under the care of a guardian during the limitations period? The first issue includes two sub-issues: (a) Does Jonah's limited intellectual ability classify him as mentally ill and (b) if so, did he have this condition at the time the cause of action accrued? To answer these questions, you will need to gain a firm grasp of this area of the law in general and locate Maine cases, and perhaps cases from other jurisdictions, that determine what it means to be mentally ill for purposes of the statute of limitations, what it means to have this condition when a cause of action accrues, and whether the appointment of a guardian makes the tolling provision inapplicable.

2.5.4. Continuing Your Research

Before continuing your research, take stock of where you are right now, what you have already discovered and what you still need to find out. Here are the preliminary questions you need to answer:

1. What area of the law is involved?
2. What is your jurisdiction? State law or federal law?
3. What law controls the outcome? Statute, regulation, or common law?

So far, you have learned (1) that you must research the law regarding statutes of limitation, specifically tolling provisions involving "mental illness" and the effect of such provisions on the appointment of a guardian; (2) that your jurisdiction is Maine and your questions will be governed by state law; and (3) that a Maine statute will control the outcome, along with cases in which the statute has been interpreted.

After that, you may want to take some time to evaluate your client's situation. Consult your notes from your interview with James and Jonah to answer the following questions:

1. Who are all the parties and things involved?
2. Where and when did the significant event(s) occur?
3. What facts do you think may be helpful to Jonah's case?
4. What facts do you think will be less helpful and perhaps irrelevant?
5. What does each party want in order to resolve the situation?
6. What outcome would seem most fair to you?
7. If you were the judge, how would you resolve this situation?

Next, you will want to begin a research log, recording the time spent, resources used, terms of art, search queries, citations to relevant materials, and whether the cases you have uncovered are still good law. You will need this research log both to document how many hours to bill your client and also to record steps you have already taken so you do not end up covering the same ground more than once, wasting time and money. Your research log might take a very simple form, like the following spreadsheet[1]:

Research step taken	How useful was it? Why?	Source(s) discovered	How useful? Why?

When listing resources you have consulted, be sure to include the full name and a proper legal citation to each resource, whether it is a case, a statute, or a secondary source. Always include the exact page, section, or paragraph you have consulted. Do not just put the overall title of the case, statute, or article. As explained earlier, the exact page, section, or paragraph is called a "pin cite." Including pin cites in legal citation is absolutely critical. The pin cite tells you or, later, the reader of your memo how to locate the referenced content and will avoid unnecessary aggravation later on. Finally, be sure to indicate that you are writing a direct quote, not paraphrasing, every time you write down the words exactly as they appear in a document or copy and paste a block of text from an electronic source. Always use quotation marks to identify direct quotes in your notes. Otherwise, you may forget that those words were not your own later when including them in your memo, which will result in plagiarism, even if that plagiarism was unintentional. Furthermore, enclosing important words and concepts in quotation marks shows that what you are saying comes from a respected authority, such as a court or law review article, infusing those words with more credibility and persuasiveness than if you had been the author.

Going back to Jonah's claim, because you have never had a case like this before, you decide to begin your research by consulting secondary sources to gain an understanding of the reasons for the tolling provision and what the legislature had in mind when creating this exception to the statute of limitations. You also want to find out what the term "mental illness" generally signifies in legal terms, what it means for a cause of action to accrue, and what effect having a guardian has on his ward's legal rights.

---

1. Thanks to Sue Liemer, Professor of Law and Director of Lawyering Skills at Southern Illinois University School of Law, for this simple, yet effective research log template.

2.6. Using Secondary Sources

2.6.1. Legal Dictionaries and Other Reference Books

Legal dictionaries and thesauruses can be helpful in defining terms and leading you to relevant case law. *Black's Law Dictionary* has been used by law students and practicing attorneys for decades. Available in hard copy or electronically on Westlaw, consulting such a dictionary can be a quick way to immerse yourself in a legal issue.

For example, when you look up "statute of limitations" in *Black's Law Dictionary*,[2] you find the following definition: "a statute establishing a time limit for suing in a civil case, based on the date when the claim accrued (as when the injury occurred or was discovered). The purpose of such a statute is to require diligent prosecution of known claims, thereby providing finality and predictability in legal affairs and ensuring that claims will be resolved while evidence is reasonably available and fresh." This definition both explains the meaning of the concept and provides an explanation of the rationale for enacting statutes of limitation.

Turning to the definition for "tolling statute," you find that it is a "law that interrupts the running of a statute of limitations in certain situations, as when the defendant cannot be served with process in the forum jurisdiction."[3] Although the dictionary does not list "mental illness" as one of the situations in which the running of the statute of limitations would be interrupted, when you look up "mental illness," you find the following definition: "A disorder in thought or mood so substantial that it impairs judgment, behavior, perceptions of reality, or the ability to cope with the ordinary demands of life."[4] That definition begins to give you an idea of what the Maine legislature might have intended when it enacted the tolling provision. It might have intended to suspend the statute of limitations for people whose mental problems impair their judgment or make it difficult for them "to cope with the ordinary demands of life."

Thus, simply consulting a legal dictionary has given you the first clue about how the tolling provision might apply to Jonah. Although you may have thought initially that the words "mental illness" meant something more like schizophrenia or bi-polar disorder, you can now see that having a mental problem that makes it more difficult to make judgments or to cope

---

2. *Black's Law Dictionary* 1546 (9th ed., 2009). Although *Black's Law Dictionary* is widely known, other excellent law dictionaries exist, such as *The Wolters Kluwer Bouvier Law Dictionary* (Stephen Michael Sheppard gen. ed., Wolters Kluwer Law & Business 2012). This two-volume law dictionary provides extensive coverage of many legal terms and concepts.

3. *Id.* at 1625.

4. *Id.* at 1075.

with the ordinary demands of life can also be seen as a form of mental illness in the legal sense. Applying this definition, you begin to form an argument in your mind that Jonah was mentally ill at the time of his surgery, based on his limited ability to cope with the ordinary demands of life at that time. Perhaps, because of his limited intellectual ability, he also had impaired judgment.

Other legal dictionaries are available in hard copy and on line, including *Ballantine's Law Dictionary* (available on LexisNexis), *The Law Guide* (TheLaw.com), *The Wolters Kluwer Bouvier Law Dictionary* (available through a mobile app), and *Nolo Plain English Law Dictionary.*

Legal thesauruses can also be helpful at all stages of the research and writing process. *Burton's Legal Thesaurus*[5] provides synonyms, definitions, parts of speech, associated legal concepts, foreign phrases, and translations. When you look up the word "toll,"[6] you find entries for four different meanings of the word. Two entries are for nouns meaning "effect" and "tax." The other two entries are for verbs meaning "exact payment" and "stop." From what you have already read, you know that the entry for the verb meaning "stop" is the one that relates to Maine's tolling provision. Here is what the entry provides: "TOLL (Stop), verb: arrest, block, check, cut off, embar, estop, frustrate, halt, hinder, hold back, impede, inhibit, interrupt, limit, obstruct, put a stop to, restrain, restrict, stay, suspend, thwart. ASSOCIATED CONCEPTS: toll a statute of limitations." Seeing all the different meanings of toll as well as the synonyms for the meaning of "toll" that relate to the tolling provision helps you to grasp what it means to toll the statute of limitations.

A Dictionary of Modern Legal Usage, by Bryan A. Garner,[7] provides guidance on all sorts of questions legal writer face, such as distinguishing between similar but distinct legal terms, identifying and avoiding "legalese," correcting grammatical errors, and framing legal issues. When you look up "statute of limitations,"[8] you find a reference to the related term "repose." Turning to the entry on "repose,"[9] you learn that a statute of repose "sets up a legal defense" that differs from a statute of limitations because it "bars a suit a fixed number of years after the defendant acts in some way (as by manufacturing a product), whereas *limitation* bars an action if the plaintiff does not file suit within a set period of time from the date when the cause of action accrues."[10] Now you will know the difference between a statute of repose and a statute of limitations as you

---

5. *Burton's Legal Thesaurus* (3d ed., Mc-Graw Hill 1998).
6. *Id.* at 513.
7. Bryan A. Garner, *A Dictionary of Modern Legal Usage* (2d ed., Oxford University Press 1995)
8. *Id.* at 831.
9. *Id.* at 759.
10. *Id.* at 530.

Ethics Alert: Excessive Redundancy, Verbosity, and Legalese

A United States District Court in Florida admonished an attorney for submitting a motion that exceeded the page limit of 25 pages, by crossing out sections and changing words in the introduction to the motion, demonstrating how the motion might have been improved. The court asserted that "a modicum of informed editorial revision easily reduces the motion to twenty-five pages without a reduction in substance." Later in the opinion, the court gave the attorney an additional week to submit more concise motion, instructing the attorney to concentrate on the "elimination of redundancy, verbosity, and legalism."

Belli v. Hedden Enterprises, Inc., 2012 WL 3255086 at **1-2 (M.D. Fla. Aug. 7, 2012).

look for cases in which the Maine statute of limitations has been interpreted.

Flipping through the book, you encounter the entry for "legalese"[11] and learn that it should be avoided. This discovery surprises you because you thought you had attended law school, in part, to learn how to speak legal language. You find out, however, that legalese, rather than being the language of the law, is "a scourge of the profession," with its "verbocity," "endless tautologies," and "saids and aforesaids." According to Garner, even Thomas Jefferson railed against lawyers' attempts to use legalese to make statutes "more plain," which ended up rendering them "more perplexed and incomprehensible, not only to common readers, but to the lawyers themselves."[12] Based on this entry, you begin to understand the value of using plain English to explain legal concepts, even complicated ones, not only to clients, but even to judges and other lawyers.

Bieber's Dictionary of Legal Abbreviations, which is available on LexisNexis, provides the meaning of legal abbreviations. Because you do not need to look up the meaning of any legal abbreviations at this point, you move on to other secondary sources.

---

11. *Id.* at 516.
12. *Id.*

2.6.2. Legal Encyclopedias

Legal encyclopedias are large, multi-volume sets containing information on every area of law. Like any encyclopedia, a legal encyclopedia provides an introduction and overview of particular areas of law, but legal encyclopedias offer something else that is equally important to the legal researcher: lists of citations to relevant primary sources, including all landmark cases, organized by jurisdiction, and citations to other useful secondary sources. There are three types of legal encyclopedias: (1) national (or general) encyclopedias, specifically *American Jurisprudence, Second Edition* (called "AmJur"), and *Corpus Juris Secundum* (called "CJS"); state encyclopedias; and subject-specific encyclopedias, like *Moore's Federal Practice* and *Federal Practice and Procedure* by Wright and Miller.

AmJur and CJS, which report national trends on legal topics, are both arranged alphabetically by topic and use a general index for the set as a whole, as well as individual indexes for each topic. The print versions are both updated by pocket parts. CJS, however, focuses more on case law and provides cross references to West Key Numbers, a system for finding cases on particular topics of law, while AmJur focuses more on federal statutes and regulations. AmJur features a Table of Statutes and Rules Cited for the set and for each volume. The most recent volumes of AmJur have references to West Key Numbers. Other publications associated with AmJur include *American Jurisprudence Forms*, *American Jurisprudence Proof of Facts*, *American Jurisprudence Trials*, and *American Jurisprudence Pleading & Practice*.

Many states have their own encyclopedias, such as *New York Jurisprudence, Maryland Law Encyclopedia, Michigan Law and Practice*, and *California Jurisprudence*. State encyclopedias follow the format of the national encyclopedias, providing an overview of areas of law, focusing on state distinctions, cases, statutes, and state-specific secondary sources.

In researching Jonah's claim, you find that Maine does not have its own encyclopedia, so you decide to check AmJur and CJS for background on the tolling issue. In section 209, Volume 51 (Limitation of Actions), of AmJur 2d, you discover a discussion of "What constitutes incompetency or incapacity—Particular conditions." There, you learn that "courts have held that persons may be found 'insane,' and therefore entitled to the tolling of a statute of limitations, as a result of . . . severe and permanent brain damage from birth," along with other conditions that are not relevant to Jonah's situation. Furthermore, you find out that courts have held that "mental incapacity or incompetency or an unsound mind" was not sufficient to toll the statute of limitations on the basis of "impaired judgment alone." Unfortunately, no Maine cases were cited.

In section 211 of the same volume you find a discussion of the effect on a tolling provision of the appointment of a guardian. Although some courts have held "that once a guardian is appointed for an incompetent . . . , the limitation period commences, there is also authority holding that the appointment of a guardian . . . does not have the effect of starting the running of a period of limitation tolled by virtue of the disability of mental incompetency." No Maine cases are cited for this proposition, but you are encouraged that courts frequently find that the tolling is still applicable, even when a guardian has been appointed for a mentally incompetent person. Because you may not be able to find a Maine case on this point, you carefully record the names of the cases cited in AmJur. Although those cases can never be mandatory authority in a Maine court, they might prove to be persuasive authority, especially if the holdings represent the prevailing view.

2.6.3. Restatements of the Law

The Restatements of the Law were first produced in 1923 by a group of prominent judges, lawyers, and law professors, who were concerned with the growing complexity and uncertainty of American law. They formed the American Law Institute (ALI) and began to describe in the Restatements the law that had been adopted in the majority and minority of jurisdictions. Originally they intended simply to describe the law as it existed at the time. Over the years, however, the Restatements began to include trends in the law, reflecting where the ALI thought the law was heading.

The Restatements may serve as persuasive authority for courts to consult when deciding how to rule on matters of law that have not previously come up in their jurisdictions. There are three series of Restatements. The first series, which covers 1923-1944, reported on the law of agency, conflict of laws, contracts, judgments, property, restitution, security, torts, and trusts. The second series, from 1957 to the present, also covers the law of foreign relations, landlord/tenant relations, and donative transfers. The third series, 1986 to the present, also covers laws governing lawyers, mortgages, servitudes, wills and donative transfers, suretyship and guarantee, apportionment of liability in tort claims, products liability, the prudent investor rule in trusts, and unfair competition.

Table 2-1: Restatement Topics

Restatement Topics		
First Series (1923-1944)	**Second Series (since 1957)**	**Third Series (Since 1986)**
Agency	Agency	Agency
Conflict of laws	Conflict of laws	Employment law
Contract	Contracts	Foreign relations of the U.S.
Judgments	Foreign relations	International commercial arbitration (TD)
Property	Property: landlord/tenant	Law governing lawyers
Restitution	Property: donative transfers	Law of American Indians (TD)
Security	Torts	Property (mortgages)
Torts	Trusts	Property (servitudes)
Trusts		Property (wills & donative transfers)
		Restitution & unjust enrichment
		Suretyship & guarantee
		Torts (apportionment of liability)
		Torts (liability for Economic harm)
		Torts (liability for physical and emotional harm)
		Torts (products liability)
		Trusts
		Unfair competition

Restatements are divided into sections with a concise statement of the law followed by explanatory comments and illustrations. In recent editions, the comments and illustrations are followed by Reporter's Notes, which provide background information on the development of the section.

Appendix volumes of the Restatements can be used to find cases in which various Restatements have been cited. Restatements are available in hard copy and on online at LexisNexis and Westlaw.

Unfortunately, the Restatements do not prove helpful to you when researching Jonah's issue because they do not cover the issue of tolling a statute of limitations for mental illness.

2.6.4. Treatises

Treatises are books providing an in-depth treatment of a single legal subject, like property or torts. They can be multi-volume sets of books, textbooks, or shorter monographs. A treatise generally includes a table of contents, table of cases, index, and, for the print versions, supplementation by pocket parts, softbound supplements, or loose-leaf pages. Treatises are also available online at LexisNexis and Westlaw.

When you checked the library for a treatise that would address the issue of tolling the statute of limitations for mental illness, you found several treatises with promising titles, including *Mental Impairment and Legal Incompetency*, by Allen, Ferster, and Weihofen; *Disabled Persons and the Law: State Legislative Issues*, by Sales, Powell, and Van Duizend; and *The Statutes of Limitation Saving Statutes*, by Ferguson. You also found a chapter on statutes of limitations, including tolling and saving statutes, in *Civil Rights and Civil Liberties Litigation: The Law of Section 1983*, by Sheldon Nahmod. When you looked to see whether any Maine cases were discussed, you found a federal case, *Douglas v. York County*, 433 F.3d 143 (1st Cir. 2005), in which the United States Court of Appeals for the First Circuit applied Maine law in holding that the plaintiff did not satisfy the test for "mental illness" laid out by the Maine Supreme Judicial Court—"an overall inability to function in society."

2.6.5. American Law Reports

The *American Law Reports* (A.L.R.) series is a set of volumes, almost like an encyclopedia, containing essays, published in chronological order, as legal issues arise. In 1919, A.L.R. editors began selecting recent cases of note and publishing them along with essays providing in-depth analyses of the issues raised in those cases, including references to virtually all relevant case law and other secondary sources on the same topics. The essays, called "annotations," are often lengthy and expansive. Finding a recent A.L.R. annotation on the topic of your research can be a gold mine. Even if it is on a related topic, it can provide you with insight into the area of law and many relevant cases. One goal of legal research is to find a reputable authority that has already researched and written extensively about the legal issue you are researching. The A.L.R. can sometimes be that authority. Although not all topics are covered in an A.L.R. annotation, finding an annotation on your topic can point you in the right direction and save you an enormous amount of time, energy, and frustration.

Each A.L.R. annotation contains an essay accompanied by a case on point, followed by a summary, table of contents, article outline, and an index for the annotation if it is lengthy. Next come citations to relevant statutes and cases along with numerous secondary sources that might be helpful for further research. The A.L.R. is contained in six series, organized chronologically.

In addition to the A.L.R., there are two series of A.L.R. Federal, covering topics in federal law. Like the A.L.R., A.L.R. Federal is arranged chronologically, beginning in 1969. Before 1969, federal topics were often included in the A.L.R. One index covers both the A.L.R. and A.L.R. Federal. The A.L.R. and A.L.R. Federal are available in print and on Westlaw and LexisNexis. The print volumes are kept up to date by replacement volumes, pocket parts, and supplements.

While researching Jonah's case, you take a look at the A.L.R.s in the law library in the hope of finding something helpful. After looking for annotations on the three issues in Jonah's case—(1) what it means to be "mentally ill" for purposes of the statute of limitations, (2) what it means to have this condition when a cause of action accrues, and (3) whether the appointment of a guardian makes the tolling provision inapplicable—you strike pay dirt.

1. WHAT IT MEANS TO BE "MENTALLY ILL"

The first annotation you find, which was written by Michele Meyer McCarthy, J.D., deals with what it means to be "mentally ill" for purposes of a tolling provision. The annotation is entitled, "When is Person, Other than One Claiming Posttraumatic Stress Syndrome or Memory Repression, Within Coverage of Statutory Provision Tolling Running of Limitations Period on Basis of Mental Disability." It begins on page 697 of Volume 23 of A.L.R.6th. Originally published in 2007, it has been updated weekly to 2013. (See Illustration 2-4.)

The annotation covers cases in which courts decided when a person, other than one claiming posttraumatic stress syndrome or memory repression, is covered by a tolling provision on the basis of mental disability. The article outline includes three sections on "Mentally ill persons": section 15—"Basis for tolling held established," section 16—"Basis for tolling held supportable," and section 17—"Basis for tolling held not established or supportable." The annotation index contains references to both

23 A.L.R.6th 697

WHEN IS PERSON, OTHER THAN ONE
CLAIMING POSTTRAUMATIC STRESS
SYNDROME OR MEMORY REPRESSION,
WITHIN COVERAGE OF STATUTORY
PROVISION TOLLING RUNNING OF
LIMITATIONS PERIOD ON BASIS OF MENTAL
DISABILITY

by
Michele Meyer McCarthy, J.D.

In an attempt to avoid the statute of limitations in an action in which the defendant has asserted the same as a bar to the action, a plaintiff may argue that the statute of limitations was tolled pursuant to state statutory law. Numerous states have statutes providing that the statute of limitations applicable to an action is tolled when the person entitled to bring the action is under a specified mental disability at the time that the cause of action accrues. Whether an individual's mental condition is sufficient to toll the statute of limitations under a state's tolling statute depends on a variety of factors. For example, in Storm v. Legion Ins. Co., 2003 WI 120, 265 Wis. 2d 169, 665 N.W.2d 353, 23 A.L.R.6th 939 (2003), the court found that genuine issues of material fact as to whether the patient was mentally ill, for the purposes of the statute tolling limitations period due to mental illness, Wis. Stat. Ann. § 893.16(1), and precluded summary judgment in favor of the physicians on limitations grounds in the medical malpractice action. This annotation covers cases discussing when a person, other than one claiming posttraumatic stress syndrome or memory repression, is within the coverage of a statutory provision tolling the running of the applicable limitations period on the basis of a mental disability.

Storm v. Legion Ins. Co. is fully reported at page 939, infra.

697

Illustration 2-4: A.L.R. Annotation

"Mentally ill persons" (sections 15, 16, and 17) and "Mental retardation" (Sections 4, 11, 13, 14, and 19). Next you go to the annotation table of cases, laws, and rules, where you find the following citations for Maine: Maine's tolling statute, Me. Rev. Stat. Ann. Tit. 14, § 853; and three cases, *Bowden v. Grindle*, 675 A.2d 958 (Me. 1960); *Dasha v. Maine Medical Center*, 665 A.2d 993 (Me. 1995); and *Douglas v. York County*, 433 F.3d 143 (1st Cir. 2005).

In section 1, the scope of the annotation is described as follows: "This annotation collects and discusses state and federal cases in which the courts have determined whether the mental condition of a person entitled to bring a cause of action comes within the meaning of state statutes providing for the tolling of the applicable statute of limitations when a person is suffering from a mental disability."

Turning to section 15, you are pleased to see that the annotation begins with a Maine case, *Bowden v. Grindle*, 675 A.2d 968 (Me. 1996), when discussing the meaning of the term "mental illness" in Maine's tolling statute. According to the annotation, the court in *Bowden*, ruled that the term "mental illness refers to an overall inability to function in society that prevents plaintiffs from protecting their legal rights." To support its holding that the plaintiff in the case was suffering from "a mental disability sufficient to toll the statute of limitations," the court pointed to evidence that she "suffered from psychiatric problems, including depression and anxiety, for which she had been hospitalized and medicated for decades and the effects of which had prevented her from making an informed rational judgment about conveying her property, and that her cognitive thinking was impaired, that her problem of dependency rendered her helpless, and that there were times when she had difficulty cooking her own meals, leaving the house, and driving."

Finding this case, and the annotation's interpretation of it, is very helpful to you at this point in your research. You realize that you are going to have to think about how you can make Jonah's intellectual disability and difficulty in performing everyday activities compare favorably with the plaintiff in the *Bowden* case.

Reading on, you find other cases where courts did and did not find people mentally ill for the purposes of the tolling statutes in different jurisdictions. Looking for common themes, you find that most of the time, a person was considered mentally ill if she could not appreciate and act upon her legal rights, manage her affairs, or take care of herself.

In section 17, another case based on Maine law confirms your growing understanding of what it takes to be considered mentally ill: *Douglas v. York County*, 433 F.3d 143 (1st Cir. 2005). In *Douglas*, the United States Court of

Appeals for the First Circuit, applying Maine law, held that a gang-rape victim, who had been diagnosed with chronic depression and bipolar disorder, was not mentally ill for the purposes of Maine's tolling provision because she still possessed the "overall ability to function in society" and had asserted her legal rights in other cases.

2. WHAT IT MEANS TO BE MENTALLY ILL "WHEN A CAUSE OF ACTION ACCRUES"

Regarding the second issue—what it means to be mentally ill when the cause of action accrues—you find an A.L.R. annotation right on point. This annotation, found in the 41 volume of A.L.R.2d, beginning on page 726 and written by M.O. Regensteiner, is called, "Time of existence of mental incompetency which will prevent or suspend running of statute of limitations." The annotation was originally published in 1955 and has been updated to the present.

In the annotation table of cases, you find three cases applying Maine law: *Chasse v. Mazerolle*, 580 A.2d 155 (Me. 1990); *McCutchen v. Currier*, 94 Me. 362, 47 A. 923 (1900); and *Priestman v. Canadian Pacific Ltd.*, 782 F. Supp. 681 (D. Me. 1992) (applying Maine law). (See Illustration 2-5.)

According to the "Scope," section 1 of the annotation, the annotation considers the time at which "mental incompetency must exist in relation to the accrual of the cause of action." In section 2, the annotation asserts as a well-settled principle that "mental incompetency must exist at the time the cause of action accrued, and that an incompetency arising after the statute has commenced to run will not suspend its operation." In support of that principle, the annotation includes cases in section 3 in which courts consistently held that "subsequent disabilities cannot be tacked upon the first disability so as to prevent or suspect the operation of the statute of limitations," and in section 4, that "[m]ental incompetency resulting from, or closely following," the injury constituting the cause of action cannot qualify as mental illness for purposes of the tolling provision.

Based on the legal principles explained in the cases cited in 41 A.L.R.2d 726, you now understand that whatever intellectual disabilities Jonah had when the injury occurred and the cause of action accrued are the ones that will be taken into account in determining whether he was mentally ill for the purposes of the tolling statute. Any depression or other mental problems he experienced later will not come into play in the determination.

Kan. Stat. Ann. § 77-201(31). See § 7

Biritz v. Williams, 262 Kan. 769, 942 P.2d 25 (1997) — § 7

Gillmore v. Gillmore, 91 Kan. 707, 139 P. 386 (1914) — § 19

Gilmore v. Gregg, 1993 WL 100209 (D. Kan. 1993) (applying Kansas law) — § 8

Jenkins v. Jenkins, 94 Kan. 263, 146 P. 414 (1915) — § 19

Lowe v. Surpas Resource Corp., 253 F. Supp. 2d 1209 (D. Kan. 2003) (applying Kansas law) — § 8

Owens v. Kansas City, 125 Kan. 533, 264 P. 730 (1928) — § 8

Kentucky

Ky. Rev. Stat. Ann. § 413.170(1). See § 6

Heizer v. Cincinnati, New Orleans and Pacific Ry. Co., 172 S.W.3d 796 (Ky. Ct. App. 2004) — § 11

Southeastern Kentucky Baptist Hosp., Inc. v. Gaylor, 756 S.W.2d 467 (Ky. 1988) — § 6

Stair v. Gilbert, 209 Ky. 243, 272 S.W. 732 (1925) — § 4

Louisiana

Harsh v. Calogero, 615 So. 2d 420 (La. Ct. App. 4th Cir. 1993) — § 3

Maine

Me. Rev. Stat. Ann. tit. 14, § 853. See §§ 15, 17

Bowden v. Grindle, 675 A.2d 968 (Me. 1996) — § 15

Dasha v. Maine Medical Center, 665 A.2d 993 (Me. 1995) — § 3

Douglas v. York County, 433 F.3d 143 (1st Cir. 2005) (applying Maine law) — § 17

Maryland

Md. Code Ann., Cts. & Jud. Proc. § 5-201. See § 11

Decker v. Fink, 47 Md. App. 202, 422 A.2d 389 (1980) — § 11

McDonald v. Boslow, 363 F. Supp. 493 (D. Md. 1973) (apparently applying Maryland law) — § 11

O'Hara v. Kovens, 60 Md. App. 619, 484 A.2d 275 (1984) — § 3

Russo v. Ascher, 76 Md. App. 465, 545 A.2d 714 (1988) — § 11

Massachusetts

Mass. Gen. Laws Ann. ch. 260, § 7. See §§ 8, 14

Riley v. Presnell, 409 Mass. 239, 565 N.E.2d 780 (1991) — §§ 8, 14

Street v. Vose, 936 F.2d 38 (1st Cir. 1991) (applying Massachusetts law) — §§ 8, 14

Illustration 2-5: A.L.R. Table of Cases

3. WHETHER THE APPOINTMENT OF A GUARDIAN MAKES THE TOLLING PROVISION INAPPLICABLE

Finally, you are fortunate to find an A.L.R. annotation on the last remaining issue: whether it makes a difference that James was appointed Jonah's guardian. The annotation, which begins on page 159 of Volume 111 of A.L.R.5th, was originally published in 2001 and has been updated to 2013. The article is written by Michele Meyer McCarthy, J.D., like your first article, and is called, "Effect of Appointment of Legal Representative for Person under Mental Disability on Running of State Statute of Limitations against Such Person." You learn in section 1(a) that this annotation "collects and discusses cases in which courts have determined the effect of the appointment of a legal representative for a person under a mental disability on the operation of a state statutory provision tolling the running of the applicable limitations period on the basis of a mental disability"—just what you were looking for.

First, you check the annotation table of cases, laws, and rules to see whether any Maine cases are listed. When you do not find any Maine cases there, you go to the section 2(a), "Summary and comment—Generally" to get the lay of the land. There you learn that most state tolling provisions, like the tolling provision in Maine, do not expressly address this issue. Some courts have concluded that tolling statutes continue to apply to a mentally disabled person even when that person has the benefit of a duly appointed legal representative or guardian, while others have adopted the view that such an appointment triggers the running of the statute of limitations.

When holding that the tolling ceases upon the appointment of a guardian, courts have reasoned either that the right of action has moved to the guardian or that the guardian has a legal duty to take all necessary legal action on behalf of his or her ward. Sometimes courts even look to see whether a guardian has been "reasonable and diligent in fulfilling his or her legal duty in order for the toll to cease."

In contrast, many courts have held that the appointment of a guardian does not trigger the running of an otherwise tolled statute of limitations because the right of action belongs to the mentally disabled person, not the guardian. In section 3 of the annotation, the author lists courts in the following jurisdictions that have agreed with this approach: Alabama, Arkansas, California, Georgia, Illinois, Mississippi, Missouri, and Oklahoma.

In sections 4 and 5, you learn that some courts in other states have held that the appointment of a guardian for a mentally disabled person does not have the effect of removing the disability in question and, as a result, does not cause the statute of limitation to begin running again. Such states include Arizona, Indiana, Kentucky, Illinois, Maryland, Massachusetts, Michigan, Minnesota, New Jersey, New York, New Mexico, Oklahoma, Rhode Island, and Washington.

In section 6, the author cites to a Florida case in which the court held that the appointment of a guardian for a mentally incompetent person did not start the running of the limitation period, "noting that the state tolling statute does not provide for the running of the statute of limitations upon the appointment of a legal representative for a plaintiff who comes within the coverage of the statute."

In section 7, however, the author points to courts in the following jurisdictions holding, without any explanation, that the limitations period begins to run upon the appointment of a legal representative for someone who is otherwise entitled to the benefit of a tolling provision because he is mentally disabled: Arkansas, California, and North Carolina.

In section 8, the author lists three cases in which courts in Alabama, Massachusetts, and New Hampshire determined that the limitation period had not run against plaintiffs solely on their mental conditions without considering that guardians had been appointed in each case.

In section 9, the following jurisdictions are listed in which courts took the view that the appointment of a guardian triggers the running of the statute of limitations: Hawaii, Kansas, New Hampshire, New York, North Carolina, and Washington.

In section 10, several cases from West Virginia are listed in which courts stated that "where there is a legal duty on the part of a representative to sue for damages done to estate of his or her incompetent," the appointment of a guardian "will trigger the running of an otherwise tolled statute of limitations if the court determines, under an objective standard, that the guardian had been reasonable and diligent in discovering the wrong perpetrated on his or her charge."

Although you still need to conduct more research on this subject, it appears from the cases cited in this A.L.R. annotation, that the appointment of James as Jonah's guardian did not trigger the running of the statute of limitations. The majority of jurisdictions that have considered this question have concluded that the appointment of a guardian should not trigger the running of the statute of limitations for a mentally disabled person. Because the vast majority of jurisdictions have taken this approach, a Maine court would likely adopt it if it were squarely presented with the question. That is good news for James and Jonah.

2.6.6. Law Reviews, Journals, and Periodicals

Articles in law reviews, journals, and periodicals are valuable secondary sources because they are written by scholars, professors, and experts who have conducted extensive research in writing their articles. For this reason, the footnotes in these articles are a rich source of citations on a particular subject. They provide background on a given subject and, if written by a recognized authority in a highly respected publication, can sometimes be used as persuasive authority.

Several print and online indexes are available to find articles on point. The most commonly used indexes are the *Index to Legal Periodicals and Books, Wilson Index to Legal Periodicals and Books, Index to Foreign Legal Periodicals*, and *Current Index to Legal Periodicals*. Periodicals can also be found on LexisNexis, Westlaw, and Hein OnLine.

Consulting several of the print and online indexes, you find a promising article on the effect of appointing a guardian on the tolling of a statute of limitations for mental incapacity: "The Guardian or the Ward: For Whom does the Statute Toll?," published in Volume 71 of the Boston University Law Review, beginning on page 575, in 1991. This article, which is exactly on point, focuses on what courts in various jurisdictions have held concerning whether the appointment of a guardian triggers the running of a statute of limitations if it had been tolled because of someone's mental illness. The author takes issue with a recent case, *O'Brien v. Massachusetts Bay Transportation Authority*, 556 N.E.2d 324 (Mass. 1989), in which the Massachusetts Supreme Judicial Court held that a statute of limitations that had been tolled due to a plaintiff's mental incompetency did not start to run upon the appointment of a guardian. Although that point of view runs counter to the argument you will need to make on Jonah's behalf, the article is extremely helpful because it identifies the position taken by the Massachusetts court as the majority position and identifies only one jurisdiction—North Carolina—that takes an opposing view.

2.7. Using Primary Sources

2.7.1. Statutes and Statutory Interpretation

You have already identified the Maine statutes that relate to the issues in Jonah's case: the Maine Health Security Act, governing medical malpractice claims, beginning at 24 M.R.S.A. § 2851; the statute of limitations requiring that medical malpractice claims be brought within three years after the cause of action accrues, 24 M.R.S.A. § 2902; and the tolling provision, allowing people who are mentally ill when the cause of action accrues to wait until the disability is removed before filing a claim, 14 M.R.S.A. § 853.

Because you have consulted an annotated code, Maine Revised Statutes Annotated, you are able to locate cases in which these statutes have been interpreted in the annotations that follow the statute. When the language in a statute is unambiguous, courts interpret the statute according to the plain, ordinary meaning of its words. Because the language in the statute of limitations for medical malpractice claims seems unambiguous, you will probably not need to look for cases interpreting its meaning. It plainly states the number of years within which claims must be brought and explains that "a cause of action accrues on the date of the act or omission giving rise to the injury."

Although the meaning of the statute of limitations seems plain on its face, the tolling provision contains the term "mental illness," for which the statute provides no definition. Also, the statute does not discuss whether the appointment of a guardian for a mentally ill person starts the statute of limitation running again. To predict how a court would apply the tolling provision to Jonah's situation, you must find analogous cases in which the court has interpreted the words of the statute, according to legislative intent, and see how the facts in those cases compare and contrast to the facts in Jonah's case.

A good place to begin your search for analogous cases is in the annotation section following the tolling provision. There you find a number of headings for various topics such as "Multiple disability," "Successive disabilities," "Removal of disability," "Discovery of sexual abuse," "Mental illness," and "Questions of fact." Only "Removal of disability," "Mental illness," and possibly "Questions of fact" appear to relate to the issues you are researching. Looking first at "Removal of disability" to see whether any cases are listed dealing with the effect of the appointment of a guardian, you are disappointed to find only one case from 1853 that deals with a different disability: the disability to sue arising from being outside the United States.

Under the heading "Mental illness," however, you find three cases that are on point. Two of the cases you already encountered in the annotation by Michele Meyer McCarthy you found in A.L.R.5th: *Douglas v. York County*, 433 F.3d 143 (1st Cir. 2005), and *Bowden v. Grindle*, 675 A.2d 968 (Me. 1996). As in the A.L.R.5th annotation, these cases are cited for the proposition that "mental illness" in the tolling provision refers to an "overall inability to function in society that prevents plaintiffs from protecting their legal rights." A third case, *McAfee v. Cole*, 637 A.2d 463 (Me. 1994), is cited for the same proposition.

According to the annotation, the plaintiff in *Douglas* was not entitled to statutory tolling of limitations periods on state and federal civil rights claims arising from gang rape on the basis of mental illness despite her chronic depression and bipolar disorder, "given her assertion of other legal rights and her employment in years following [the] attack." In *Bowden*, however, a deed grantor was found to be mentally ill at the time she executed a deed, based on expert testimony that she "suffered from psychiatric problems for which she was hospitalized and medicated for decades" and her own testimony that "she had little recollection of meeting with [an] attorney and did not know what she was signing" when executing the deed. For these reasons "experts testified that [she] was unable to make [an] informed rational judgment about [her] property due to her impaired cognitive thinking." The plaintiff's allegations in *McAfee*, however, that he had "denied and repressed all memories of sexual acts committed upon him by [the] defendant until he watched [a] television report concerning criminal charges against [the] defendant" as well as "claims of trauma and severe stress were insufficient to alert [the] court and opposing parties that mental illness under [the] statute of limitations tolling statute might be an issue."

Under the heading "Questions of fact," you find *Douglas* and *Bowden* cited for the rule that "the question of whether the statute of limitations is tolled by mental illness . . . is a question of fact" under Maine law. Several other cases are listed in which courts found that a question of fact was generated, precluding summary judgment, regarding whether the plaintiffs were mentally ill at the time their causes of action accrued: *Carlson v. Rice*, 832 F. Supp. 17 (D. Me. 1993) (involving a plaintiff's repressed memory, extreme emotional distress, and inability to engage in normal activities after being sexually abused by her father); *Priestman v. Canadian Pacific Ltd.*, 782 F. Supp. 681 (D. Me. 1992) (dealing with whether a railroad worker was mentally ill at the time his tort cause of action against the railroad accrued and whether his disability was lifted); *Morris v. Hunter*, 652 A.2d 89 (Me. 1994) (regarding whether the former client pressing a legal malpractice claim was unable to function in society and protect his legal rights).

Finding the names and citations to these cases is a good first step in understanding the law. Now, you will have to look up the cases, read them, and focus on the particular sections of the opinions where the relevant law is explained. Although the citations provided in the annotations do not include pin cites, even for quoted material, you should have no trouble finding the relevant law and including pin cites when you cite to the cases in your memo.

2.7.2. Cases

A. Finding Relevant Cases and Making Sure They Are Still Good Law

Finding one good case—a case in your jurisdiction that is right on point—is the key to uncovering a treasure trove of cases that you can use in your memo to explain the relevant legal rules and demonstrate, though analogous cases, how courts have applied those rules in past cases. Once you have that case in hand, you can look up other cases mentioned in that case and use the citation to that case to find later cases that used that case as precedent.

Up until now, you have been finding cases indirectly in secondary sources and the annotations following the tolling provision. Now it is time to identify that one good case and complete your list by looking for cases directly and making sure that the cases you have found are still good law, using the following research tools: the Maine Digest, West Digest Topic and Key Numbers, Westlaw, LexisNexis, Shepard's, and Key Cite. You will know that your research is complete when you keep seeing the same cases mentioned over and over and you determine that those cases have not been overruled.

B. Using the West Digest Topic and Key Number System

Cases are arranged chronologically in the reporters. Thus, it would be impossible to find cases relating to a particular topic without some sort of research guide that arranges cases by subject. The West Key Number Digest does just that. It organizes the law by subject, summarizes cases published in reporters, and provides citations to those summarized cases. The West Digest system includes four different sets: (1) the combined digests, which include cases from all jurisdictions, including both state and federal cases; (2) the federal digests, which include all federal cases, including United States Supreme Court cases; (3) the regional digests, which include a digest for each regional reporter; and (4) the state digests, which include a digest for each state reporter.

The digests divide the law into seven broad topics: persons, property, contracts, torts, crimes, remedies, and government. (See Illustration 2-6.) These seven broad topics are then divided into 414 digest topics, ranging alphabetically from "Abandonment and Lost Property" to "Zoning and Planning." The digest topics are divided into smaller subtopics, each of which has been assigned a "Key Number," which can be used to find cases on that subtopic in any jurisdiction.

To locate cases having to do with the meaning of "mental illness" in Maine's tolling provision, you begin by looking at the outline of the Law, to determine which of the seven main divisions of the law contain your subject matter. Under the sixth division, "Remedies," you discover the term "Limitation of Actions" under the heading "Civil Actions in General." Thus, "Limitation of Actions" will be your digest topic.

Next, you turn to the descriptive-word index (shown in Illustration 2-7), which is arranged alphabetically, and look up your digest topic, "Limitation of Actions." Under "Limitation of Actions," you find an alphabetical list of subtopics, including "Disabilities," below which you find the entry "Insanity or incompetency," followed by the abbreviation "Lim of Act," a small picture of a key, and the number "74." This means that you will be able to find all the cases that exist on the subject of insanity or incompetency, as those terms relate to the statute of limitations, under key number 74 of the digest topic "Limitation of Actions," abbreviated "Lim of Act."

Now that you know your digest topic and key number, you go to the table of cases where you find the section on "Limitation of Actions," under which all the subtopics are arranged in numerical order by key number. Under key number 74, you find a list of the following cases, most of which you have already found in the annotations accompanying the tolling provision and the secondary sources: *Rowe v. Maine*, 324 F. Supp. 2d 238 (D. Me. 2004); *Priestman v. Canadian Pacific Ltd.*, 782 F. Supp. 681 (D. Me. 1992); *Bowden v. Grindle*, 675 A.2d 968 (Me. 1996); *Dasha v. Maine Medical Center*, 665 A.2d 993 (1995); *McAfee v. Cole*, 637 A.2d 463 (Me. 1994); *Oliver v. Berry*, 53 Me. 206 (Me. 1865). You remember to consult the pocket part (see Illustration 2-8) where you find an additional, more recent case, which you have also found before: *Douglas v. York County*, 433 F.3d 143 (1st Cir. 2005).

After each citation is a brief summary of the case. Because you have not heard of *Rowe v. Maine* before, you decide to look up the case to see whether it might be useful. When you find it in the 324th Volume of the Federal Supplement, Second, on page 238, you see that it is organized like most of the other cases you have found, beginning with the heading, which contains the names of the parties, the docket number of the case (No. CIV. 04-42-B-W), the name of the court (United States District Court, D. Maine), and the date the case was decided (July 2, 2004). Then come sections called "Background" and "Holding," in which the historical and procedural history are described along with the present holding of the United States District Court for the District of Maine. Under the "Holding," you find a list of six digest topics and key numbers, three of which relate to your digest topic, "Limitation of Actions," but only one of which has your key number, 74.

OUTLINE OF THE LAW

Digest Topics are arranged for your convenience by Seven Main Divisions of Law.
Complete alphabetical list of Digest Topics with topic numbers follows this section.

---

1. **PERSONS**
2. **PROPERTY**
3. **CONTRACTS**
4. **TORTS**
5. **CRIMES**
6. **REMEDIES**
7. **GOVERNMENT**

6. REMEDIES

REMEDIES BY ACT OR AGREEMENT OF PARTIES

Accord and Satisfaction
Arbitration
Submission of Controversy

REMEDIES BY POSSESSION OR NOTICE

Liens
Lis Pendens
Maritime Liens
Mechanics' Liens
Notice
Salvage

MEANS AND METHODS OF PROOF

Acknowledgment
Affidavits
Estoppel
Evidence
Oath
Records
Witnesses

CIVIL ACTIONS IN GENERAL

Action
Declaratory Judgment
Election of Remedies
Limitation of Actions
Parties
Set-Off and Counterclaim
Venue

> The digest topics are organized into seven broad topics. The relevant topic for this issue is Remedies. Remedies, as well as the six remaining broad topics are broken down into subtopics, and then into sub-subtopics. For example the topic "Remedies" is broken down into the subtopic "Civil Actions in General" and this is further broken down into several other sub-subtopics, including "Limitation of Actions," the topic that is relevant to the issue at hand.

Illustration 2-6: Digest Topics

Following this list of digest topics and key numbers comes a list of the attorneys arguing the case and finally, at the bottom of the page, the "Order Affirming Recommended Decision," followed by the name of the judge issuing the opinion (Woodcock, District Judge). Please note that it is not until the bottom of the page, following the heading "Order Affirming

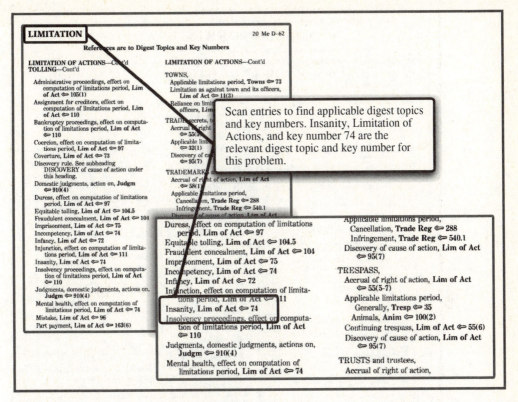

LIMITATION   20 Me D-62

References are to Digest Topics and Key Numbers

LIMITATION OF ACTIONS—Cont'd
TOLLING—Cont'd

Administrative proceedings, effect on
    computation of limitations period, Lim
    of Act ☞ 105(1)
Assignment for creditors, effect on
    computation of limitations period, Lim
    of Act ☞ 110
Bankruptcy proceedings, effect on computa-
    tion of limitations period, Lim of Act
    ☞ 110
Coercion, effect on computation of limita-
    tions period, Lim of Act ☞ 97
Coverture, Lim of Act ☞ 73
Discovery rule. See subheading
    DISCOVERY of cause of action under
    this heading.
Domestic judgments, action on, Judgm
    ☞ 910(4)
Duress, effect on computation of limitations
    period, Lim of Act ☞ 97
Equitable tolling, Lim of Act ☞ 104.5
Fraudulent concealment, Lim of Act ☞ 104
Imprisonment, Lim of Act ☞ 75
Incompetency, Lim of Act ☞ 74
Infancy, Lim of Act ☞ 72
Injunction, effect on computation of limita-
    tions period, Lim of Act ☞ 311
Insanity, Lim of Act ☞ 74
Insolvency proceedings, effect on computa-
    tion of limitations period, Lim of Act
    ☞ 110
Judgments, domestic judgments, actions on,
    Judgm ☞ 910(4)
Mental health, effect on computation of
    limitations period, Lim of Act ☞ 74
Mistake, Lim of Act ☞ 96
Part payment, Lim of Act ☞ 163(6)

LIMITATION OF ACTIONS—Cont'd

TOWNS,
    Applicable limitations period, Towns ☞ 73
    Limitation as against town and its officers,
        Lim of Act ☞ 11(3)
    Reliance on limitations period by town and its
        officers, Lim
TRADE secrets, t
    Accrual of right
    ☞ 55(
    Applicable limita
    ☞ 32(1)
    Discovery of ca
    ☞ 95(7)
TRADEMARKS a
    Accrual of right of action, Lim of Act
    ☞ 58(1
    Applicable limitations period,
        Cancellation, Trade Reg ☞ 288
    Infringement, Trade Reg ☞ 540.1
    Discovery of cause of action, Lim of Act

> Scan entries to find applicable digest topics
> and key numbers. Insanity, Limitation of
> Actions, and key number 74 are the
> relevant digest topic and key number for
> this problem.

Duress, effect on computation of limitations
    period, Lim of Act ☞ 97
Equitable tolling, Lim of Act ☞ 104.5
Fraudulent concealment, Lim of Act ☞ 104
Imprisonment, Lim of Act ☞ 75
Incompetency, Lim of Act ☞ 74
Infancy, Lim of Act ☞ 72
Injunction, effect on computation of limita-
    tions period, Lim of Act ☞ 311
Insanity, Lim of Act ☞ 74
Insolvency proceedings, effect on computa-
    tion of limitations period, Lim of Act
    ☞ 110
Judgments, domestic judgments, actions on,
    Judgm ☞ 910(4)
Mental health, effect on computation of
    limitations period, Lim of Act ☞ 74

Applicable limitations period,
    Cancellation, Trade Reg ☞ 288
    Infringement, Trade Reg ☞ 540.1
Discovery of cause of action, Lim of Act
    ☞ 95(7)

TRESPASS,
    Accrual of right of action, Lim of Act
    ☞ 55(5-7)
    Applicable limitations period,
        Generally, Tresp ☞ 35
    Animals, Anim ☞ 100(2)
    Continuing trespass, Lim of Act ☞ 55(6)
    Discovery of cause of action, Lim of Act
    ☞ 95(7)

TRUSTS and trustees,
    Accrual of right of action,

Illustration 2-7: Descriptive-Word Index

Recommended Decision" that the opinion actually begins. Other than the heading, everything else is has been added by West Publishing to help the legal researcher and should never be cited as part of the opinion. For example, the entry containing your digest topic and key number looks like this: "3. Limitation of Actions [key] 74(1) Mental incompetence is not a per se reason to toll the statute of limitations." If you wanted to quote this in your memo, you would not cite the first page of the opinion for this legal proposition. You would go to the number 3 in brackets on page 240 of the opinion and cite to what the court stated there: "Mental incompetence is not a *per se* reason to toll the statute of limitations." *Rowe v. Maine*, 324 F. Supp. 2d 238, 240 (D. Me. 2004). You would never cite the first page of the opinion, page 238, for this proposition because it only appeared in what is called a "headnote" there (see Illustration 2-9); it did not appear in the actual opinion until two pages later, on page 240. That is the page you would need to cite in your memo if you were going to quote or paraphrase that proposition.

After reading the opinion, you decide you will not need to use this case in your memo because it is a federal case, dealing with a federal statute of limitations and the doctrine of "equitable tolling," not the statutory tolling

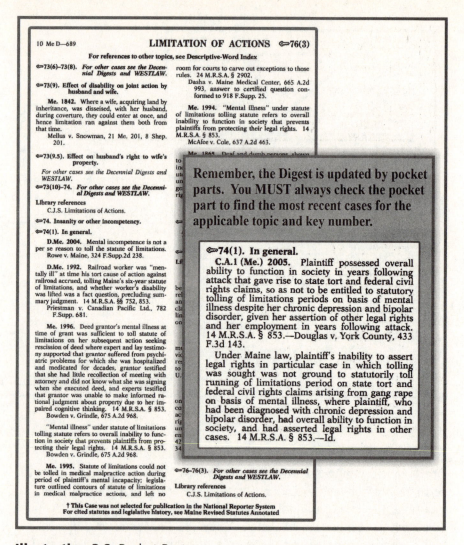

Illustration 2-8: Pocket Part

provision at issue in Jonah's case. On page 239 of the opinion, you learn that "[t]he doctrine of equitable tolling provides that in exceptional circumstances, a statute of limitations may be extended for equitable reasons not acknowledged in the statute creating the limitations period." On the following page, the court ruled that "mental incompetence is not a *per se* reason to toll the statute of limitations," as stated in headnote 3. Because the Maine tolling provision specifically states that the statute of limitations will be tolled for mental illness, you realize that the doctrine of equitable tolling has no relevance to Jonah's situation and you can set aside the *Rowe* case.

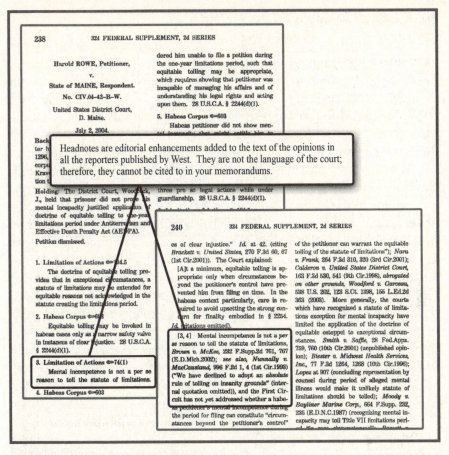

Illustration 2-9: Case Headnotes

 ETHICS ALERT: Inadequate Legal Research

A United States District Court in Georgia denied an attorney's claim of "excusable neglect" after the attorney failed to uncover controlling authority, finding that the attorney, a member of a 350-attorney law firm with "the most modern legal research facilities, including computer-assisted legal research services," would have discovered the case by simply Shepardizing a prior decision in his own case. According to the court, "the use of basic research techniques such as the West Key Number System, Westlaw, or Lexis would have identified the possible relevance" of the case.

Stephens v. Kemp, 602 F. Supp. 960, 965 (M.D. Ga. 1984).

C. Using Westlaw and LexisNexis

In addition to using the hardbound Maine Digest to find cases, you can also search for cases electronically using Westlaw and LexisNexis.[13] Because West established the Key Number System, you can search for cases on Westlaw using the digest topic and key numbers you have found for the issue you are researching: tolling the statute of limitations for mental illness. The digest topic number for "Limitation of Actions" is 241, and the key number for "insanity or other incompetency" is 74.

After signing onto Westlaw, go to "WestlawClassic," choose Maine Cases as your database and enter "me-cs" in the space provided at the bottom left of the screen. Then select "Key Numbers" at the top of the screen, which will take you automatically to the next screen. At the center of the next screen, select "West Key Number Digest Outline," where you can enter your digest topic and key numbers at the bottom right of the screen, as follows: 241k74. Then hit "Go," which brings you a screen where your digest topic and key number request has been converted to a search: LIMITATION OF ACTIONS 241k74 Insanity or other incompetency. After you select "Search" at the bottom left of the screen, you come to a list of Maine cases dealing with that topic: *Bowden v. Grindle*, 675 A.2d 968 (Me. 1996); *Dasha v. Maine Medical Center*, 665 A.2d 993 (Me. 1995); *McAfee v. Cole*, 637 A.2d 463 (Me. 1994); *Oliver v. Berry*, 53 Me. 206 (Me. 1865).

You decide to see if you can find any Maine cases dealing with the guardian issue by using the West Key Number system. Because this topic does not seem to be included in the Maine Digest, you look at the headnotes in *Barton-Mallow Company, Inc.*, 556 N.E.2d 324 (Ind. 1990), in which the Supreme Court of Indiana held that the appointment of a guardian did not remove a mentally ill man's disability for purposes of tolling the statute of limitations. The headnote that included that holding has the title: "Limitation of Actions Key 74(2)." You notice that the headnotes in the cases you found regarding the tolling of the statute of limitations for mental illness had the Key Number 74(1). When you run a search for Maine cases with the digest topic and key numbers 241K(2), you discover that none exist. Thus, you now know for certain that you will have to use cases from other jurisdictions in the section of your memo dealing with the effect of the appointment of a guardian.

LexisNexis does not employ the same Key Number System as Westlaw, but the cases do have numbered headnotes, as well as a case summary

---

13. Other major, fee-based electronic legal databases include Loislaw, Bloomberg Law, and Casemaker. Legal researchers can also find cases, statutes, and other legal resources at no charge on state and federal court websites.

and core terms reported before the opinion begins. At the beginning of *Bowden v. Grindle*, 675 A.2d 968 (Me. 1996), for example, headnote 1 includes the following information: "If a person is mentally ill when the cause of action accrues she may bring an action within the statutorily prescribed time limit after the disability is removed. Me. Rev. Stat. Ann tit. 14, § 853 (Supp. 1995). Pursuant to the tolling statute mental illness refers to an overall inability to function in society that prevents plaintiffs from protecting their legal rights." (See Illustration 2-10.)

Knowing how to cite to the correct page of a case when viewing the print version is easy and straightforward. You just look at the top of the page for the page number. Also, in the print version, you can tell the difference between a headnote number and a paragraph number. Although both are enclosed in brackets, only the paragraph number is preceded by a paragraph sign. The same is true about headnote numbers and paragraph numbers in cases appearing on Westlaw. To find the page numbers on Westlaw, however, look for a number preceded by an asterisk (*). Once you find a page number preceded by an asterisk, you know that everything that appears after that page number appears on that page until you reach another page number preceded by an asterisk. Then you will be moving on to the next page. On Lexis/Nexis, the paragraph number is in brackets, following the letter "P" rather than the paragraph symbol. The headnote number is underlined and in italics, following the letters "HN." The page number appears in brackets. Unlike on Westlaw, however, all three numbers do not appear on one screen. You must select either the screen with the headnotes and paragraph numbers or the screen with headnotes and page numbers. (See Illustration 2-11.)

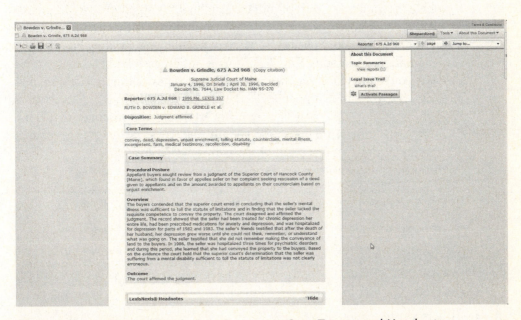

Illustration 2-10: LexisNexis Case Summary, Core Terms, and Headnote

LEWISTON DAILY SUN v. UNEMPLMT. INS. COM'N

Cite as 733 A.2d 344 (Me. 1999)

PRINT VERSION

Me. 347

PAGE NUMBER

1)(E) (1988). The ... vens was providing goods rather than services and thus the test was inapplicable. We disagree.

[3] [¶ 10] The following facts, as found by the Commission and supported by competent evidence, demonstrate that Stevens provided a mixture of both goods and services:

The employing unit provided the claimant with a letter of agreement concerning their employment rel... November 13, 1990. In th... employing unit informs the ... his duties will include attending town meetings and other local events in a particular geographical territory at the employing unit's request for the purpose of taking photographs and preparing articles to be used in the employing unit's newspapers.

. . . .

The employing unit assigned leads to the claimant. It suggested stories to the claimant that it was interested in publishing. The claimant could choose whether or not to accept such assign-

prove all three prongs of the test. Because we find that the Commission did not err in holding that the Sun failed to prove that Stevens was customarily engaged in an independently established trade, occupation, profession, or business, *see* 26 M.R.S.A. § 1043... not consider the othe... est.

[¶ 12] The Commission found as fact, supported by competent evidence, that Stevens had no previous experience as a ... he answered the Sun's ad ... t and that the Sun trained Stevens to improve his writing ability and write in a style espoused by the Sun. The Commission also found that Stevens introduced himself as a reporter for the Sun when interviewing people, that he did not advertise nor hold himself out as a freelance reporter, and that he did not perform reporting services for any other newspaper or magazine.

HEADNOTE NUMBER & PARAGRAPH NUMBER

[6] [¶ 13] A person is independently established when he has a proprietary interest in his occupation such that he can "operate without hindrance from any

WESTLAW VERSION

t least in part, the Commission properly applied the statutory test.

4 **5** [¶ 11] The Sun next contends that even if the test applied, Stevens's services did not constitute employment. If an employer fails to satisfy any of the three prongs of the test, the worker is deemed an employee and the other prongs of the test need not be consid... *Employment Ins. Comm'n*, 1998 ME 177, ¶ 7, 714 A.2d 818, 821; *Hasco Mfg. Co. v. ...*, 415, 185 A.2d 442, 443 (1962). The Commission held that the Sun failed to prove ... hat the Commission did not err in holding that the Sun failed to prove that Stevens ... y established trade, occupation, profession, or business, *see* 26 M.R.S.A. § 1043(11)(E)(3), we need not consider the other two prongs of the test.

HEADNOTE NUMBER & PARAGRAPH NUMBER

[¶ 12] The Commission found as fact, supported by competent evidence, that Stevens had no previous experience as a reporter when he answered the Sun's ad for a journalist and that the Sun trained Stevens to improve his writing ability and write in a style espoused by the Sun. The Commission also found that Stevens introduced himself as a reporter for the Sun when interviewing people, that he did not advertise nor hold himself out as a freelance reporter, and that h... for any other newspaper or magazine.

STAR PAGINATION

6 [¶ 13] A person is independently established when he has a proprietary interest in his occupation such that he can "operate without hindrance from any source." *Hasco Mfg. Co. v. Maine Employment Sec. Comm'n*, 158 Me. 413, 419, 185 A.2d 442, 445 (1962). Although a proprietary interest need not be established by a place of business or a mailing address, "at the very least such workers must hold themselves out to some community of potential customers as independent tradesmen involved in a particular craft." *Nyer v. Maine Unemployment Ins. Comm'n*, 601 A.2d 626, 628 (Me.1992) (footnote omitted); *see also Vector Mktg. Corp. v. Maine Unemployment Ins. Comm'n*, 610 A.2d 272, 275 (Me.1992) (holding that when sales persons were prohibited from selling competing products for a year after the expiration of their contracts and sold only the employing unit's products they did not have a proprietary interest in their occupation).

[¶ 14] On the unique facts of this case, because Stevens did not have prior experience as a reporter, received his only training *348 from the Sun, did not advertise his services as a reporter, and did not perform such services for any other newspaper or magazine, the facts do not compel a result contrary to that reached by the Commission that Stevens was not customarily engaged in an independently established profession.

The entry is:

Judgment affirmed.

Illustration 2-11: Star Pagination

Because Stevens provided services, at least in part, the Commission properly applied the statutory test.

LEXIS VERSION I s that even if the test applied, Stevens's services did not constitute employment. HN4 If an employer fails to satisfy any of the three prongs of the test, the worker is deemed an employee and the other prongs of the test need not be considered. *See McPherson Timberlands, Inc. v. Unemployment Ins. Comm'n*, 1998 ME 177, P7, 714 A.2d 818, 821; *Hasco Mfg. Co. v. Maine Employment Sec. Comm'n*, 158 Me. 413, 415, 185 A.2d 442, 443 (1962). The Commission held that the Sun failed to prove all three prongs of the test. Because we find that the Commission did not err in holding that the Sun failed to prove that Stevens was customarily engaged in an independently established trade, occupation, profession, or business, *see* 26 M.R.S.A. § 1043(1l)(E)(3), we need not consider the other two prongs of the test.

The Commission fo HEADNOTE NUMBER npetent evidence, that Stevens had no previous experienc ered the Sun's ad for a journalist and that the Sun trained Stevens to improve his writing ability and write in a style espoused by the Sun. The Commission also found that Stevens introduced himself as a reporter for the Sun when interviewing people, that he did not advertise nor hold himself out as a freelance reporter, and that he did not perform reporting services for any other newspaper or magazine.

HN6 A person is independently established when he has a proprietary interest in his occupation such that he can "operate without hindrance from any source." *Hasco Mfg. Co. v. Maine Employment Sec. Comm'n*, 158 Me. 413, 419, 185 A.2d 442, 445 (1962). Although a proprietary interest need not be established by a place of business or a mailing address, "at the very least such workers must hold themselves out to some community of potential customers as independent tradesmen involved in a particul_____ *Unemployment Ins. Comm'n*, 601 A.2d 626, 628 (Me. 1992) (footno PAGE NUMBER *ector Mktg. Corp. v. Maine Unemployment Ins. Comm'n*, 610 A.2d 272, 273 (Me. 1992) (holding that when sales persons were prohibited from selling competing products for a year after the expiration of their contracts and sold only the employing unit's products they did not have a proprietary interest in their occupation).

On the unique facts of this case, because Stevens did not have prior experience as a reporter, received his only training **[348]** from the Sun, did not advertise his services as a reporter, and did not perform such services for any other newspaper or magazine, the facts do not compel a result contrary to that reached by the Commission that Stevens was not customarily engaged in an independently established profession.

The entry is:

Judgment affirmed.

Illustration 2-11: (Continued)

Because Stevens provided services, at least in part, the Commission properly applied the

LEXIS VERSION II

ntends that even if the test applied, Stevens's services did not constitute employment. *HN5* If an employer fails to satisfy any of the three prongs of the test, the worker is deemed an employee and the other prongs of the test need not be considered. *See McPherson Timberlands, Inc. v. Unemployment Ins. Comm'n, 1998 ME 177, P7, 714 A.2d 818, 821; Hasco Mfg. Co. v. Maine Employment Sec. Comm'n, 158 Me. 413, 415, 185 A.2d 442, 443 (1962).* The Commission held that the Sun failed to prove all three prongs of the test. Because we find that the Commission did not err in holding that the Sun failed to prove that Stevens was customarily engaged in an independently established trade, occupation, profession, or business, *see 26 M.R.S.A. § 1043(1l)(E)(3),* we need not consider the other two pro

PARAGRAPH NUMBER & HEADNOTE NUMBER

[P12] The Comm_____y competent evidence, that Stevens had no previous experien_____d the Sun's ad for a journalist and that the Sun trained Stevens to improve his writing ability and write in a style espoused by the Sun. The Commission also found that Stevens introduced himself as a reporter for the Sun when interviewing people, that he did not advertise nor hold himself out as a freelance reporter, and that he did not perform reporting services for any other newspaper or magazine.

[P13] *HN6* A person is independently established when he has a proprietary interest in his occupation such that he can "operate without hindrance from any source." *Hasco Mfg. Co. v. Maine Employment Sec. Comm'n, 158 Me. 413, 419, 185 A.2d 442, 445 (1962).* Although a proprietary interest need not be established by a place of business or a mailing address, "at the very least such workers must hold themselves out to some community of potential customers as independent tradesmen involved in a particular craft." *Nyer v. Maine Unemployment Ins. Comm'n, 601 A.2d 626, 628 (Me. 1992)* (footnote omitted); *see also Vector Mktg. Corp. v. Maine Unemployment Ins. Comm'n, 610 A.2d 272, 275 (Me. 1992)* (holding that when sales persons were prohibited from selling competing products for a year after the expiration of their contracts and sold only the employing unit's products they did not have a proprietary interest in their occupation).

[P14] On the unique facts of this case, because Stevens did not have prior experience as a reporter, received his only training from the Sun, did not advertise his services as a reporter, and did not perform such services for any other newspaper or magazine, the facts do not compel a result contrary to that reached by the Commission that Stevens was not customarily engaged in an independently established profession.

The entry is:

Judgment affirmed.

Illustration 2-11: (Continued)

Bowden v. Grindle, 675 A.2d 968 (Me. 1996), appears to be the "one good case" you have been seeking. Now that you have found that case in an annotation to a statute and various secondary sources and looked it up on Westlaw or LexisNexis, you can use the headnotes that appear in Westlaw and LexisNexis to find other cases on point. For example, after learning about *Bowden v. Grindle*, 675 A.2d 968 (Me. 1996), in section 15 of the A.L.R.6th Annotation by Michele Meyer McCarthy, you use the citation to locate the case on Westlaw and LexisNexis. On Westlaw, in headnote 2, you discover the digest topic and key number needed to find all the other Maine cases containing the following definition of "mental illness" (Limitation of Actions, key 74(1)): An "overall inability to function in society that prevents plaintiffs from protecting their legal rights." On LexisNexis, headnote 1 contains the same definition and can be used to search the entire LexisNexis database for all the other Maine cases containing that headnote.

You can also find cases on Westlaw and LexisNexis by searching their databases using search terms describing what you are seeking. To find out whether you have found all the cases dealing with the definition of "mental illness" for purposes of the tolling provision, you construct a search using the terms "statute of limitations," "tolling," and "mental illness" to find cases that include those words. Once you find one good case on point, you can mine that case for other cases in which courts have determined what is meant by "mental illness" or whether the appointment of a guardian makes a difference. When you find additional cases within the text of the one good case you have found, you can get to them easily by clicking on the citations to those cases, called "jump cites," which appear in blue and are "live" links. Clicking on a jump cite will take you to another case, where you can repeat the process. For example, as you expected, *Bowden v. Grindle*, 675 A.2d 968 (Me. 1996), is among the cases you find after running your search. Scanning down the text of the opinion, you find a reference in blue to page 466 of *McAfee v. Cole*, cited as follows with the pin cite, *McAfee v. Cole*, 637 A.2d 463, 466 (Me. 1994). When you click on the jump cite, page 466 of *McAfee v. Cole* appears on your computer screen. You can then read *McAfee v. Cole* and mine it for additional cases on point.

You can mine a case in print as well, but you will have to actually look up the cases you find in reporters if you are working with printed materials. When you read a case on Westlaw or LexisNexis, you can jump quickly from one case to the next, which can make your research more efficient.

Westlaw and LexisNexis have developed new platforms that make searching for legal materials even easier. Called WestlawNext and LexisAdvance, these research platforms provide many helpful tools and allow you to use natural language to search all available databases at once. You can then narrow down the results of your search and focus on the information that is most relevant. Westlaw and LexisNexis representatives are available at all times to help you decide which research platform would be best for your particular research problem and to help you retrieve the documents that would be most relevant to your legal question.

D. *Making Sure Your Cases Are Still Good Law*

Another important job that is easier to accomplish on Westlaw and LexisNexis is checking to see whether the cases you have found are still good law. Making this determination is essential. You do not want to submit a memo to a law partner or a brief to a judge that relies on cases that have been overruled. To check on the status of a case, you must use a "citator."

A citator is a list of all the authorities citing a particular case, statute, or legal authority. Frank Shepard began publishing the first citator in 1873 as a series of books indexed to different jurisdictions, called *Shepard's Citations*. In 1996, *Shepard's* was bought by LexisNexis, which soon released an online version of the Shepard's Citation Service. Although the print versions of *Shepard's* remain on the shelves in libraries, they are not as easy to use as the online version. Either version allows you to determine whether a case, statute, or other legal authority has been overturned, reaffirmed, questioned, or cited in later cases.

On LexisNexis, every case and statute bears a "Shepardize" link in its header. When clicked, you can bring up a full *Shepard's* report on the case and statute, which explains the status of the case using plain English phrases like "followed by" or "questioned by" or "overruled," rather than the sometimes cryptic abbreviations that appear in the print version.

Westlaw uses a different citation-checking service called "KeyCite," which uses "status flags" to indicate that information for a document is available. A red flag at the top left of the first page of a case indicates that a case is no longer good law on one particular point of law determined in that case. The case may still be good law on the point of law that you are researching, however. You must read the case carefully to determine why the red flag marks that case. A red flag also signals a statute that has been amended or repealed. A yellow flag indicates that a case has some negative history but has not been overruled. A blue "H" indicates that a case has some history, a green "C" indicates that citing material exists, and a purple quotation mark indicates that the reference directly quotes the cited material. KeyCiting a case on Westlaw is just as easy as Shepardizing it on LexisNexis. It is just a click away. Because it is so easy to use online citators, almost no one uses printed volumes any more.

For example, a yellow flag appears at the top of the first page of *McAfee v. Cole*, along with a message that says, "Distinguished by *Douglas v. York County*, 433 F.3d 143 (1st Cir. 2005)." When you click on

ETHICS ALERT: Failure to Shepardize

A United States District Court in Iowa found the government's brief "most unsatisfactory, indeed misleading, in that it failed to cite" a critical decision. The court pointed to the brief as an example of "the kind of gross oversight that can result from failure to update a 'canned' brief." According to the court, merely Shepardizing the cases in the brief would have revealed the important decision. Whether the government knew of the case and intentionally failed to cite it or was negligent in failing to find and discuss it, the court sternly stated that it expected more from the government.

United States v. Barnes, 912 F. Supp. 1187, 1189 n.1 (N.D. Iowa 1996).

the yellow flag, which indicates that there has been some negative treatment of the case, you are taken to a screen that describes the "Negative Citing Reference" as *Douglas v. York County*, in which the United States Court of Appeals for the First Circuit stated that the "[i]nability to assert claims in one case was not inability to function that could toll limitations based on mental illness." Because this rule does not have any significance in Jonah's case, and no red flag indicated that *McAfee v. Cole* had been overruled, you know that the case is still good law.

Citators can also be a helpful tool in finding cases on point. If you Shepardize or KeyCite a good case, you can find other good cases in which your original good case has been cited. In that way, you can build your list of good cases and complete your research. For example, you can Shepardize *McAfee v. Cole*, 637 A.2d 463 (Me. 1994), to find any other cases in which the court applied the definition of mental illness stated in *McAfee*: "an *overall inability* to function in society that prevents plaintiffs from protecting their legal rights." *See McAfee v. Cole*, 637 A.2d 463, 466 (Me. 1994) (emphasis in original). Then you can read those cases and determine whether any of them factual scenarios that are similar to Jonah's situation, which would make them good analogous cases to use in your memo to show how the court has applied the definition in the past.

Using all the techniques described above, you research the second major issue in Jonah's case: whether the appointment of James as his guardian had any effect on the tolling of the statute of limitations. You decide to start by looking for one good case for the majority position and one good case for the minority position by re-reading Michele Meyer McCarthy's article in the A.L.R.5th: "Effect of Appointment of Legal Representative for Person Under Mental Disability on Running of State Statute of Limitations Against Such Person." This is a good place to begin because the author did extensive research on the subject and listed many cases on point.

There you find several promising cases in which courts adopted the majority view:

Sullivan ex rel. Wrongful Death Beneficiaries of Sullivan v. Chattanooga Medical Investors, L.P., 221 S.W.3d 506 (Tenn. 2007).

Weaver v. Edwin Shaw Hosp., 819 N.E.2d 1079 (Ohio 2004).

Barton-Malow Co. v. Wilburn, 556 N.E.2d 324 (Ind. 1990).

O'Brien v. Massachusetts Bay Transportation Authority, 556 N.E.2d 324 (Mass. 1989)

Sahf v. Havasu City Association for the Retarded and Handicapped, 721 P.2d 1177 (Ariz. App. 1986).

You also find a good case in which the Supreme Court of North Carolina adopted the minority view:

Johnson v. Pilot Life Insurance Company, 7 S.E.2d 475 (N.C. 1940).

Some of these cases were also cited in the Boston University Law Review, "The Guardian or the Ward: for Whom does the Statute Toll?," including *Barton-Malow Co. v. Wilburn*, 556 N.E.2d 324 (Ind. 1990); *O'Brien v. Massachusetts Bay Transportation Authority*, 556 N.E.2d 324 (Mass. 1989); and *Johnson v. Pilot Life Insurance Company*, 7 S.E.2d 475 (N.C. 1940). In the law review article, only North Carolina courts were recognized as consistently recognizing the minority view.

2.7.3. Organizing What You Have Found

After KeyCiting and Shepardizing these cases to determine whether any better cases exist and also to determine whether the cases you have found are still good law, you are ready to begin planning your memo. Before beginning to write the memo, you need to assess the secondary sources, statutes, and cases you have found, eliminating any that are not helpful and organizing those that are helpful in a way that makes them easy to access as you are preparing an outline for your memo. You set aside any cases or secondary sources that did not turn out to be on point and then identify those resources you definitely want to use in your memo.

Next, you may decide to brief some of your cases, especially the ones that seem most promising. Below, following the case itself, is a case brief for *Bowden v. Grindle*, 675 A.2d 968 (Me. 1996).

Bowden v. Grindle, 675 A.2d 968 (Me. 1996)

PROCEDURAL HISTORY:

Grantor of a property deed sued grantees for rescission of the deed in 1990. Maine Superior Court rescinded the deed. Grantees appealed to the Law Court.

FACTS:

Grantor conveyed title to her farm in April 1984, reserving a life estate. Grantor had been treated for chronic depression all her life and was hospitalized for depression in 1982 and 1983. After her husband's death in 1983, she became suicidal. She took medications and was hospitalized at times. She did not remember signing the deed conveying the farm to the grantees. Medical testimony established that she had trouble preparing meals, driving a car, and venturing

968 Me.   **675 ATLANTIC REPORTER, 2d SERIES**

tion. Identical words in different *parts* of the same statute are presumed to have the same meaning. *Sullivan v. Stroop,* 496 U.S. 478, 484, 110 S.Ct. 2499, 2503, 110 L.Ed.2d 438 (1990). So much more so for identical words in the same *section.* Had the Legislature intended the same words to have different meanings within the same statutory provision, it could have stated that intention. Moreover, a statute must be read in its entirety, so that a harmonious result intended by the Legislature can be reached. *Delano v. City of S. Portland,* 405 A.2d 222, 227 (Me.1979); *In re Belgrade Shores, Inc.,* 359 A.2d 59, 61 (Me.1976). Had the Legislature intended the same words to have different meanings within the same statutory provision, it could have stated that intention.

The Assessor's construction impermissibly is skewed to increase the amount of taxes realized at the expense of comporting with the unitary business concept. Pursuant to that concept, Maine taxes income of corporations that do business across state lines by apportioning the income of the entire unitary business to determine what part of the income is attributable to Maine. The Assessor's construction attributes to Maine business activity that is not truly related to this state, i.e., sales in other states. The Superior Court correctly analyzed the issue:

> Under the unitary business concept, the income of a functionally integrated business enterprise is aggregated and then apportioned to reflect the amount of income of the entire unitary business that is attributable to Maine. The income is apportioned among Maine and other states in which the unitary business operates based on the relative level of property, payroll and sales of the unitary business in those states. Property, payroll and sales are thought to be reliable indicators of the level of business activity of the unitary business.

The Assessor's interpretation of the apportionment provisions follows the unitary business principle in all respects except when applying the throwback rule.

In so doing, the Assessor undermines the function of Maine's combined reporting/formula apportionment method of taxation by reducing the accuracy and reliability of the sales factor as a measure of the business activity of a unitary business. Sales by the unitary business that actually occurred in other states are counted as Maine sales.

(Citations omitted.)

Even though the language of section 5211 was enacted when UDITPA dealt only with a single taxpayer, on the subsequent enactment of section 5244 and the adoption of the unitary combined reporting, UDITPA became applicable to all members of the unitary business group, and the language of section 5244 implicitly was amended so that "the taxpayer" would mean the entire unitary business group throughout section 5211. *See* 1 J. Hellerstein & W. Hellerstein, STATE TAXATION ¶ 9.21[1][a] (1993).

I would affirm the Superior Court judgment.

Ruth D. BOWDEN

v.

Edward B. GRINDLE et al.

Law Docket No. HAN–95–270.

Supreme Judicial Court of Maine.

Submitted Jan. 4, 1996.

Decided April 30, 1996.

Grantor of deed of property brought claim against grantees for rescission of deed, and grantees brought counterclaim seeking damages for labor and materials used to improve property. The Superior Court, Hancock County, Mead, J., entered judgment against grantors, and both parties appealed. The Supreme Judicial Court, Dana, J., 651 A.2d 347, vacated and remanded with instructions. On remand, the Superior Court entered judgment for grantor and grantees appealed. The Supreme Judicial Court held that: (1) grantor's mental illness at time of grant was sufficient to toll statute of limitations on her subsequent action seeking rescission of deed; (2) sufficient evidence sup-

Illustration 2-12: *Bowden v. Grindle* Opinion

BOWDEN v. GRINDLE   Me.   **969**
Cite as 675 A.2d 968 (Me. 1996)

ported court's finding that grantor lacked requisite mental capacity to deed land; and (3) damages award of $3674 plus costs was supported by competent evidence.

Affirmed.

1. Limitation of Actions ⬅74(1)

Deed grantor's mental illness at time of grant was sufficient to toll statute of limitations on her subsequent action seeking rescission of deed where expert and lay testimony supported that grantor suffered from psychiatric problems for which she was hospitalized and medicated for decades, grantor testified that she had little recollection of meeting with attorney and did not know what she was signing when she executed deed, and experts testified that grantor was unable to make informed rational judgment about property due to her impaired cognitive thinking. 14 M.R.S.A. § 853.

2. Limitation of Actions ⬅74(1)

"Mental illness" under statute of limitations tolling statute refers to overall inability to function in society that prevents plaintiffs from protecting their legal rights. 14 M.R.S.A. § 853.

See publication Words and Phrases for other judicial constructions and definitions.

3. Limitation of Actions ⬅199(1)

Whether person is mentally ill within meaning of provision allowing tolling of statute of limitations on action for mental illness is question of fact. 14 M.R.S.A. § 853.

4. Appeal and Error ⬅1008.1(5), 1010.1(4)

Supreme Judicial Court will not set aside trial court's factual findings unless they are clearly erroneous, that is, there is no competent evidence in record to support them.

5. Appeal and Error ⬅994(3), 1012.1(2)

Weight of evidence and credibility of witnesses is within exclusive province of factfinder.

6. Deeds ⬅211(1)

Sufficient evidence supported court's finding that grantor lacked requisite mental capacity to deed land; medical testimony revealed that at time of conveyance grantor was not able to make informed rational judgment about conveying her farm, her cognitive thinking was impaired, her dependency problem rendered her helpless, and anyone she depended on may have received deed to her property. Restatement (Second) of Property § 34.5.

7. Deeds ⬅68(1.5)

Grantor's mental incompetency alone is sufficient to rescind deed. Restatement (Second) of Property § 34.5.

8. Implied and Constructive Contracts ⬅112

Damages award of $3,674 plus costs on claim for unjust enrichment to grantees of deed who had taken care of land, after court ordered rescission of grant of deed to land to grantees, was supported by competent evidence in the record; grantees were reimbursed for expenses which represented quantifiable benefits retained by landowner such as insurance, lime, firewood, well, soil test, and taxes but value of hay producing fields could not be included in damage award as improvement to property as value had not been proven.

9. Appeal and Error ⬅1013

Damage award will be disturbed only if there is no rational basis to support it, that is, no competent supporting evidence in record.

10. Implied and Constructive Contracts ⬅110

Recovery under doctrine of unjust enrichment is measured by value of benefits that plaintiff proves are actually received and retained by defendant.

11. Implied and Constructive Contracts ⬅110

Cost of improvements, such as value of work, labor, services, and materials furnished, is evidence that may be considered in determining value of benefit conferred for purposes of unjust enrichment damages.

Illustration 2-12: (Continued)

Barry K. Mills, Hale & Hamlin, Ellsworth, for Plaintiff.

William N. Ferm, Ferm, McSweendy & Collier, Ellsworth, for Defendant.

Before WATHEN, C.J. and ROBERTS, GLASSMAN, CLIFFORD, RUDMAN, DANA, and LIPEZ, JJ.

DANA, Justice.

Edward B. Grindle and Prudence E. Grindle appeal from the judgment entered in the Superior Court (Hancock County, *Mead, J.*) in favor of Ruth D. Bowden on her complaint seeking rescission of a deed given to the Grindles and on the amount awarded to the Grindles on their counterclaim based on unjust enrichment. The Grindles contend that the court erred in concluding that Bowden's mental illness was sufficient to toll the statute of limitations, in finding that Bowden lacked the requisite competence to convey the property, and in its computation of the damages awarded to them on their counterclaim. Finding no error, we affirm the judgment.

Bowden conveyed title to her farm in Blue Hill to the Grindles on April 3, 1984, reserving a life estate to herself. Six years and three months after this conveyance Bowden commenced an action seeking the rescission of the deed on the basis that in 1984 she lacked the mental capacity to convey her land. In the alternative, she claimed that the conveyance was the result of undue influence by the Grindles. The Grindles asserted the statute of limitations as an affirmative defense and counterclaimed, seeking damages for labor and material used to improve the property and for the return of various items.

Following the Grindles request for a jury trial the parties and the court agreed that the jury's verdict would be advisory on the equitable counts and binding on the issues triable of right to a jury. The jury found

that Bowden had not commenced her action within the statute of limitations and awarded a clock to the Grindles on their counterclaim. The court concluded that it was bound by the jury's determinations and entered a judgment on all counts for the Grindles. Bowden appealed and the Grindles cross-appealed. Holding that the trial court erred when it considered itself bound by the advisory jury's verdict, we vacated the judgment.[1] *See Bowden v. Grindle,* 651 A.2d 347 (Me.1994).

On remand the Superior Court found that Bowden's claim was not time barred because Bowden was legally incompetent during the relevant period thus tolling the statute of limitations. The court also found that Bowden lacked the requisite competence to convey the property and entered a judgment in her favor on her claim for rescission of the deed. The court entered a judgment in favor of the Grindles on their counterclaim for unjust enrichment and awarded damages.

The record discloses the following: Ruth and Millard Bowden had no children and Edward Grindle, their nephew, lived with them off and on when he was growing up. Bowden was dependent on her husband who had complete responsibility for the finances and operation of their farm. Bowden had been treated for chronic depression her entire life, had been prescribed medications for anxiety and depression, and was hospitalized for depression for parts of December 1982 and January 1983. After she was released she received psychiatric treatment and medication as an out-patient. In September 1983 Millard died. The medical testimony revealed that after her husband's death Bowden's condition became acute and suicidal. Bowden's friends testified that her depression grew worse and she could not think, remember or understand what was going on. She does not remember much of what happened during the year following her hus-

---

1. We concluded that a statute of limitations defense when used to bar an equitable action is not an issue triable of right by a jury and therefore the court erred when it considered itself bound by the jury's finding that Bowden's claim was barred by the statute of limitations. *Bowden v. Grindle,* 651 A.2d 347, 349–50 (Me.1994). We also determined that the Grindles' counterclaim labeled *quantum meruit* was in fact an equitable claim for unjust enrichment and thus not triable of right by a jury. *Id.* at 349–51. Therefore we held that the court also erred when it considered itself bound by the jury's determinations on the Grindles' counterclaim for unjust enrichment. *Id.* at 350–51.

Illustration 2-12: (Continued)

band's death. She took medications and was hospitalized "off and on."

Bowden does not remember discussing with the Grindles that she would convey the farm to them. Her recollection of meeting with an attorney to execute documents relating to the conveyance was similarly vague. Bowden's friend arranged for Bowden to meet with an attorney to settle her husband's estate. In the Spring of 1984 Bowden contacted her friend about arranging another appointment with the attorney. Bowden testified that she had no recollection of signing the deed conveying her farm to the Grindles and that she did not know what she was signing. She also had no recollection of signing a power of attorney she gave the Grindles. She did have a recollection, however, of asking the attorney to prepare the power of attorney after having been told it would be a good idea. She testified that she did not retain the attorney to prepare the deed and power of attorney although she was billed and paid for the legal services of drafting a will and a quitclaim deed. In the years following the conveyance Bowden continued to take medication and was hospitalized again in 1986. In 1986 Bowden learned of the conveyance in a conversation with a friend.

Edward Grindle testified that he was aware Bowden was taking medication but denied having knowledge of the reason or of the fact that Bowden was undergoing psychiatric care and had been suicidal. Edward characterized Bowden's emotional and medical condition after her husband's death as "very good for someone that had just lost their husband...." Prudence Grindle testified that she found Bowden very depressed on occasion and believed she was being treated for anxiety and depression. Edward acknowledged that Bowden was in a position of dependency on him and his wife after her husband's death and that he was the only male figure and close relative in her life. The Grindles testified that several times after her husband's death Bowden initiated discussions about conveying her farm to them but they did not accept her offer until April 1984. Bowden delivered the deed to the Grindles. Edward testified that he recorded the deed in 1986 despite Bowden's

request that he not record the deed because it would cause trouble in the family.

I.

[1–4] The Grindles first contend that the court erred in concluding that Bowden's mental illness was sufficient to toll the statute of limitations. If a person is mentally ill when the cause of action accrues she may bring an action within the statutorily prescribed time limit after the disability is removed.   14 M.R.S.A. § 853 (Supp.1995). Pursuant to the tolling statute mental illness refers to "an *overall inability* to function in society that prevents plaintiffs from protecting their legal rights." *McAfee v. Cole*, 637 A.2d 463, 466 (Me.1994) (citations omitted). Whether a person is mentally ill within the meaning of 14 M.R.S.A. § 853 is a question of fact. *Morris v. Hunter*, 652 A.2d 80, 82 (Me.1994). We will not set aside a trial court's factual findings unless they are clearly erroneous, that is, there is no competent evidence in the record to support them. *F.D.I.C. v. Proia*, 663 A.2d 1252, 1254 (Me. 1995).

The expert and lay testimony supports the court's determinations that Bowden had suffered from psychiatric problems for which she had been hospitalized and medicated for decades and that her depression and anxiety were most acute after her husband's death in 1983. There was evidence that Bowden's thinking was impaired, that she could not remember, and that she experienced suicidal thoughts. Bowden testified that she had little recollection of meeting with the attorney and she did not know what she was signing when she executed the deed. Medical experts explained that memory loss is consistent with depression when a person becomes so preoccupied that the person's actions may not have registered. In the opinions of the experts, Bowden in 1984 was not able to make an informed rational judgment about conveying her property because she was experiencing the effects of her depression at that time, her cognitive thinking was impaired, and her problem of dependency rendered her helpless. The medical testimony also suggested that anyone she formed a

Illustration 2-12: (Continued)

dependency on might have received a deed to her property.

[5] Although there was conflicting testimony regarding Bowden's ability to drive and cook for herself, the medical testimony confirmed that there were times when Bowden had difficulty cooking her own meals, leaving the house, and driving. The weight of the evidence and credibility of witnesses is within the exclusive province of the factfinder. *State v. Sargent*, 656 A.2d 1196, 1200 (1995).

In 1986 Bowden was hospitalized three times for psychiatric disorders and during this period she learned from her friend that she had conveyed her property to the Grindles. The evidence reveals that Bowden's disability was not removed until her condition began to change in 1986 or 1987 when her condition began to improve. Bowden filed her complaint in July 1990 within six years from the time the disability was removed.

The court found that the medical testimony supported the conclusion that Bowden was legally incompetent during the period in question and concluded that the statute of limitations was tolled during this period. Based on the evidence the court's implicit determination that Bowden was suffering from a mental disability sufficient to toll the statute of limitations is not clearly erroneous.

II.

[6, 7] After concluding that Bowden's incompetence tolled the statute of limitations, the court found it also impaired her capacity to make the disputed transaction. A grantor's incompetency alone is sufficient to rescind a deed. *Bragdon v. Drew*, 658 A.2d 666, 668–69 (Me.1995); *see also* RESTATEMENT (SECOND) OF PROPERTY § 34.5 (1992) ("A mentally incompetent person cannot make a valid ... inter vivos donative transfer."). The Grindles, however, contend that the court did not focus on the appropriate standard for assessing a grantor's competence or capacity to convey the property. They argue that Bowden had the capacity to convey the

property because she was "able to understand what [s]he is about." *Hovey v. Chase*, 52 Me. 304, 317 (1863).

In *Bragdon* we quoted with approval section 15 of the RESTATEMENT (SECOND) OF CONTRACTS (1981) which provides in relevant part:

(1) A person incurs only voidable contractual duties by entering into a transaction if by reason of mental illness or defect

(a) he is unable to understand in a reasonable manner the nature and consequences of the transaction, or

(b) he is unable to act in a reasonable manner in relation to the transaction and the other party has reason to know of his condition.

Bragdon, 658 A.2d at 668. There is sufficient evidence to support the court's finding that Bowden lacked the requisite mental capacity to deed the land. *Id.* The medical testimony reveals that at the time of the conveyance Bowden was not able to make an informed rational judgment about conveying her farm to the Grindles, her cognitive thinking was impaired, her dependency problem rendered her helpless, and anyone she depended on may have received a deed to her property.

III.

[8] Finally, the Grindles contend that the court awarded inadequate damages on their counterclaim for unjust enrichment by failing to compensate them adequately for their labor and money spent in the restoration of Bowden's hay fields. They contend that Bowden retained the benefit of the income potential of the fields.

[9–11] "A damage award will be disturbed only if there is no rational basis to support it, that is, no competent supporting evidence in the record." *McCain Foods, Inc. v. Gervais*, 657 A.2d 782, 783 (Me.1995). "'Recovery under the doctrine of unjust enrichment is measured by the value of the benefits that the plaintiff proves are actually received and retained by the defendant.'"[2]

---

2. To prevail on a claim for unjust enrichment the following elements must be proved: the plaintiff

conferred a benefit on the defendant; an appreciation or knowledge by the defendant of the

Illustration 2-12: (Continued)

NADEAU v. RAINBOW RUGS, INC.   Me. **973**
Cite as 675 A.2d 973 (Me. 1996)

ERA–Northern Assocs. v. Border Trust Co.,
662 A.2d 243, 246 (Me.1995) (citation omitted). The cost of improvements, such as the
value of the work, labor, services, and materials furnished, is evidence that may be considered in determining the value of the benefit conferred. *A.F.A.B., Inc. v. Old Orchard
Beach,* 639 A.2d 103, 106 (Me.1994) (citations
omitted).

The court awarded the Grindles damages
in the amount of $3,674, plus costs. The
court determined that the amount of damages based on the Grindles' expenses for the
following items represented quantifiable benefits retained by Bowden: insurance, lime,
firewood, well, soil test, and taxes. There is
competent evidence in the record to support
the court's damage award. The Grindles
produced receipts and testified regarding
these expenses. The Grindles, however, did
not prove the value of the hay producing
fields that they contend Bowden retained.
See ERA–Northern Assocs., 662 A.2d at 246.
Bowden did not make any profit as a result
of Edward's work renovating the fields.
Furthermore, because he did not keep records of the hours he worked, the Grindles
were required to estimate the amount of the
time expended to improve the property. *See
Williams v. Ubaldo,* 670 A.2d 913, 917 (Me.
1996) (damages are not recoverable when
uncertain or speculative). Based on a review
of the evidence the court was not compelled
to award the Grindles a greater amount of
damages on their counterclaim for unjust
enrichment.

Judgment affirmed.

All concurring.

Joyce NADEAU f/k/a Joyce Recker

v.

RAINBOW RUGS, INC.

Supreme Judicial Court of Maine.

Argued Jan. 3, 1996.

Decided May 7, 1996.

Former employee brought hostile work
environment sexual harassment action
against employer. The Superior Court,
Cumberland County, Mills, J., found employer liable, and employer appealed. The Supreme Judicial Court, Wathen, C.J., held
that: (1) given unique circumstances, single
incident of supervisor's sexual harassment of
employee was sufficient to establish hostile
work environment sexual harassment; (2) as
a matter of first impression, employer could
be held liable for supervisor's hostile work
environment sexual harassment of employee;
and (3) employee could recover attorney fees
incurred in preliminary action before Human
Rights Commission.

Affirmed.

1. Civil Rights ⚖145
Discriminatory behavior that is sufficiently severe or pervasive creates hostile or
abusive working environment. 5 M.R.S.A.
§ 4572, subd. 1, par. A.

2. Civil Rights ⚖145
Standard for determining whether conduct is actionable as hostile work environment harassment requires objectively hostile
or abusive environment, one that reasonable
person would find hostile or abusive, as well
as victim's subjective perception that environment is abusive. 5 M.R.S.A. § 4572,
subd. 1, par. A.

3. Civil Rights ⚖145
Although many cases considering hostile
environment harassment claims involve pat-

ERA–Northern Assocs. v. Border Trust Co., 662
A.2d 243, 245 (Me.1995) (citing *Bowden,* 651
A.2d at 350).

benefit; and the defendant's acceptance or reten-
tion of the benefit was under such circumstances
as to make it inequitable for the defendant to
retain the benefit without payment of its value.

Illustration 2-12: (Continued)

beyond her home at that time. She continued taking medication after the conveyance and was hospitalized again in 1986, the year a friend told her about the conveyance. After that, her condition began to improve. In July 1990, six years and three months after the conveyance, she sought its rescission.

ISSUE:

Was grantor mentally ill at the time of the conveyance, tolling the six-year statute of limitations?

HOLDING:

Yes. The statute of limitations was tolled until her disability was removed in 1986.

RATIONALE:

Grantor was mentally ill at the time of the conveyance as she "was not able to make an informed rational judgment about conveying her property because she was experiencing the effects of her depression at that time."

Using your research log and case briefs, you are able to tell which cases relate to which issues you have been researching: Issue 1—What it means to be mentally ill when the cause of action accrued; and Issue 2—Whether the appointment of a guardian affects the tolling of the statute of limitations. A good place to start would be to divide the secondary sources, cases, and statutes into two piles or two electronic folders, one for everything you have found that relates to Issue 1 and the other for everything you have found that relates to Issue 2. Your piles, labeled Issue 1 and Issue 2, would contain the following:

Issue 1: What it means to be mentally ill when the cause of action accrued

Meaning of "mentally ill":

Cases found in secondary source, Michele Meyer McCarthy, J.D., *When Is Person, Other than One Claiming Posttraumatic Stress Syndrome or Memory Repression, Within Coverage of Statutory Provision Tolling Running of Limitations Period on Basis of Mental Disability*, 23 A.L.R.6th 697 (2007 & Supp. 2013)

Bowden v. Grindle, 675 A.2d 968 (Me. 1996)

Douglas v. York County, 433 F.3d 143 (1st Cir. 2005)

Cases listed in annotations from tolling provision:

Douglas v. York County, 433 F.3d 143 (1st Cir. 2005).

Bowden v. Grindle, 675 A.2d 968 (Me. 1996)

McAfee v. Cole, 637 A.2d 463 (Me. 1994)

Morris v. Hunter, 652 A.2d 89 (Me. 1994)

Cases found in key number 74 search:

Douglas v. York County, 433 F.3d 143 (1st Cir. 2005)

Rowe v. Maine, 324 F. Supp. 2d 238 (D. Me. 2004) (not helpful)

Priestman v. Canadian Pacific Ltd., 782 F. Supp. 681 (D. Me. 1992)

Bowden v. Grindle, 675 A.2d 968 (Me. 1996)

Dasha v. Maine Medical Center, 665 A.2d 993 (Me. 1995)

McAfee v. Cole, 637 A.2d 463 (Me. 1994)

Oliver v. Berry, 53 Me. 206 (Me. 1865)

When the cause of action accrued (timing):

M.O. Regensteiner, "Time of existence of mental incompetency which will prevent or suspend running of statute of limitations," 41 A.L.R.2d 726 (1955 & Supp. 2013)

Priestman v. Canadian Pacific Ltd., 782 F. Supp. 681 (D. Me. 1992)

Chasse v. Mazerolle, 580 A.2d 155 (Me. 1990)

McCutchen v. Currier, 94 Me. 362, 47 A. 923 (1900)

Issue 2: Effect of appointment of guardian

Majority view: The appointment of a guardian has no effect on the tolling provision.

Weaver v. Edwin Shaw Hosp., 819 N.E.2d 1079, 1083-1085 (Ohio 2004) (concluding that the appointment of a guardian has no effect on the tolling provision because "the statute does not mention the effect of a guardian's appointment" and citing opinions of state courts adopting the majority rule from Alabama, Arizona, California, Massachusetts, Michigan, New York, Nebraska, and Washington, and federal courts adopting the majority opinion applying Michigan, Missouri, New Mexico, and Nevada state law).

Michele Meyer McCarthy, Effect of Appointment of Legal Representative for Person Under Mental Disability on Running of State Statute of Limitations Against Such Person, 111 A.L.R.5th 159 § § 4-7 (2001 & Supp. 2013) (adding state courts adopting the majority rule from Arkansas, Florida, Georgia Illinois, Indiana, Kentucky, Maryland, Minnesota, Mississippi, New Jersey, Oklahoma, and Rhode Island and federal courts adopting the majority rule applying Illinois and Oklahoma state law).

Colo. Rev. Stat. 13-81-103(1)(a): The Colorado tolling provision expressly provides for the statute of limitations to run after a guardian is appointed.

Barton-Malow Co. v. Wilburn, 556 N.E.2d 324, 325 (Ind. 1990) (concluding that "the statutory language is clear and unambiguous [and the] appointment of a guardian does not alter the fact of mental unsoundness," it does not terminate the legal disability").

Sullivan ex rel. Wrongful Death Beneficiaries of Sullivan v. Chattanooga Med. Investors, L.P., 221 S.W.3d 506, 511 (Tenn. 2007) (concluding that because the claim belongs to "the person who suffered the legal wrong," not the legal guardian, the statute of limitations is tolled for as long as that person is under the legal disability of "unsound mind").

Sahf v. Havasu City Assn. for the Retarded and Handicapped, 721 P.2d 1177, 1182 (Ariz. App. 1986) (holding that a mentally incompetent person's disability was not removed when a guardian was appointed based on legislative intent, asserting that the legislature considered not only a mentally disabled person's inability to sue when enacting the tolling statute, but also the disabled person's difficulties in testifying and providing information to a court).

Minority view: The appointment of a guardian triggers the running of the statute of limitations when the guardian has the right or legal duty to pursue legal action on behalf of a ward.

McCarthy, 111 A.L.R.5th at § § 9-10 (citing state courts adopting the minority rule from Hawaii, Kansas, New Hampshire, New York, North Carolina, Washington, and West Virginia).

Johnson v. Pilot Life Ins. Co., 7 S.E.2d 475, 477 (N.C. 1940) (reasoning that the "policy of repose which underlies statutes limiting the time in which actions may be brought would be imperfectly expressed if these statutes did not apply to all those who might bring such actions, and actions which might be brought in their behalf," like a guardian who has a duty "to bring suit, when necessary").

2.7.4. Getting Ready to Write

One of the biggest challenges of legal research and writing is knowing when it is time to stop researching and begin writing. Knowing that Ms. Walker is depending on you to find all the relevant statutes and cases that relate to Jonah's case before beginning to analyze the law places a heavy burden on your shoulders. You are probably hesitant to stop your search for cases, fearing you may have missed something.

Although you can never know for certain that you have found all the relevant cases, there comes a time when you must stop researching and start planning your memo. Luckily, you can always conduct more research, even after you begin writing, if you find you need additional material. In addition, you should Shepardize or KeyCite your cases right before you hand in your memo to make sure those cases are still good law.

Because researching the law is an art as well as a science, you will have to rely on your intuition somewhat in knowing when to stop researching and start preparing to write. One of the ways you can tell that you have completed the research process is when the same cases keep coming up over and over again, especially when you find citations to those cases in support of recent holdings. When you look at the list of cases you have created, you begin to understand that courts have used the same definition for "mentally ill" and consistently cited to the same cases for that definition, all of which you have found. You have also found the cases on which courts have relied for the meaning of "when the cause of action accrues." As for the question of whether the appointment of a guardian removes a plaintiff's disability and starts the limitations period running, you have found a reliable secondary source, the A.L.R.5th annotation, written by Michele Meyer McCarthy, that describes the majority and minority rules and lists cases from all the jurisdictions in which courts have considered the question. You have also found representative cases in which courts have gone both ways, which you have established are still good law. Although you may want to conduct some more research after you begin writing your memo, you seem to have found everything you need to get started. The time has come to stop researching the issues and begin thinking about what you want to say in your memo.

Chapter 3

Legal Analysis

3.1. Getting Organized

By now, with so much information swirling around in your head, it is time to get your thoughts down on paper. Do not be overwhelmed by this prospect. The important step at this point is to find some method of managing your research and your thoughts. Whether you use a chart or some other method, you need to start writing down what you are finding for several reasons. First, many people get writer's block at this point. They sit down to write and do not know where to start. Using a chart or some other method of breaking down the information will give you a way to visualize your analysis before you actually start writing your document. Once you have developed a plan or your memo, the writing process will be more manageable.

Start by reviewing what you have learned in your research and applying it to the facts of Jonah's situation. Remember that most legal analysis consists of the same basic components: (1) identifying the issues; (2) understanding the relevant legal rules; (3) describing previous cases that explain the legal rules or illustrate how those rules have been applied to specific facts in the past; (4) applying the legal framework to your client's situation; and (5) reaching a conclusion about the likely outcome. You will need to consider each of these components when analyzing the issues in Jonah's case.

3.2. Finalizing Your Understanding of the Issues

You have already identified and refined your understanding of the issues throughout the research process. Before you even began your research, you had to think about what you wanted to know. You knew that to determine whether Jonah could sue the hospital, you needed to consider any preliminary procedural questions, such as whether the statute of limitations for his medical malpractice claim had already expired. When you learned that the statute of limitations for Jonah's claim had already expired, you refined your understanding of the issue further by focusing on (1) whether the limitations period has been tolled because of Jonah's mental disabilities and (2) whether James's appointment as Jonah's guardian affects the potential tolling of the statute of limitations. You also determined that to answer the first issue, you need to consider two sub-issues: (a) whether James's mental disabilities classify him as mentally ill and (b) if so, whether he had this condition at the time the cause of action accrued.

Before you started your research, you would not have been able to identify all of the issues and sub-issues involved in answering the question of whether the statute of limitations had expired. Throughout your research process, however, you used what you were learning about the legal rules and how they had been applied in the past to refine the issues into two separate questions, one with sub-questions that you must analyze. Because you have two distinct questions—one involving whether the statute of limitations has been tolled and the other involving the effect of James's appointment as Jonah's guardian—be aware that they will require two distinct analyses. Thus, at this point, the framework for your legal analysis looks something like this:

Overall Question: Has the statute of limitations expired for Jonah's medical malpractice claim?

1. Under the tolling provision, is the statute of limitations tolled by Jonah's limited intellectual ability?
   a. Does Jonah's limited intellectual ability classify him as mentally ill?
   b. Did Jonah have this condition at the time the cause of action accrued?
2. Does the tolling provision still apply if Jonah was under the care of a guardian during the limitations period?

3.3. Finding the Rules

Now that you have refined your issues, you need to identify and understand the legal rules relating to each issue. This is a critical component of your legal analysis because the legal rules are the principles that will guide any court in its analysis of Jonah's claim. To determine the legal rules that apply to Jonah's claim, start with the statutory provisions you found. The relevant language in section 2902 states:

> § 2902. Statute of limitations for health care providers and health care practitioners. Actions for professional negligence shall be commenced within 3 years after the cause of action accrues. For the purposes of this section, a cause of action accrues on the date of the act or omission giving rise to the injury.

Think about what this rule is telling you: A lawsuit based upon a medical malpractice claim must be started within three years from the date that someone did something (or failed to do something) that resulted in the injury.

By applying this rule to Jonah's situation, you have already determined that unless the three-year statute of limitations is tolled, Jonah's medical malpractice claim is too late and will not be allowed. That is why you looked at the tolling provisions in Maine's statutes when you were conducting your research. You decide to analyze your first issue thoroughly before addressing the second issue regarding the effect of James's appointment as guardian.

The relevant tolling provision you found explains that the statute of limitations may be tolled when a person entitled to bring an action under section 2902 is "mentally ill . . . when the cause of action accrues." Note that this rule sets forth two elements that must be satisfied in order for the rule to apply: (1) a person must be "mentally ill" and (2) that condition must have been present when the cause of action accrued. You notice how these two elements directly relate to the two sub-issues you have identified in (a) and (b) in your framework for your analysis:

---

a. Does Jonah's limited intellectual ability classify him as mentally ill?
b. Did Jonah have this condition at the time the cause of action accrued?

Because the process of legal analysis involves going back and forth among the various components, what you learn by identifying and understanding the rules informs the way you refine your issues and determine which facts are legally significant. Before conducting your research, you could not have identified these two sub-issues or known which facts would be important. You had to wait until you found the rule setting forth the two elements required for the statute of limitations to be tolled.

Now that you have identified the two elements that are required to toll the statute of limitations for Jonah's medical malpractice claim, you might want to create a chart to help you visualize your analysis. In the first column, list each element that is required under the tolling statue, the applicable legal rule. If your legal rule involved a list of factors to be considered or a balancing test, the first column would list each individual factor or the interests to be balanced.

Elements Required to Toll Statute of Limitations				
A person must be "mentally ill"				
When the cause of action accrues				

Although you have identified the elements that must be satisfied, you may be wondering what they mean. You look at the tolling provision in the statute again, but it does not provide a definition for "mentally ill" or "when the cause of action accrues." Oftentimes, though, other parts of a statute may provide definitions for terms. Fortunately, you recall that the section of the statute that sets forth the statute of limitations for medical malpractice claims contains a definition for "when the cause of action accrues." You look back at section 2902 and see that you are correct: It states that a cause of action accrues "on the date of the act or omission giving rise to the injury." This definition is a legal rule that helps you to understand the meaning of one of your elements. In your chart, create a category for "Rules" next to the "Elements" column. Here you can put the rules that further define and clarify the elements.

Elements Required to Toll Statute of Limitations	Rules			
A person must be "mentally ill"				
When the cause of action accrues	"A cause of action accrues on the date of the act or omission giving rise to the injury." 24 Me. Rev. Stat. § 2902 (2013).			

You are pleased to have found clarification of when a cause of action accrues, but you cannot find anything in the statute that provides a definition of when a person is "mentally ill." Because you know that the legal rules are not found only in the statutes, you turn to your research notes to see if you can learn how "mentally ill" has been defined by the courts. You remember reading an annotation in the A.L.R. that dealt with what it means to be "mentally ill" for purposes of a tolling provision. You quickly find the annotation in your research notes and congratulate yourself not only for writing down the annotation author's name, but also for including in your notes all of the Maine cases listed there. You look through your collection of cases and find one of the cases listed in the annotation. To determine whether this case provides a definition of "mentally ill," you skim the headnotes that appear before the opinion begins. Because the headnotes tell you the legal principles that are discussed in the opinion, they are a great place to look to see what legal rules are involved in the case. Headnote 1 includes the following information:

> If a person is mentally ill when the cause of action accrues she may bring an action within the statutorily prescribed time limit after the disability is removed. Me. Rev. Stat. Ann tit. 14, § 853 (Supp. 1995). Pursuant to the tolling statute mental illness refers to an overall inability to function in society that prevents plaintiffs from protecting their legal rights.

This looks promising, so you find the headnote in the opinion and read what the opinion says about it. It is almost identical to the annotation headnote, except it contains more citations.

> If a person is mentally ill when the cause of action accrues she may bring an action within the statutorily prescribed time limit after the disability is removed. 14 M.R.S.A. § 853 (Supp. 1995). Pursuant to the tolling statute mental illness refers to "an *overall inability* to function in society that prevents plaintiffs from protecting their legal rights." *McAfee v. Cole*, 637 A.2d 463, 466 (Me. 1994) (citations omitted). Whether a person is mentally ill within the meaning of 14 M.R.S.A. § 853 is a question of fact. *Morris v. Hunter*, 652 A.2d 80, 82 (Me. 1994).

You carefully read the parts of the opinion in which this language appears to confirm that it is indeed a rule and not a dictum in the opinion. Attorneys need to be careful not to present dicta as legal rules in a legal memorandum or brief. As explained earlier, dicta may be presented as persuasive legal authority, but not as mandatory authority. You are pleased to have found a rule to help you understand what "mentally ill" means and you insert this rule into your chart. Be sure to provide full citations to legal authority, including pin cites, in your chart. This will save valuable time and effort later when you are actually writing your memo.

Elements Required to Toll Statute of Limitations	Rules			
A person must be "mentally ill"	Definition: "overall inability to function in society that prevents plaintiffs from protecting their legal rights." *Bowden v. Grindle*, 675 A.2d 968, 971 (Me. 1996); *McAfee v. Cole*, 637 A.2d 463, 466 (Me. 1994).			
When the cause of action accrues	"A cause of action accrues on the date of the act or omission giving rise to the injury." 24 Me. Rev. Stat. § 2902 (2013).			

While you are pleased to have this additional rule, the opinion does not provide a list of factors to consider in determining whether one has the "overall inability to function in society." You realize that you will need to study your cases to find specific examples of the types of facts that influence that determination.

3.4. Identifying Analogous Cases

As you turn to your stack of cases, keep in mind how you will use those cases. You are looking for specific examples of how the law has been applied previously to different factual situations. Seeing how the law has been applied previously should help you understand how the law works in action. You should also be looking for ways in which the prior case is similar to or different from Jonah's situation. Using previous cases in your legal analysis provides support for your arguments, giving you precedent to point the court towards, and helps you to make a prediction, knowing that courts abide by the principle of *stare decisis*.

Remember that *stare decisis* requires that the court stand by its previous decisions, absent a compelling reason to deviate from the precedent. Because of this, identifying how Jonah's situation is similar to or different from previous cases is a way to predict the outcome because a judge will base his or her conclusion on how the precedent established in those previous cases will apply to Jonah's situation.

As you study the cases, look for meaningful similarities or differences. You may see many similarities and differences that have no significance in terms of the legal analysis. Those are not the ones that will be useful to you. You are looking for those commonalities or distinctions that matter to the analysis.

Be creative when thinking about the cases; do not discard a case simply because it does not initially appear to be on point with Jonah's situation. You can make many different kinds of analogies: Narrow analogies compare closely parallel facts, while broad analogies compare more general commonalities or characteristics. Narrow analogies can be made when you find a close match between the facts in the prior case and Jonah's situation. Narrow analogies are the stronger type of analogy and the ones you should use if you want the court to rule the same way in your case as it did in the prior case. If you can show the court that Jonah's situation is very similar to the situation in the prior case, the court will likely follow the prior case and rule in Jonah's favor. Broad analogies, however, can still be useful. Broad analogies would be used when the previous case is not a close match to Jonah's situation, but you are trying to convince the court that the case still might be helpful. Broad analogies require additional thought because you need to identify the common characteristics between the prior case and Jonah's case. This requires studying the case and the court's rationale to find an analogy or distinction that will help convince the court to rule in Jonah's favor.

You start your review of possible analogous cases with *Bowden v. Grindle*, 675 A.2d 968, 971 (Me. 1996), the case in which the court defined the term "mental illness" as "an overall inability to function in society that prevents plaintiffs from protecting their legal rights." To support its holding that the plaintiff in the case was suffering from "a mental disability sufficient to toll the statute of limitations," the court pointed to evidence that she "suffered from psychiatric problems, including depression and anxiety, for which she had been hospitalized and medicated for decades and the effects of which had prevented her from making an informed rational judgment about conveying her property, and that her cognitive thinking was impaired, that her problem of dependency rendered her helpless, and that there were times when she had difficulty cooking her own meals, leaving the house, and driving." The court also noted that she had suffered from memory losses.

You review what you know about Jonah. He is able to care for his basic needs: He can cook simple meals and shower and dress himself; however, he is unable to drive. You recognize some immediate similarities and distinctions between the plaintiff in *Bowden* and Jonah: The plaintiff in *Bowden* could cook and drive, though she had difficulty doing both at times; Jonah can cook, but cannot drive at all. You note that the court's rationale for its holding focuses on the woman's inability to make an "informed rational judgment." This rationale will be a key factor in the court's future decisions about whether someone is mentally ill. Because of the useful reasoning and close match in some of the facts, this case seems like it would be useful in analyzing whether Jonah is mentally ill for purposes of the tolling statute.

Finding one case, like *Bowden*, that you can use for both rule and analogous-case purposes provides a good foundation for your legal analysis. Sometimes one case will contain good legal rules, but not analogous facts. Finding a case that provides both is especially helpful. To keep track of this case and to help visualize your analysis, you create a third column in your chart in which to include the details of any analogous cases you might use.

You read through another case that does not seem very useful. The facts are quite different, and the court does not explicitly articulate its rationale. Although a court's rationale is sometimes implicit in an opinion rather than explicitly stated, you cannot discern the basis on which the court made its decision and decide to set it aside.

Next you pick up *Chasse v. Mazerolle*, 580 A.2d 155 (Me. 1990), in which the plaintiff was mentally disabled and sued her doctor to recover damages for wrongful sterilization. The court concluded "that evidence of [the plaintiff's] marriage and divorce more than two years prior to the filing of her claim . . . [gave] no indication that [she] possessed sufficient competence to comprehend and exercise her legal rights. . . . " The court explained that "the legal standard of competency varies for different purposes." You spend some time thinking about how you might use this case. The facts are not as close a match as those in *Bowden*; you know that Jonah has never been married and, thus, the factual comparison seems weak. Yet, the court's rationale focused on whether the plaintiff possessed sufficient competence to comprehend and exercise her legal rights, a factor that seems important in Jonah's case, too. It is also helpful that the court's statement that the legal standard can vary for different purpose sounds like a legal rule that you should include in the rules section of your chart. For these reasons, you enter this case into your chart, with the legal rule in the rules section and the facts and rationale in the analogous cases section.

You read the headnotes, case summaries, and facts sections of some more cases, but your assessment of them is that they are not useful for your analysis of when someone is mentally ill. Thus, you move on to the second element, which requires that the condition of mental illness exist when the cause of action accrues. The definition provided by the statute seems clear, and you think you can apply it to Jonah's claim without looking for cases

Elements Required to Toll Statute of Limitations	Rules	Analogous Cases		
A person must be "mentally ill"	Definition: "overall inability to function in society that prevents plaintiffs from protecting their legal rights." *Bowden v. Grindle*, 675 A.2d 968, 971 (Me. 1996); *McAfee v. Cole*, 637 A.2d 463, 466 (Me. 1994).	Case 1: *Bowden v. Grindle*, 675 A.2d 968, 971-72 (Me. 1996). Relevant conclusion: plaintiff was mentally ill.

Relevant facts: Even though plaintiff could drive and cook by herself on occasion, she had difficulty performing those functions or even leaving her house at times. She also had a long history of psychiatric problems, including depression and anxiety, for which she had been hospitalized and medicated for decades. Evidence showed that her cognitive thinking was impaired. She had memory lapses.

Relevant Rationale: Because of these limitations, she was not capable of making an "informed rational judgment" to convey her property. | | |
| When the cause of action accrues | "A cause of action accrues on the date of the act or omission giving rise to the injury." 24 Me. Rev. Stat. § 2902 (2013). | | | |

that further explain this rule. Nonetheless, you review the cases you had put in a pile for the timing issue to see if you have missed anything. You determine that none of the cases provide further clarification or explanation of the rule. At this point, you decide to take a break from reading cases to

Elements Required to Toll Statute of Limitations	Rules	Analogous Cases		
A person must be "mentally ill"	Definition: "overall inability to function in society that prevents plaintiffs from protecting their legal rights." *Bowden v. Grindle*, 675 A.2d 968, 971 (Me. 1996); *McAfee v. Cole*, 637 A.2d 463, 466 (Me. 1994).	Case 1: *Bowden v. Grindle*, 675 A.2d 968, 971-72 (Me. 1996). Relevant conclusion: plaintiff was mentally ill. Relevant facts: Even though plaintiff could drive and cook by herself on occasion, she had difficulty performing those functions or even leaving her house at times. She also had a long history of psychiatric problems, including depression and anxiety, for which she had been hospitalized and medicated for decades. Evidence showed that her cognitive thinking was impaired. She had memory lapses. Relevant Rationale: Because of these limitations, she was not capable of making an "informed rational judgment" to convey her property.		

Elements Required to Toll Statute of Limitations	Rules	Analogous Cases		
	The "legal standard of competency varies for different purposes." *Chasse v. Mazerolle*, 580 A.2d 155, 157 (Me. 1990).	*Chasse v. Mazerolle*, 580 A.2d 155, 157 (Me. 1990). Conclusion: Mental competence for marriage or divorce does not mean competence to bring a lawsuit. Rationale: "no indication that [the plaintiff] possessed sufficient competence to comprehend and exercise her legal rights."		
When the cause of action accrues	"A cause of action accrues on the date of the act or omission giving rise to the injury." 24 Me. Rev. Stat. § 2902 (2013).			

think about how the legal rules and analogous cases you have identified apply to Jonah's situation.

3.5. Applying the Legal Framework

Before you can apply the legal framework to Jonah's situation, you must be sure you understand the relevant legal rules as well as the rationales of your analogous cases. Any confusion you may have about the rules will result in a muddled analysis of how those rules apply to Jonah's claim. You believe you have a good understanding of the legal rules, and your chart has helped you to see the distinct parts of the rules. Now that you understand the legal framework, you should be able to identify which facts are legally significant. Legally significant facts are those facts that are most critical to the legal analysis. They are the facts that a court would consider significant either in deciding what law applies or in determining the outcome of an issue.

You have already identified some legally significant facts when you were looking for your analogous cases. When you read *Bowden*, where the plaintiff could cook and drive but had difficulty doing so at times, you thought about the facts that Jonah can cook but cannot drive. To help you keep track of which facts you decide are significant, you add two more columns to your chart—one for the legally significant facts and one for the irrelevant facts. This is not to say that the irrelevant facts will have no value when you are writing your memo; there are several other types of facts that you will need to think about when you write your memo, but for now, the only facts you are concerned with are the ones that are necessary to the legal analysis. Because you will use the facts about Jonah's cooking and driving capabilities by comparing them to the facts in *Bowden*, you label them as legally significant facts.

You know that for the tolling provision to apply, you must show that Jonah has an overall inability to function in society that prevents him from protecting his legal rights. You think about what you know about Jonah: Jonah was born with a mental disability. He is 30 years old and now lives with his brother James, who was declared Jonah's legal guardian on March 15, 2009. Jonah is able to care for his own basic needs. In addition to preparing simple meals, Jonah is able to shower and dress himself. Because of his mental disability, however, he has not been able to learn to how to drive a car; read beyond a third-grade level; or perform any complex intellectual

Elements Required to Toll Statute of Limitations	Rules	Analogous Cases	Jonah's Facts— Significant	Jonah's Facts— Irrelevant
A person must be "mentally ill"	Definition: "overall inability to function in society that prevents plaintiffs from protecting their legal rights." *Bowden v. Grindle*, 675 A.2d 968, 971 (Me. 1996); *McAfee v. Cole*, 637 A.2d 463, 466 (Me. 1994).	Case 1: *Bowden v. Grindle*, 675 A.2d 968, 971-72 (Me. 1996). Relevant conclusion: plaintiff was mentally ill. Relevant facts: Even though plaintiff could drive and cook by herself on occasion, she had difficulty performing those functions or even leaving her house at times.	• Can prepare simple meals • Cannot drive	

Elements Required to Toll Statute of Limitations	Rules	Analogous Cases	Jonah's Facts— Significant	Jonah's Facts— Irrelevant
		She also had a long history of psychiatric problems, including depression and anxiety, for which she had been hospitalized and medicated for decades. Evidence showed that her cognitive thinking was impaired. She had memory lapses. Relevant Rationale: Because of these limitations, she was not capable of making an "informed rational judgment" to convey her property.		
	The "legal standard of competency varies for different purposes." *Chasse v. Mazerolle*, 580 A.2d 155, 157 (Me. 1990).	*Chasse v. Mazerolle*, 580 A.2d 155, 157 (Me. 1990). Conclusion: Mental competence for marriage or divorce does not mean competence to bring a lawsuit. Rationale: "no indication that [the plaintiff] possessed sufficient competence to comprehend and exercise her legal rights."		
When the cause of action accrues	"A cause of action accrues on the date of the act or omission giving rise to the injury." 24 Me. Rev. Stat. § 2902 (2013).			

tasks, like balancing a checkbook. Before his surgery, Jonah was an out-standing athlete, lived semi-independently in a group home, and was able to hold down a job he loved performing janitorial services at a daycare center. He was happy with his life. Since the surgery, however, Jonah has fallen into a deep depression.

Of these facts, you think several relate to the issue of whether Jonah has an overall inability to function in society that keeps him from protecting his legal rights: He can care for his basic needs, and he was able to live semi-independently and work before his surgery; however, he reads only at a third-grade level and cannot perform any complex intellectual tasks, like balancing a checkbook.

You are tempted to identify the fact that Jonah was an outstanding athlete as a significant fact as well because it conjures up an image of Jonah healthy, active, and capable. You quickly dismiss this fact, however, because you realize that it does not speak to his mental capabilities; it only speaks to his physical capabilities, which have nothing to do with his ability to understand his legal rights. This fact may be important later, if you end up litigating the medical malpractice claim, but it is not legally significant with regard to his mental competence.

Likewise, you start to put Jonah's depression into the significant facts on your chart, but you think of the second element—that the condition must have existed at the time the act that caused the injury occurred—and realize that his depression did not exist at the time of the surgery, which was the act that caused his injury. Again, this fact could be crucial in proving that Jonah suffered severe injuries, but not in proving that he was mentally ill at the time of the surgery.

Similarly, you decide that you do not need to include the fact that Jonah now lives with James, who is his guardian, as this happened after the surgery. Although the fact that James is Jonah's guardian may factor into your analysis of how the guardianship affects the tolling provision, you know that you are not yet analyzing that issue. To the issue of whether the tolling provision applies at all, the fact of James's guardianship after the surgery is irrelevant.

This reminds you that even though you do not need to spend much time analyzing the second element, you should apply the legal rule to the facts to establish that Jonah's condition existed at the time the act caused his injury. Therefore, you add to the second element in your chart the facts about when Jonah developed his mental disability and the date of the surgery that caused his injury. Because Jonah has had his mental disability since the time he was born, you conclude that the second element is satisfied. Now your chart looks full and you are doing a terrific job of keeping the elements as distinct analyses.

This organized approach to analyzing Jonah's situation is proving helpful. As you look at the significant facts you identified, you can see

Elements Required to Toll Statute of Limitations	Rules	Analogous Cases	Jonah's Facts— Significant	Jonah's Facts— Irrelevant Legally (may be emotionally significant)
A person must be "mentally ill"	Definition: "overall inability to function in society that prevents plaintiffs from protecting their legal rights." *Bowden v. Grindle*, 675 A.2d 968, 971 (Me. 1996); *McAfee v. Cole*, 637 A.2d 463, 466 (Me. 1994).	Case 1: *Bowden v. Grindle*, 675 A.2d 968, 971-72 (Me. 1996). Relevant conclusion: plaintiff was mentally ill. Relevant facts: Even though plaintiff could drive and cook by herself on occasion, she had difficulty performing those functions or even leaving her house at times. She also had a long history of psychiatric problems, including depression and anxiety, for which she had been hospitalized and medicated for decades. Evidence showed that her cognitive thinking was impaired. She has memory lapses. Relevant Rationale: Because of these limitations, she was not capable of making an "informed	• Can prepare simple meals • Cannot drive • Reads at third-grade level • Can shower and dress himself • Lived semi-independently before surgery • Worked as a janitor before surgery	• Outstanding athlete • Depressed after surgery • Lives with James since surgery • James was appointed legal guardian of Jonah on March 15, 2009

Elements Required to Toll Statute of Limitations	Rules	Analogous Cases	Jonah's Facts—Significant	Jonah's Facts—Irrelevant Legally (may be emotionally significant)
		rational judgment" to convey her property.		
	The "legal standard of competency varies for different purposes." *Chasse v. Mazerolle*, 580 A.2d 155, 157 (Me. 1990).	*Chasse v. Mazerolle*, 580 A.2d 155, 157 (Me. 1990). Conclusion: Mental competence for marriage or divorce does not mean competence to bring a lawsuit. Rationale: "no indication that [the plaintiff] possessed sufficient competence to comprehend and exercise her legal rights."		
When the cause of action accrues	"A cause of action accrues on the date of the act or omission giving rise to the injury." 24 Me. Rev. Stat. § 2902 (2013).	Case 1: none	• Mentally disabled since birth • Surgery on February 4, 2009	

the interplay between the components of legal analysis. Before you did any research, you thought you knew which facts were important, but as you learned about the legal rules and read prior cases, you gained a better understanding of which facts are actually the most legally significant. Without knowing the facts, you would never be able to identify an issue to start your research to identify the law. At the same time, without understanding the law, you could not know which facts are the legally significant ones. This process of facts leading to the law and the law then applying to facts is central to legal analysis.

Now that you have identified the legally significant facts, you need to consider which of them are helpful to Jonah and which support the hospital's position. The best facts for Jonah are those that show that he has a reduced ability to function in society or comprehend his legal rights. Those facts are his inability to drive; read beyond a third-grade level; or perform complex intellectual tasks, like balancing a checkbook. His capabilities seem less than the woman in *Bowden*, who could perform ordinary functions but had difficulty doing so. The fact that Jonah is competent in some respects, such as being able to prepare simple meals and bathe himself, does not mean that he is competent to understand his legal rights. The woman in *Chasse* had been married and divorced, but that was not evidence of her competency to exercise her legal rights. On the other hand, Jonah lived semi-independently and held down a job as a janitor before the surgery. The hospital could use those facts to argue that Jonah has the ability to function in society. The hospital might also distinguish Jonah's mental state at the time of the surgery from the woman in *Bowden*: unlike her, Jonah was not suffering from depression at the time of the surgery nor is there any indication that he was ever hospitalized or medicated for psychiatric problems. Although you have fully considered both sides of the legal analysis regarding the issue of whether Jonah is mentally ill for purposes of the tolling provision, your legal analysis is not complete. You still must consider one final component of legal analysis: your conclusion.

3.6. The Conclusion

The final component of legal analysis is the conclusion. What do you think the likely outcome is and why do you think so? Your conclusion should make sense based upon your analysis and your assessment of the strengths and weaknesses of your case. Because your analysis will be used to make decisions about how to advise Jonah, you need to be completely objective in reaching your conclusions. If you believe the likelihood of a court ruling in Jonah's favor is weak, you must say so. Based upon your analysis of the strengths and weaknesses in Jonah's case, though, you believe that a court would likely conclude that he had a limited ability to function in society and comprehend his legal rights at the time of his surgery and was, thus, mentally ill at the time the cause of action accrued.

3.7. Repeating the Process

Remember that when you started looking at your legal rules, you chose to fully analyze the first issue before addressing the issue of whether James's appointment as guardian affects the tolling provision. Thus, you need to repeat the process of legal analysis for that issue. You have already identified the issue, so you consider the legal rules. You know from your research that the relevant Maine statutes do not say anything about this issue, and that the Maine Law Court has not yet addressed it. In your research, however, you found an A.L.R. annotation entitled, "Effect of Appointment of Legal Representative for Person under Mental Disability on Running of Statute of Limitations against Such Person." You pull out the A.L.R. annotation from your stack of materials to review and are reminded that the majority view is that the appointment of a guardian has no effect on the tolling of the statute of limitations. You decide to create a simple table for this issue, listing the states that follow the majority rule on one side and those that do not on the other.

Majority Rule	Minority Rule
Alabama	Colorado
Arkansas	Hawaii
Arizona	Kansas
California	Washington
Florida	West Virginia
Georgia	
Illinois	
Indiana	
Kentucky	
Maryland	
Massachusetts	
Michigan	
Minnesota	
Mississippi	
New Jersey	
New York	
Nebraska	
Ohio	
Oklahoma	
Rhode Island	
Washington	

You read through the A.L.R. and cases and see that although many states follow the majority rule, they do so for a variety of reasons. You identify the different types of rationale and organize the decisions around those.

Rationale for Majority Rule	States
The tolling provision did not state that the SOL would begin to run upon such an appointment.	Indiana—*Barton-Malow Co. v. Wilburn*, 556 N.E.2d 324, 325 (Ind. 1990) Ohio—*Weaver v. Edwin Shaw Hosp.*, 819 N.E.2d 1079, 1083-1085 (Ohio 2004)
The claim belongs to "the person who suffered the legal wrong," not the legal guardian; therefore, the statute of limitations is tolled for as long as that person is under the legal disability of "unsound mind."	Tennessee—*Sullivan ex rel. Wrongful Death Beneficiaries of Sullivan v. Chattanooga Med. Investors, L.P.*, 221 S.W.3d 506, 511 (Tenn. 2007)
Legislative Intent: evidence that the legislature considered not only a mentally disabled person's inability to sue when enacting the tolling statute, but also the disabled person's difficulties in testifying and providing information to a court.	Arizona—*Sahf v. Havasu City Assn. for the Retarded and Handicapped*, 721 P.2d 1177, 1182 (Ariz. App. 1986).

Next, you identify the rationale for the minority view.

Rationale for Minority Rule	States
Statute expressly provides that appointment of guardian starts the running of the statute of limitations.	Colorado—Colo. Rev. Stat. 13-81-103(1)(a).
Appointment of a guardian triggers the running of the statute of limitations when the guardian has the right or legal duty to pursue legal action on behalf of a ward.	Michele Meyer McCarthy, *Effect of Appointment of Legal Representative for Person Under Mental Disability on Running of State Statute of Limitations Against Such Person*, 111 A.L.R.5th 159 §§ 9-10 (2001 & Supp. 2013)

Looking at the rationales for each side, you identify a strong rationale you can use to argue that a Maine court should follow the majority rule: The Maine statute is silent on the issue, like the statutes in Ohio and Indiana. You also decide that you can use the other reasoning to argue that the claim belongs to Jonah and not to his guardian, and that the purpose of the tolling provision relates not only to his difficulty in bringing suit, which could potentially be remedied by the appointment of a guardian, but also to his difficulty in testifying and providing information to a trial court. Although you recognize that the hospital could argue that the underlying purpose of the statute of limitations would be undermined if it did not apply to James, Jonah's legal guardian, who had the duty to bring suit on Jonah's behalf, you think that a court would adopt the majority rule. You have some confidence in your conclusion because of the number of states that have taken this approach. Your analysis is now complete and you are ready to begin writing the memo.

Chapter 4

Writing the Objective Memorandum

4.1. Prewriting: The Outline

Before you start writing the memo itself, you decide to create an outline of the analysis to help you get the large-scale organization of your memo in place and to identify any gaps that may still exist in your research and analysis. You begin by taking what you have found so far about the issue of whether Jonah is mentally ill for purposes of the statute of limitations and put it into a rough outline. It will look something like this:

1. IS JONAH "MENTALLY ILL" WITHIN THE MEANING OF THE TOLLING PROVISION?

RULES

"Mental illness under the tolling statute refers to an *overall inability* to function in society that prevents plaintiffs from protecting their legal rights." *McAfee v. Cole*, 637 A.2d 463, 466 (Me. 1994) (emphasis in original).

The "legal standard of competency varies for different purposes." *Chasse v. Mazerolle*, 580 A.2d 155, 157 (Me. 1990).

ANALOGOUS CASES

Chasse v. Mazerolle, 580 A.2d 155 (Me. 1990): Evidence that a mentally "retarded" woman had previously gotten married and divorced did not preclude her claim of mental illness for purposes of the tolling provision. The Court concluded that such evidence did not indicate that she "possessed sufficient competence to comprehend and exercise her legal right" to withhold consent to a sterilization procedure arranged by her parents. (Page 157)

Bowden v. Grindle, 675 A.2d 968 (Me. 1996): A severely depressed woman with memory lapses was found to be mentally ill for purposes of the tolling provision even though she could drive and occasionally cooked for herself because she had difficulty performing those functions or even leaving her house. Because of these limitations, the Court found that she did not possess an overall ability to function in society and, therefore, was not capable of making an "informed rational judgment" to convey her property. (Pages 971-972)

You could also extend this basic outline by including the arguments you plan to make when you apply the law and precedent to your facts. Regardless, if your outline includes at least the rules and the potentially useful analogous cases, with full citations to all legal sources, writing the memo will be a much easier process. Everything you need will be right in your outline. You will not need to spend time paging through all the individual authorities and searching for things when you are deep in the writing process.

4.2. Choosing the Memo Structure: Understanding Your Reader's Expectations

Now that you have researched and analyzed Jonah's issue and created an outline of the rules and useful cases, it is time to start writing. But what is the best way to present your analysis? Remind yourself of who your audience is and for what purpose you are writing the memo. Recall that Ms. Walker, one of the senior partners in your firm, has asked you to write a memo that she will use to make strategic decisions about the case. Your memo may also be used as the starting point for drafting many other documents as the case unfolds, such as client letters to James and Jonah, letters to other attorneys, and memoranda of law to accompany motions in a trial court. Thus, the tone of your memo must be objective because you need to provide Ms. Walker with an analysis that takes into account not just the strengths of Jonah's case, but also any areas of weakness. The purpose of the memo is not to advocate for Jonah, but to provide the information needed to make rational decisions about his case, which includes weighing the relative strength of each side of the analysis.

If you do not already know, you will need to check with Ms. Walker regarding her preferences for format and length of the memo. From firm to firm, memos may vary in length, format, and even overall organization of the legal analysis. Ms. Walker informs you that she would like you to present your analysis in a formal office memo that is no longer than ten pages.[1] She prefers that you use 14-point font because her eyesight is not what it used to be. She encourages you to look at previous office memos to get a sense of the overall format and organization to which she is accustomed. Even though the content of the previous memos will be different from the one you'll write about Jonah's situation, using previous memos as models for format and overall organization can be very helpful.

From the previous memos, you can see that Ms. Walker expects to see these sections in the memo: Heading, Statement of Facts, Question Presented, Brief Answer, and Discussion. Therefore, you know you should include all of those sections in your memo. Now that you have considered your audience and the purpose, tone, and format of the memo, it is time to get to work.

4.3. Writing the Memo

4.3.1. The Heading

The heading should be relatively straightforward. It contains information that tells the reader to whom the memo is addressed, who wrote the memo, the date, and what the memo is about. As with other aspects of the memo, your firm may have specific information that is required to be entered into the "re:" line, such as a case number, the client's name, and the subject of the memo. The heading in your memo about Jonah's case should look something like this:

TO: Ellen Walker
FROM: [Your name]
DATE: March 6, 2013
RE: Jonah Malloy; File #22-3665; Maine's tolling provision, 14 M.R.S. § 853
         (2013); mental illness exception to the statute of limitations

---

1. Although supervisors rarely assign a specific page limit for objective memos, it is important to understand your particular supervisor's expectations. She may want a short summary of a subject or a much longer discussion. Sometimes, a supervisor may not even want a formal memo, just a quick e-mail with an answer to a legal question. Your job is to give her what she wants, not to try to impress her with a lengthy dissertation when she simply needs a concise summary of the law and how it applies to a client's situation.

4.3.2. The Statement of Facts

Before writing your Statement of Facts (or Facts) section, you need to determine which facts to include. To do this, consider the different types of facts that exist: legally significant, contextual, emotionally significant, and unknown.

First, the legally significant facts are those that are needed to determine what law applies or to determine the outcome when the law is applied to the facts. You have already identified some of the legally significant facts when you created the chart while analyzing the cases you have found: Jonah cannot drive; read beyond a third-grade level; or perform complex intellectual tasks, like balancing a checkbook. Jonah can prepare simple meals and bathe himself; Jonah lived semi-independently and held down a job as a janitor before his surgery; and to your knowledge, Jonah has not been hospitalized or medicated for psychiatric problems.

Properly identifying all of the legally significant facts will often be a back-and-forth process between the Facts section and the Discussion section. Any facts you are relying on to support the arguments you are making in your Discussion are facts that are legally significant and should be included in your Facts section. Because understanding which facts are important requires an understanding of which facts you use in your analysis, many people write the Facts section after they have written the Discussion section. Others write an initial fact statement that is refined after the analysis is completed. Either way, before turning in your memo, you should compare your Facts section to your Discussion section and make sure that any fact used in the Discussion section is introduced in the Facts section.

Next, contextual facts are those facts that are needed to tell the story and provide the context for the legally significant facts. These include background information and any relevant procedural history.

Third, your situation may include emotionally significant facts. These facts are those that might appeal to the emotions of a judge or jury hearing your case, and could make a judge or jury want to rule in your favor (or rule against you).

Finally, as you gain an understanding of the legal framework for your issue, you may realize that facts exist that you do not know and that could affect the outcome of the case. These are your unknown facts. If an unknown fact might be a legally significant one, you should state in your Facts section what it is you do not know that might affect the outcome.

Now that you have thought about the facts you should include, you need to write the Statement of Facts section of your memo. Usually, the most effective organization for this section is to present the facts in either a chronological or topical scheme (or some combination of the two). Try to identify the parties at the beginning and indicate which party is your client. State the facts accurately in a neutral, objective tone. Because this is objective writing, the reader should not be able to tell what your prediction about the case will be from the Facts section; thus, you should not present the facts in a way that favors one side over the other. Include only the facts; do not include legal conclusions, which answer the legal question. Remember to cross-check your facts in the Statement of Facts with those used in the Discussion section so that you include all of the legally significant facts. Do not make up facts or make assumptions about the facts. In either the first or last sentence of the Facts section, identify the nature of the dispute.

For the memo you will write about Jonah's situation, the Statement of Facts should be concise and focused on the legally significant facts, the background facts, and any emotional facts.

Example

STATEMENT OF FACTS

James Malloy, would like to know whether his brother, Jonah, can bring a claim against Maine General Hospital for inadequate care that may have resulted in Jonah's physical disability. On February 4, 2009, Jonah had knee surgery that resulted in the amputation of his leg below the knee. Jonah, who is 30 years old, now lives with James, who was declared Jonah's legal guardian on March 15, 2009. Although Jonah was born with a mental disability, he has always been able to care for his own basic needs. For example, he can prepare simple meals for himself and shower and dress himself. Because of his mental disability, however, he has not been able to learn to how to drive a car, read beyond a third-grade level, or perform any complex intellectual tasks, like balancing a checkbook.

Before the surgery, Jonah was an outstanding athlete who was able to hold down a job he loved, performing janitorial services at a daycare center, and live semi-independently in a group home. He was happy with his life. Since the surgery, however, Jonah has fallen into a deep depression.

 ETHICS ALERT: Misstatement of the Facts

The United States Court of Appeals for the Seventh Circuit affirmed sanctions against a company whose attorneys misstated the facts about a collective bargaining agreement the company had signed. The court reduced the requested attorney fees and imposed sanctions in the amount of $7,025.

Teamsters Local No. 579 v. B&M, 882 F.2d 274, 280-81 (7th Cir. 1989).

4.3.3. Question(s) Presented

Your job in the Question Presented section of your memo is to present the legal question along with the controlling law and the legally significant facts. Unless you have a pure question of law, you will need to include the legally significant facts because they are critical to answering the legal question. To ensure that you address each component of the question, use this format as a template for your Question Presented section:[2]

Under [state the controlling law],
Did / Is / Can [ask the legal question]
When [explain the legally significant facts]?

You may vary this format as needed to help with the flow of your question, but you should be sure that you have included the necessary three components in the Question Presented: the controlling law, the legal question, and the legally significant facts.[3] If you have more than one legal question, include more than one question in the Question Presented section. For example, in Jonah's case, two questions must be answered. Therefore, you will have two questions in your Questions Presented section.

QUESTIONS PRESENTED

1. Under Maine's provision for tolling the three-year statute of limitations for medical malpractice claims, can a 30-year-old man bring a medical malpractice claim against a hospital after more than three years have passed when, at the time of the surgery resulting in his physical injuries, he had a mental disability such that he was unable to read beyond a third-grade level; learn to drive a car; or perform complex intellectual tasks, like balancing a checkbook; but he was able to live semi-independently in a group home, hold down a janitorial job, and prepare for his own basic needs at home?

---

2. Laurel Currie Oates & Anne Enquist, *The Legal Writing Handbook* 127 (4th ed. Aspen Publishers 2006).

3. Some legal writers prefer other formats for the Question Presented, such as beginning with the word "whether" or using several sentences rather than putting all the components into one question. These alternate formats are fine, as long as they include the three necessary components and are clear and comprehensible to the reader.

2. Under Maine's tolling provision, will the statute of limitations still be
    tolled for a 30-year-old man if he is found to be mentally ill at the time
    the cause of action accrued when a guardian was appointed for him
    before the limitations period expired?

Because you are writing an objective memo, your question should not
imply the answer you would like, nor should it include any legal conclusions. A legal conclusion is a conclusion about an issue that the court has to
decide. For example, including a legal conclusion in the first Question Presented could result in a question that looks like this.

---

1. Under Maine's provision for tolling the three-year statute of limitations
    for medical malpractice claims, can a 30-year-old man bring a medical
    malpractice claim against a hospital after more than three years have
    passed when, at the time of the surgery resulting in his physical inju-
    ries, he was mentally ill?

Saying that the man was "mentally ill" in this question is a legal conclusion. Whether he was mentally ill or not is the legal question that needs
to be determined. Instead of stating the legal conclusion, the properly written question contains the underlying facts that the court will use to answer
the legal question.

When you start writing a question that contains a lot of legally significant facts, you may think that the question will turn into a run-on sentence.
This can be avoided by using parallel construction and proper punctuation
in the question. Just because your question is long does not necessarily
mean that it is ungrammatical.

4.3.4. Brief Answer(s)

For every question presented, you should include a brief answer that
explains how you think the issue will likely be resolved and your reasoning
for this prediction. Hence, if you have two questions presented, you should
have two brief answers. The purpose of the Brief Answer section is to provide
a quick synopsis of your conclusion and rationale, which is helpful to any
busy legal reader, who may not have time to read the entire memo at that
moment but wants to understand your basic analysis and conclusion. The
Brief Answer section is similar to an abstract for a thesis or other scholarly
paper. Like the abstract, which is a short summary used to help a reader
quickly understand the purpose and content of a paper, the Brief Answer
section is a short summary intended to help a legal reader quickly grasp
the essence of your legal analysis and the reasons for your conclusion.

The Brief Answer section should be concise. It should succinctly communicate your complex legal analysis. You do not need to explain everything that is in your Discussion section. That would undermine the purpose of having a *brief* answer. Remember that you are using the Brief Answer section to answer the questions laid out in the Question Presented section. Look at your Question Presented section to see what you are asking. Then, answer each question presented in one or two words, stating the likely outcome, followed by a statement of the relevant rule or legal principle and an explanation of how it applies to your facts. In each brief answer, you should make a prediction of a likely outcome, not offering a guaranteed result. Always provide a brief summary of the rationale for your prediction. Citation to legal authority is generally not needed in the Brief Answer section.

For Jonah's memo, you have two questions in your Questions Presented section; therefore, your Brief Answers section should have two distinct answers, addressing each question separately.

BRIEF ANSWERS

1. Probably. Jonah would likely meet both requirements of the tolling provision, which requires that he be "mentally ill . . . when the cause of action accrues." First, he would probably be found "mentally ill" because his limited ability to care for himself, read, or perform complex intellectual tasks suggests that he is not competent to function independently in society and, thus, under Maine law, he is not competent to file a lawsuit on his own. Second, his mental disability existed at the time he underwent surgery, which was when the cause of action accrued.

2. Probably. Although this issue has not been raised in Maine, the majority of jurisdictions have found that the appointment of a guardian does not make the tolling provision for mental illness inapplicable.

4.3.5. Discussion

A. How to Organize Your Legal Analysis

The Discussion section is the real substance of your memo because it is where you present your legal analysis. Remember that your legal analysis consists of five different components: the issue, the law, examples, application of the law to your facts, and your conclusion. Now, you must present these components in a logical, concise manner.

By reviewing other memos written for Ms. Walker, you determine that she is expecting you to use the IRAAC organization system (Issue, Rules, Analogous Cases, Application, Conclusion) for presenting your legal analysis. You should have one complete IRAAC for *each* issue that you address in your memo because each issue will have its own distinct legal analysis. Before you get to the individual issues, however, you should start your Discussion section with an "orienting section."

B. The Orienting Section—Setting the Stage

Your orienting section helps your reader by conveying the big picture. Start by explaining the broadest legal principles (overall rules). Next, dismiss parts of the rules that your memo will not need to address. Finally, identify the elements that your memo will analyze, listing what must be established and providing a preview of the order in which the disputed elements will be addressed in your memo.

Because you are trying to determine whether Jonah can bring his claim, the logical place to start your orienting section is by explaining the timeframe in which he may normally bring a claim.

Maine has a three-year statute of limitations for medical malpractice claims. 24 M.R.S. § 2902 (2013). The relevant statutory language requires that malpractice claims "be commenced within three years after the cause of action accrues," and explains that "a cause of action accrues on the date of the act or omission giving rise to the injury." *Id.* Unless this statute is tolled, Jonah's claim will be barred because his cause of action is more than three years old.

Your first sentence provides the logical starting place in the analysis, explaining that the statute of limitations for medical malpractice claims is generally three years. Then, you apply that general rule to Jonah's claim, indicating that his claim will be time barred unless the statute of limitations is tolled for some reason.

Next, you need to explain when the statute of limitations will be tolled. Notice how you are going from the most general rule—the statute of limitations that generally applies—to the more specific rule, defining the circumstances in which the statute of limitations will be tolled.

A separate Maine statute provides that the statute of limitations may be tolled when a person entitled to bring an action under section 2902 "is mentally ill . . . when the cause of action accrues." 14 M.R.S. § 853 (2013). Therefore, Jonah can bring a claim only if he is found to be "mentally ill" within the meaning of the tolling provision and if the onset of Jonah's mental disability meets the timing requirement of the tolling provision.

Again, you have stated the legal rule and then indicated what must be shown in Jonah's circumstances. Note that the legal rule regarding tolling has two elements: For the statute of limitations to be tolled, a person must be (1) mentally ill and (2) must have been so when the cause of action accrued. The sentence that follows the rule provides a transition by showing how the elements are the conditions that must be met in order for Jonah's claim to be tolled.

Next, you must dismiss the elements of this rule that are not at issue. You know that Jonah has been mentally disabled from birth; thus, his condition was present at the time the cause of action accrued, so there is no need to analyze that element of the rule. What you do not know is whether Jonah's mental disability qualifies as "mentally ill" to satisfy that element of the rule. Therefore, you can dispense with one element of the rule and let your reader know that you will be analyzing the second element.

There can be no dispute that the onset of Jonah's mental disability meets the timing requirement of the tolling provision because he was mentally disabled from birth. Thus, Jonah will only have to establish that his mental disability qualifies him as "mentally ill" within the meaning of the tolling provision. He will also have to show that the tolling provision continues to apply even though James was appointed as his legal guardian.

Notice that the first sentence dispenses with one element while the second sentence sets the reader up for an analysis of the second element. Your final sentence addresses the second major issue: whether the appointment of James as Jonah's guardian will make a difference. In this way, you have introduced the two questions that you must analyze in your memo: (1) whether Jonah is mentally ill within the meaning of the tolling provision, and (2) whether James's appointment as his legal guardian will affect the tolling provision. Because they are two distinct questions, you will present two legal analyses. Thus, you should divide your analysis into two parts, each with its own subheading within the Discussion section. Each of these subheadings will be the start of a separate legal analysis, each of which will have its own IRAAC structure. If you had three questions, you would have three subheadings with three IRAACs. For your memo, your overall structure after the orienting section will look something like this:

1. **Is Jonah "mentally ill" within the meaning of the tolling provision?** (IRAAC)
   - Provide the Rules relating to the issue (IRAAC)
   - Explain how the law has been previously interpreted and applied in Analogous Cases (IRAAC)
   - Apply the legal framework to the facts of Jonah's case for this issue (IRAAC) by describing the arguments each side would make.
   - Conclude. Predict the likely outcome for this issue (IRAAC) by explaining what a court would likely do and why.
2. **Did James's appointment as Jonah's legal guardian remove Jonah's legal disability under the tolling provision and trigger the running of the statute of limitations?** (IRAAC)
   - Provide the Rules relating to this second issue (IRAAC)
   - Explain the Analogous Cases for this issue (IRAAC)
   - Apply the legal framework to the facts of Jonah's case for this issue (IRAAC) by describing the arguments each side would make.
   - Conclude. Predict the likely outcome for this issue (IRAAC) by explaining what a court would likely do and why.

C. Writing the Sections in the IRAAC

1. Issue

You have already identified the two issues to be discussed in the memo you are writing about Jonah's situation. Now, state the issues in the form of a question. Number each issue and use bold font, single-spaced for these subheadings. Your issue statements should match up with the issues you identified in your orienting section. For example, your orienting section for Jonah's memo ends as follows:

Thus, Jonah will only have to establish that his mental disability qualifies him as "mentally ill" within the meaning of the tolling provision. He will also have to show that the tolling provision continues to apply even though James was appointed as his legal guardian.

This sets up two conditions that must be met, or two issues to explore in the memo. Therefore, your issues statements should match the conditions set forth in the orienting section:

1. **Is Jonah "mentally ill" within the meaning of the tolling provision?**
2. **Did James's appointment as Jonah's legal guardian remove Jonah's legal disability under the tolling provision and trigger the running of the statute of limitations?**

When you have the overall structure in place, address each issue in turn. Finish the IRAAC for the first issue before moving onto the second.

2. Rules for the First Issue

After you have stated the issue, you should explain the relevant law—in other words, you must present the rules. You have already identified the rules when you analyzed the cases and completed your chart. Now you have to explain them to your audience. A large part of your job is to think about what the rules mean and how they fit together, so you can explain this to your reader. Remember that you should avoid placing large chunks of quoted material into your memo. When you do that, you force the reader to sift through the material and figure out what it means and how it is all connected. Your job is to guide the reader through the material in a way that is clear, concise, precise, and logical.

To help keep your rules concise, avoid cluttering your sentences with unnecessary introductory language before each rule. Some examples of this are "The Maine Supreme Court held that" or "Section 32 of Title 14 of the Maine Revised Statutes provides that." In both of these instances, the introductory language is simply telling the reader where the rule comes from (a particular court or a statute). But the reader can understand where the rule comes from by reading the citation that follows the sentence. Compare the following two examples explaining the same rules.

Uses unnecessary introductory language:

The Law Court has held that "mental illness" is an "overall inability to function in society that prevents plaintiffs from protecting their legal rights." *McAfee v. Cole*, 637 A.2d 463, 466 (Me. 1994). The Law Court also explained that "the legal standard of competency varies for different purposes." *Chasse v. Mazerolle*, 580 A.2d 155, 157 (Me. 1990).

Eliminates unnecessary introductory language:

"Mental illness" is defined as an "overall inability to function in society that prevents plaintiffs from protecting their legal rights." *McAfee v. Cole*, 637 A.2d 463,

466 (Me. 1994). Furthermore, the "legal standard of competency varies for different purposes." *Chasse v. Mazerolle*, 580 A.2d 155, 157 (Me. 1990).

The introduction about which court held these things is not needed because the citation includes the court's abbreviation in parentheses: "(Me.)." This tells the reader which court articulated the rule without you having to include it in your explanation. Your job is to state the relevant rule accurately and indicate, through citation, the important information about which court decided the case, the date the case was decided, and where the case can be found.

 ETHICS ALERT: Inaccurate Statements of the Law

A United States District Court in California admonished the government for citing an outdated version of the applicable statute in a social security disability benefits case. According to the court, the government's motion misleadingly relied on the text as it read before it was amended in 1980 when the word "may" was substituted for "shall" and a "good cause" requirement was added. The court concluded that the "government's moving papers [had] thus deliberately misstate[d] the applicable law and ignore[d] the express command of the statute," violating "counsel's certification under Fed. R. Civ. P. 11 that the motion 'is well grounded in fact and is warranted by existing law.'"

Larkin v. Heckler, 584 F. Supp. 512, 513 (N.D. Cal. 1984)

3. Analogous Cases

Recall that material from Analogous Cases section is different from statements of rules. Descriptions of analogous cases show how a rule has been interpreted or provide the underlying rationale of the rule. The Analogous Cases section also provides examples of specific factual situations where the rules have previously been applied.

For your memo about Jonah's situation, you have already identified two cases to use as analogous cases: *Chasse v. Mazerolle* and *Bowden v. Grindle*. Both had facts that you thought you could use to analogize to Jonah's situation. Keep in mind that you want to focus the reader on the relevant holding, legally significant facts, and the court's rationale.

Example:

For example, evidence that a mentally "retarded" woman had previously gotten married and divorced did not preclude her claim of mental illness for purposes of the tolling provision. *Id.* The Court concluded that such evidence did not indicate that she "possessed sufficient competence to comprehend and exercise her legal right" to withhold consent to a sterilization procedure arranged by her parents. *Id.* Similarly, a severely depressed woman with memory lapses was found to be mentally ill for purposes of the tolling provision even though she could drive and occasionally cooked for herself because she had difficulty performing those functions or even leaving her house. *Bowden v. Grindle*, 675 A.2d 968, 971-72 (Me. 1996). Because of these limitations, the Court found that she did not possess an overall ability to function in society and, therefore, was not capable of making an "informed rational judgment" to convey her property. *Id.*

4. Application

The Application section is where you apply the rules and cases that you have explained to the facts of your case. In the Application section of your memo, you need to analyze both sides of the issue. Thus, you will summarize the arguments that Jonah could make and then the arguments that the hospital could make. Present all of Jonah's arguments together and all of the hospital's arguments together. When you start Jonah's arguments, start with a topic sentence that makes an assertion related to the issue. The first issue in your memo is whether Jonah is "mentally ill" for purposes of the tolling provision. Therefore, you should start his arguments by asserting that he could argue that he meets the definition for "mental illness." This broad assertion lets the reader know what the paragraph will be about and everything that follows will be reasoning that supports the assertion. This also will help keep you from making your Application section just a series of case comparisons. While case comparisons can be helpful support for your overall assertion, if you just make your Application section a series of case comparisons, you may end up repeating the same argument over and over again, and may leave out other important arguments that could be made by just using the facts or policy considerations.

You do, however, want to use the cases for support wherever they would be helpful. Because you have already explained the cases in the Analogous Case section, you do not need to explain them fully again or cite to them in your Application section. But you should point out to the reader what it is about the particular case that you think is meaningfully similar to or different from your own case. Thus, you will end up repeating a portion of the case when you explain what it is you are comparing. For example, Jonah would compare his limitations—not being able to live independently; learn to drive; read beyond a third-grade level; or perform complex intellectual tasks, like balancing a checkbook—to the limitations of the plaintiff in *Bowden*, who could perform ordinary functions with difficulty, yet did not have the capacity to convey her property. To help the reader understand how you think Jonah's case and the *Bowden* case are similar, you must point out the specific similarities. You should not assume that your reader sees the same similarities that you see; thus, you must make your thoughts clear to the reader. For the same reason, you should be methodical in going through your application. Do not leave the arguments at broad, conclusory assertions; instead, be specific, use the facts, and connect all of the dots in your argument for your reader.

When you are finished with Jonah's arguments, you should do the same thing for the hospital's arguments,[4] starting with a topic sentence that asserts the hospital's main point as it relates to the issue statement.

Example:

Jonah could argue that he meets the definition of mental illness articulated in *McAfee* because his severely limited abilities at the time of the operation show that he did not possess an overall ability to function in society. Jonah would compare his limitations—not being able to live independently; learn to drive; read beyond a third-grade level; or perform complex intellectual tasks, like balancing a checkbook—to the limitations of the plaintiff in *Bowden*, who could perform ordinary functions with difficulty, yet did not have the capacity to convey her property. Jonah would also compare himself to the mentally disabled plaintiff in *Chasse*, whose previous marriage and divorce had no bearing on whether she could protect her legal rights: The fact that Jonah is competent in some respects, such as his ability to perform the basic tasks of living and hold a janitorial position at the time of the operation, does not establish that he is competent to pursue a lawsuit.

The hospital would argue that Jonah does not meet the requirement for mental illness in *McAfee* because he is able to read and function fairly well even outside the home while working at the daycare center. The hospital would distinguish Jonah's mental state at the time of the operation from that of the plaintiff in *Bowden*, who suffered from severe depression and memory loss at the time the cause of action accrued, affecting her ability to make an informed judgment about a legal matter. The hospital would contend that, unlike the plaintiff in *Bowden*, Jonah's limitations do not preclude him from understanding and protecting his legal rights. For these reasons, the hospital would argue that Jonah is not mentally ill under the tolling provision.

---

4. There is no set rule about which parties' arguments should be presented first. In determining the order of the arguments, consider what seems more logical, in light of your conclusion.

5. Conclusion

After you have analyzed both sides of the issue in your Application section, write a conclusion that relates to the issue statement. Look back at the question you asked in your issue statement to make sure you are answering that question in your conclusion. Write a simple paragraph that explains what you think the likely outcome will be and the basic rationale for your prediction. You should not state the conclusion as a guarantee. It is your best guess as to the likely outcome based upon your analysis of the issue.

Example:

A court would probably find that Jonah is incapable of protecting his legal rights without significant assistance and, thus, his condition meets the definition of mentally illness laid out in *McAfee*: possessing an "overall inability to function in society that prevents plaintiffs from protecting their legal rights." In accordance with the ruling in *Chasse* that different levels of mental competency are required for different purposes, a court would be unlikely to decide that Jonah's ability to read at a third-grade level, attend to his basic needs at home, and work as a janitor in a daycare center means that he is competent to bring a lawsuit.

D. IRAAC for the Second Issue

Once you have finished presenting the legal analysis for one issue, you will need to repeat the process of organizing and presenting a legal analysis for each of your remaining issues. Here, you have only one remaining issue.

Did James's appointment as Jonah's legal guardian remove Jonah's legal disability under the tolling provision and trigger the running of the statute of limitations?

You already know from your research that the Maine Law Court has not addressed this issue. Therefore, unlike the first issue where you were analyzing what the law means, under Maine precedent, for this issue you will need to analyze what the law in Maine should be. How you talk about the rules and analogous cases will look different in this section. Because there is no controlling rule in your state, you will need to explain what other jurisdictions do—the majority and minority rules. The clearest way to present this is to write a topic sentence that explains the majority rule and then cite to sources that support that topic sentence.

Example:

Although the Maine Supreme Judicial Court has not considered whether the appointment defeats the application of the tolling provision, an "overwhelming majority of courts . . . have concluded that the appointment of a guardian has no effect on the tolling of the statute of limitations." *Weaver v. Edwin Shaw Hosp.*, 819 N.E.2d 1079, 1083-85 (Ohio 2004) (citing opinions of state courts adopting the majority rule from Alabama, Arizona, California, Massachusetts, Michigan, New York, Nebraska, and Washington, and federal courts adopting the majority opinion applying Michigan, Missouri, New Mexico, and Nevada state law). *See also* Michele Meyer McCarthy, *Effect of Appointment of Legal Representative for Person Under Mental Disability on Running of State Statute of Limitations Against Such Person*, 111 A.L.R.5th 159 § § 4-7(2001 & Supp. 2013) (adding state courts adopting the majority rule from Arkansas, Florida, Georgia Illinois, Indiana, Kentucky, Maryland, Minnesota, Mississippi, New Jersey, Oklahoma, and Rhode Island and federal courts adopting the majority rule applying Illinois and Oklahoma state law). In Colorado, however, the tolling provision expressly provides for the statute of limitations to run after a guardian is appointed. Colo. Rev. Stat. 13-81-103(1)(a).

Next, in your analysis of this issue, you will use the analogous cases very differently than you did in the first issue. In the first issue, you used the analogous cases to make factual comparisons to and distinctions from Jonah's situation. For this issue, however, the facts of the other cases are not that important. Instead, knowing the underlying rationale and any policy considerations for the majority and minority rules will be more useful in crafting an argument for Maine to adopt one rule over the other. Thus, your Analogous Case section here should focus on explaining the reasoning that supports the rules in the other states rather than the facts of each of the cases.

To present this information clearly, you should use topic sentences that explain each rationale and then cite to the cases that support that rationale. Thus, instead of explaining case by case, you will be explaining concept by concept (each individual rationale) and providing the supporting citation after the explanation. This presentation will help your reader follow your analysis. If you just started explaining case after case in great detail, your reader would quickly lose track of your analysis and feel overwhelmed by the amount of information. You would be making your reader do the work of figuring out what the cases have in common for rationale. But processing and synthesizing this information is your job as a legal writer. Fortunately, you have already done this work when you created the chart of the rationale for these cases while you were reading them. Take a look at the charts you created.

Rationale for Majority Rule	States
The tolling provision did not state that the SOL would begin to run upon such an appointment.	Indiana—*Barton-Malow Co. v. Wilburn*, 556 N.E.2d 324, 325 (Ind. 1990) Ohio—*Weaver v. Edwin Shaw Hosp.*, 819 N.E.2d 1079, 1083-85 (Ohio 2004)
The claim belongs to "the person who suffered the legal wrong," not the legal guardian; therefore, the statute of limitations is tolled for as long as that person is under the legal disability of "unsound mind."	Tennessee—*Sullivan ex rel. Wrongful Death Beneficiaries of Sullivan v. Chattanooga Med. Investors, L.P.*, 221 S.W.3d 506, 511 (Tenn. 2007)
Legislative intent: evidence that the legislature considered not only a mentally disabled person's inability to sue when enacting the tolling statute, but also the disabled person's difficulties in testifying and providing information to a court.	Arizona—*Sahf v. Havasu City Assn. for the Retarded and Handicapped*, 721 P.2d 1177, 1182 (Ariz. App. 1986).

Rationale for Minority Rule	States
Statute expressly provides that appointment of guardian starts the running of the statute of limitations.	Colorado—Colo. Rev. Stat. 13-81-103(1)(a).
Appointment of a guardian triggers the running of the statute of limitations when the guardian has the right or legal duty to pursue legal action on behalf of a ward.	Michele Meyer McCarthy, *Effect of Appointment of Legal Representative for Person Under Mental Disability on Running of State Statute of Limitations Against Such Person*, 111 A.L.R.5th 159 §§ 9-10 (2001 & Supp. 2013)

Using these charts, you can easily craft topic sentences that explain the various rationales and considerations that you already identified in the left-hand column. You might explain a couple of the cases in greater detail to illustrate what you have stated in your topic sentence, but the topic sentence will help the reader understand the significance of any cases you discuss more fully.

Example:

Some courts hold that the appointment of a guardian does not remove a mentally incompetent adult's legal disability because the tolling provision did not state that the statute of limitations would begin to run upon such an appointment. *See Barton-Malow Co. v. Wilburn*, 556 N.E.2d 324, 325 (Ind. 1990). In *Barton-Malow*, the Supreme Court of Indiana interpreted a tolling provision that provides: "Any person being [of unsound mind] when the cause of action accrues may bring his action within two years after the disability is removed." *Id.* (quoting Ind. Code § 34-1-2-5). Concluding that "the statutory language is clear and unambiguous [and the] appointment of a guardian does not alter the fact of mental unsoundness," it does not terminate the legal disability." *Id.* Declining to consider the parties' contentions regarding statutory construction, the court added, "We do not construe a statute that is unambiguous." *Id. Accord Weaver*, 819 N.E.2d at 1082 (concluding that the appointment of a guardian has no effect on the tolling provision because "the statute does not mention the effect of a guardian's appointment").

Other courts have reached the same conclusion, but for a different reason, concluding that because the claim belongs to "the person who suffered the legal wrong," not the legal guardian, the statute of limitations is tolled for as long as that person is under the legal disability of "unsound mind." *See e.g. Sullivan ex rel. Wrongful Death Beneficiaries of Sullivan v. Chattanooga Med. Investors, L.P.*, 221 S.W.3d 506, 511 (Tenn. 2007).

Adopting yet another rationale, the Court of Appeals of Arizona, Division 1, Department D, held that a mentally incompetent person's disability was not removed when a guardian was appointed based on legislative intent, asserting that the legislature considered not only a mentally disabled person's inability to sue when enacting the tolling statute, but also the disabled person's difficulties in testifying and providing information to a court. *Sahf v. Havasu City Assn. for the Retarded and Handicapped*, 721 P.2d 1177, 1182 (Ariz. App. 1986).

Some courts, however, have taken the view that the appointment of a guardian triggers the running of the statute of limitations when the guardian has the right or legal duty to pursue legal action on behalf of a ward. McCarthy, 111 A.L.R.5th at §§ 9-10 (citing state courts adopting the minority rule: Hawaii, Kansas, New Hampshire, New York, North Carolina, Washington, and West Virginia). *See e.g. Johnson v. Pilot Life Ins. Co.*, 7 S.E.2d 475, 477 (N.C. 1940) (reasoning that the "policy of repose which underlies statutes limiting the time in which actions may be brought would be imperfectly expressed if these statutes did not apply to all those who might bring such actions, and actions which might be brought in their behalf," like a guardian who has a duty "to bring suit, when necessary").

Finally, you will need to apply the rules and rationales by crafting an argument for why Maine should adopt the majority rule. Unlike in the first issue, you will not be making arguments by analogy here. Instead, focus on the reasoning and include policy considerations in the argument. As in the first issue, you will also need to anticipate what arguments the hospital might make. When you are finished, make a prediction about which rule you think a Maine court would adopt and why. This is your conclusion for the second issue.

Example:

Jonah would argue that the majority rule should be adopted in Maine for the three reasons set out above: The Maine tolling provision does not provide for an exception if a guardian is appointed; the claim belongs to him and not to his guardian; and the purpose of the tolling provision relates not only to his difficulty in bringing suit, which could potentially be remedied by the appointment of a guardian, but also his difficulty in testifying and providing information to a trial court.

The hospital would argue for the minority position, contending that the underlying purpose of the statute of limitations would be undermined if it did not apply to James, Jonah's legal guardian, who had the duty to bring suit on Jonah's behalf.

The court would probably adopt the view taken by the majority of jurisdictions in concluding that the appointment of James as Jonah's guardian did not trigger the running of the statute of limitations for Jonah's medical malpractice claim against the hospital. Because Maine's tolling provision states nothing about the effect of appointing a guardian, the court is likely to see the claim as belonging to Jonah, who would continue to be disabled even after James's appointment as guardian for the purposes of the tolling provision.

4.4. Reviewing Your Work

You are finished writing the first draft of your memo, but the draft is not finished yet. You should fix any organizational issues before you start working on more detailed edits and polishing your work.

First, print out a copy of your memo to highlight the legal analysis to make sure you have presented it in the correct order. Remember that your first complete legal analysis begins after the orienting section of your memo. Thus, you do not need to highlight anything before the first issue in the Discussion section. If you find that your color-coded draft is out of order, you should correct the organization of your legal analysis to match the following chart.

Issue	pink
Rules	orange
Analogous Cases	yellow
Application	green
Conclusion	blue

When you are satisfied with the overall organization of your memo, review the small-scale organization. Within your first issue, do your rules, cases, arguments, and conclusion all relate to the issue statement you have written? Study the paragraphs and then the sentences to make more detailed edits. Remember that conciseness is highly valued in legal writing, so look for ways to make paragraphs and sentences more concise. Finally, proofread your entire memo carefully.

When you are finally satisfied that you have made the necessary revisions to ensure that you have a clear, concise, precise, and logical memo, and you have checked it carefully for errors, you send a copy of the finished memo to Ms. Walker.

MEMORANDUM

To: Ellen Walker
From: Your Name
Date: January 18, 2014
Re: Jonah Malloy, File #22-3665; Maine's tolling provision, 14 M.R.S. § 853 (2013); mental illness exception to statute of limitation

STATEMENT OF FACTS

James Malloy, would like to know whether his brother, Jonah, can bring a claim against Maine General Hospital for inadequate care that may have resulted in Jonah's physical disability. On February 4, 2009, Jonah had knee surgery that resulted in the amputation of his leg below the knee. Jonah, who is 30 years old, now lives with James, who was declared Jonah's legal guardian on March 15, 2009. Although Jonah was born with a mental disability, he has always been able to care for his own basic needs. For example, he can prepare simple meals for himself and shower and dress himself. Because of his mental disability, however, he has not been able to learn how to drive a car; read beyond a third-grade level; or perform any complex intellectual tasks, like balancing a checkbook.

Before the surgery, Jonah was an outstanding athlete who was able to hold down a job he loved performing janitorial services at a daycare center and live semi-independently in a group home. He was happy with his life. Since the surgery, however, Jonah has fallen into a deep depression.

QUESTIONS PRESENTED

1. Under Maine's provision for tolling the three-year statute of limitations for medical malpractice claims, can a 30-year-old man bring a medical malpractice claim against a hospital after more than three years have passed when, at the time of the surgery resulting in his physical injuries, he had a mental disability such that he was unable to read beyond a third-grade level; learn to drive a car; or perform complex intellectual tasks, like balancing a checkbook, but was able to live semi-independently in a group home, hold down a janitorial job, and prepare for his own basic needs at home?

2. Under Maine's tolling provision, will the statute of limitations still be tolled for a 30-year-old man if he is found to be mentally ill at the time the cause of action accrued when a guardian was appointed for him before the limitations period expired?

BRIEF ANSWERS

1. Probably. Jonah would likely meet both requirements of the tolling provision, which requires that he be "mentally ill . . . when the cause of action accrues." First, he would probably be found "mentally ill" because his limited ability to care for himself, read, or perform complex intellectual tasks suggests that he is not competent to function independently in society and, thus, under Maine law, he is not competent to file a lawsuit on his own. Second, his mental disability existed at the time he underwent surgery, which was when the cause of action accrued.

2. Probably. Although this issue has not been raised in Maine, the majority of jurisdictions have found that the appointment of a guardian does not make the tolling provision for mental illness inapplicable.

DISCUSSION

Maine has a three-year statute of limitations for medical malpractice claims. 24 M.R.S. § 2902 (2013). The relevant statutory language requires that malpractice claims "be commenced within three years after the cause of action accrues," and asserts that "a cause of action accrues on the date of the act or omission giving rise to the injury." *Id.* Unless this statute is tolled, Jonah's claim will be barred because his cause of action is more than three years old.

A separate Maine statute provides that the statute of limitations may be tolled when a person entitled to bring an action under section 2902 "is mentally ill . . . when the cause of action accrues." 14 M.R.S. § 853 (2013). Therefore, Jonah can bring a claim only if he is found to be "mentally ill" within the meaning of the tolling provision and if the onset of Jonah's mental disability meets the timing requirement of the tolling provision. There can be no dispute that the onset of Jonah's mental disability meets the timing requirement of the tolling provision because he was mentally disabled from birth. Thus, Jonah will only have to establish that his mental disability qualifies him as "mentally ill" within the meaning of the tolling provision and that the tolling provision continues to apply even though James was appointed as his legal guardian.

1. Is Jonah "mentally ill" within the meaning of the tolling provision?

"Mental illness" is defined as an "*overall inability* to function in society that prevents plaintiffs from protecting their legal rights." *McAfee v. Cole*, 637 A.2d 463, 466 (Me. 1994) (emphasis in original). Furthermore, the "legal standard of competency varies for different purposes." *Chasse v. Mazerolle*, 580 A.2d 155, 157 (Me. 1990).

For example, evidence that a mentally "retarded" woman had previously gotten married and divorced did not preclude her claim of mental illness for purposes of the tolling provision. *Id.* The Court concluded that such evidence did not indicate that she "possessed sufficient competence to comprehend and exercise her legal right" to withhold consent to a sterilization procedure arranged by her parents. *Id.* Similarly, a severely depressed woman with memory lapses was found to be mentally ill for purposes of the tolling provision even though she could drive and occasionally cooked for herself because she had difficulty performing those functions or even leaving her house. *Bowden v. Grindle*, 675 A.2d 968, 971-72 (Me. 1996). Because of these limitations, the Court found that she did not possess an overall ability to function in society and, therefore, was not capable of making an "informed rational judgment" to convey her property. *Id.*

Jonah could argue that he meets the definition of mental illness articulated in *McAfee* because his severely limited abilities at the time of the operation show that he did not possess an overall ability to function in society. Jonah would compare his limitations—not being able to live independently; learn to drive; read beyond a third-grade level; or perform complex intellectual tasks, like balancing a checkbook—to the limitations of the plaintiff in *Bowden*, who could perform ordinary functions with difficulty, yet did not have the capacity to convey her property. Jonah would also compare himself to the mentally disabled plaintiff in *Chasse*, whose previous marriage and divorce had no bearing on whether she could protect her legal rights: The fact that Jonah is competent in some respects, such as his ability to perform the basic tasks of living and hold a janitorial position at the time of the operation, does not establish that he is competent to pursue a lawsuit.

The hospital would argue that Jonah does not meet the requirement for mental illness in *McAfee* because he is able to read and function fairly well even outside the home while working at the daycare center. The hospital would distinguish Jonah's mental state at the time of the operation from that of the plaintiff in *Bowden*, who suffered from severe depression and memory loss at the time the cause of action accrued, affecting her ability to make an informed judgment about a legal matter. The hospital would contend that, unlike the plaintiff in *Bowden*, Jonah's limitations do not preclude him from understanding and protecting his legal rights. For these reasons, the hospital would argue that Jonah is not mentally ill under the tolling provision.

A court would probably find that Jonah is incapable of protecting his legal rights without significant assistance and, thus, his condition meets the definition of mental illness laid out in *McAfee*: possessing an "overall inability to function in society that prevents plaintiffs from protecting their legal rights." In accordance with the ruling in *Chasse* that different levels of mental competency are required for different purposes, a court would be unlikely to decide that Jonah's ability to read at a third-grade level, attend to his basic needs at home, and work as a janitor in a daycare center mean that he is competent to bring a lawsuit.

2. Did James's appointment as Jonah's legal guardian remove Jonah's legal disability under the tolling provision and trigger the running of the statute of limitations?

Although the Maine Supreme Judicial Court has not considered whether the appointment defeats the application of the tolling provision, an "overwhelming majority of courts . . . have concluded that the appointment of a guardian has no effect on the tolling of the statute of limitations." *Weaver v. Edwin Shaw Hosp.*, 819 N.E.2d 1079, 1083-85 (Ohio 2004) (citing opinions of state courts adopting the majority rule from Alabama, Arizona, California, Massachusetts, Michigan, New York, Nebraska, and Washington, and federal courts adopting the majority opinion applying Michigan, Missouri, New Mexico, and Nevada state law). *See also* Michele Meyer McCarthy, *Effect of Appointment of Legal Representative for Person Under Mental Disability on Running of State Statute of Limitations Against Such Person*, 111 A.L.R.5th 159 §§ 4-7(2001 & Supp. 2013) (adding state courts adopting the majority rule from Arkansas, Florida, Georgia Illinois, Indiana, Kentucky, Maryland, Minnesota, Mississippi, New Jersey, Oklahoma, and Rhode Island and federal courts adopting the majority rule applying Illinois and Oklahoma state law). In Colorado, however, the tolling provision expressly provides for the statute of limitations to run after a guardian is appointed. Colo. Rev. Stat. 13-81-103(1)(a).

Some courts hold that the appointment of a guardian does not remove a mentally incompetent adult's legal disability because the tolling provision did not state that the statute of limitations would begin to run upon such an appointment. *See Barton-Malow Co. v. Wilburn*, 556 N.E.2d 324, 325 (Ind. 1990). In *Barton-Malow*, the Supreme Court of Indiana interpreted a tolling provision that provides: "Any person being [of unsound mind] when the cause of action accrues may bring his action within two years after the disability is removed." *Id.* (quoting Ind. Code § 34-1-2-5). Concluding that "the statutory language is clear and unambiguous [and the] appointment of a guardian does not alter the fact of mental unsoundness," it does not terminate the legal disability." *Id.* Declining to consider the parties' contentions regarding statutory construction, the court added, "We do not construe a statute that is unambiguous." *Id. Accord Weaver*, 819 N.E.2d at 1082 (concluding that the appointment of a guardian has no effect on the tolling provision because "the statute does not mention the effect of a guardian's appointment").

Other courts have reached the same conclusion, but for a different reason, concluding that because the claim belongs to "the person who suffered the legal wrong," not the legal guardian, the statute of limitations is tolled for as long as that person is under the legal disability of "unsound mind." *See e.g. Sullivan ex rel. Wrongful Death Beneficiaries of Sullivan v. Chattanooga Med. Investors, L.P.*, 221 S.W.3d 506, 511 (Tenn. 2007).

Adopting yet another rationale, the Court of Appeals of Arizona, Division 1, Department D, held that a mentally incompetent person's disability was not removed when a guardian was appointed based on legislative intent, asserting that the legislature considered not only a mentally disabled person's inability to sue when enacting the tolling statute, but also the disabled person's difficulties in testifying and providing information to a court. *Sahf v. Havasu City Assn. for the Retarded and Handicapped*, 721 P.2d 1177, 1182 (Ariz. App. 1986).

Some courts, however, have taken the view that the appointment of a guardian triggers the running of the statute of limitations when the guardian has the right or legal duty to pursue legal action on behalf of a ward. McCarthy, 111 A.L.R.5th at §§ 9-10 (citing state courts adopting the minority rule: Hawaii, Kansas, New Hampshire, New York, North Carolina, Washington, and West Virginia). *See e.g. Johnson v. Pilot Life Ins. Co.*, 7 S.E.2d 475, 477 (N.C. 1940) (reasoning that the "policy of repose which underlies statutes limiting the time in which actions may be brought would be imperfectly expressed if these statutes did not apply to all those who might bring such actions, and actions which might be brought in their behalf," like a guardian who has a duty "to bring suit, when necessary").

Jonah would argue that the majority rule should be adopted in Maine for the three reasons set out above: The Maine tolling provision does not provide for an exception if a guardian is appointed; the claim belongs to him and not to his guardian; and the purpose of the tolling provision relates not only to his difficulty in bringing suit, which could potentially be remedied by the appointment of a guardian, but also his difficulty in testifying and providing information to a trial court.

The hospital would argue for the minority position, contending that the underlying purpose of the statute of limitations would be undermined if it did not apply to James, Jonah's legal guardian, who had the duty to bring suit on Jonah's behalf.

The court would probably adopt the view taken by the majority of jurisdictions in concluding that the appointment of James as Jonah's guardian did not trigger the running of the statute of limitations for Jonah's medical malpractice claim against the hospital. Because Maine's tolling provision states nothing about the effect of appointing a guardian, the court is likely to see the claim as belonging to Jonah, who would continue to be disabled even after James's appointment as guardian for the purposes of the tolling provision.

Chapter 5

Writing Effective Client Letters and E-Mails

Now that you have finished writing your objective memo and submitted it to Ellen Walker, you need to think about how to communicate your conclusions to James and Jonah.

Under Rule 1.4 of the Maine Rules of Professional Conduct, a lawyer must "reasonably consult with the client about the means by which the client's objectives are to be accomplished" and "explain a matter to the extent reasonably necessary to permit the client to make informed decisions." This rule, originally appearing in the American Bar Association Model Rules of Professional Conduct, has been adopted by all 50 states and the Virgin Islands. Lawyers must also correspond effectively with colleagues, both within and outside their law firms. These days, much of that correspondence is taking place in e-mail messages. Knowing how to keep your client informed through written correspondence and communicating effectively with colleagues using e-mail are skills that are essential to the ethical practice of law.

 ETHICS ALERT: Failure to Communicate with Client

The Supreme Court of Hawaii suspended a lawyer for six months after he failed to communicate with clients and respond to their inquiries. The court concluded that such "professionally unethical . . . misconduct operated to keep the clients uninformed as to the status of their cases," causing one client "to serve out additional time in prison that may not have been necessary if he had employed a reasonably competent and diligent attorney."

In re Trask, 488 P.2d 1167, 1170-71 (Haw. 1971).

5.1. Communicating with Clients: The Opinion Letter

Lawyers generally write letters to their clients to update them on the status of their cases and write opinion letters to communicate the results of legal research. James and Jonah have been waiting to hear whether Jonah may bring a lawsuit against the hospital to compensate him for the injuries he suffered after knee surgery. Now that you have researched the statute of limitations question in Jonah's case and determined how the law will probably apply, you need to update James and Jonah in an opinion letter.

Before writing the letter, however, you should consider your purpose in writing it and who will be receiving it. Your purpose is clear: You need to tell James and Jonah what will likely happen in Jonah's case. They are not interested in a lengthy, abstract discussion of the law. They just want to know whether Jonah will be able to file a claim against the hospital for the injuries he suffered after his knee surgery. In the letter, you need to explain that Jonah will probably be able to file the claim, even though more than three years have passed, because he will probably be considered "mentally ill" at the time of the surgery. You also need to inform them that James's appointment as Jonah's guardian will probably not make any difference because that appointment did not affect Jonah's disability. By explaining the law and how it applies so that James and Jonah can make informed decisions about the case, you will be complying with Rule 1.4 of the Maine Rules of Professional Conduct.

Next, you need to decide whether you are writing the letter to Jonah, a mentally disabled man who reads at a third-grade level; to James, a person of normal intelligence; or to both of them. You have to find out whether James happens to be a lawyer himself. If he is, he would have a much greater ability to understand the legal concepts underlying your conclusions; he might even want to read the memo you wrote for your law partner. Assessing your clients' level of legal sophistication will help you determine the vocabulary and depth of legal analysis to include in your letter.

Regardless of who the recipient is, you need to organize your letter carefully and adopt a respectful, professional tone. Following the internal heading and salutation, you should begin with an introductory paragraph establishing your relationship, identifying the issues, providing your opinion regarding each issue, and giving a brief rationale for each opinion. Next, you should summarize the facts on which your opinions are based and provide an explanation of the law and how it applies to the case. In the final paragraph, you should state your overall conclusions and indicate what steps should be taken next.

The format for your letter parallels the format you used in your objective memo. The heading and salutation in the client letter contain basically the same information as the heading in your memo. The statement of the issues in the introductory paragraph of the client letter mirrors the Questions Presented in the memo. Your opinions and brief rationales in the client letter should match the conclusions and rationales in the Brief Answer section of your memo. In the letter, the summary of facts on which your opinions are based must be the same as the summary in the Facts section of the memo. Your explanation of how the law applies to your clients' situation and your conclusions should be the same in the client letter as in the Discussion section of your memo. The final paragraph in the client letter reflects the overall conclusion from your memo and adds the next steps your clients should take.

5.1.1. The Introductory Paragraph

Your introductory paragraph needs to accomplish three things: It must (1) establish your relationship with your client by setting an appropriate tone, (2) identify the legal issues under consideration, and (3) communicate your opinion regarding those issues and the reasons for that opinion.

You establish the relationship with your clients and set the tone through the words you choose. You want to communicate respect for your clients and an appreciation for the situations that have caused them to seek legal counsel. Although your vocabulary and depth of analysis will vary depending on the legal sophistication of your client, your tone must always be professional, yet friendly and welcoming. Your job is to explain difficult legal concepts in an understandable way. That does not mean you are "dumbing down" the material. Rather, you are carefully choosing the words that will have the most meaning for your particular clients, showing respect for their ability to understand what you are explaining, regardless of their intellectual capacity.

Deciding how formal your letter should be depends on who your clients are and the sort of relationship you have established with them. When you know clients well or think they would appreciate a friendlier approach, you should probably use a less formal tone, addressing them by first name in your salutation: "Dear James and Jonah." If you do not know a client very well or sense that he or she would prefer a more formal approach, adjust your tone accordingly: "Dear Mr. Malloy." Either way, you must communicate professionalism and respect. If you are writing to James and Jonah together, it would be awkward to use "Mr." for both of them in the salutation: "Dear Mr. Malloy and Mr. Malloy." You would not want to differentiate between them formally addressing James as "Mr. Malloy" and Jonah informally as "Jonah." Treating Jonah differently because of his mental disability would be disrespectful. Although you have not known them long, calling them by their first names in the salutation seems like the right thing to do.

Just as you did when writing your memo, you need to make sure that everything you say in your client letter is clear, concise, and accurate. Although you do not want to appear stuffy or condescending, you do need to use formal English in explaining the law and how it applies. You should avoid contractions, slang, and colloquialisms as well as overly legalistic terminology. Your job is lay out the legal issues and explain in plain English how the law applies, providing only the depth necessary for your clients to understand their legal position. Do not talk about particular cases or concepts like the common law. Your clients are not asking you for a mini-law school class; they just want to know how the law applies to their case and why. Be sure to use correct grammar, spelling, and punctuation. You do not want to lose credibility with your clients by making careless errors. Proofread as carefully when writing a letter to a client as you would when writing to another attorney or to a judge.

Example: Tone is too informal and chatty

I checked out whether Jonah can get back at the hospital for messing up his knee. At first, I thought he couldn't do it because he was too late, but now I'm pretty sure he can.

Example: Tone is too stuffy and formal

Per your request, I have consulted relevant legal authority to ascertain whether you may pursue a cause of action against the hospital. Because Mr. Malloy was mentally ill at the time the cause of action accrued, the statute of limitations has been tolled.

Example: Tone is inconsistent, confusing, and ungrammatical

Just like you asked, I've figured out that the statute of limitations won't prevent you from suing the hospital since, under the tolling statute, Jonah was mentally ill when the cause of action accrued.

Example: Tone is consistently professional, yet friendly

As you requested, I have conducted some research to determine whether you will be able to bring a lawsuit against the hospital. Normally, a person cannot sue a hospital for medical injuries after more than three years have passed, but you will probably still be able to sue because Jonah was mentally disabled at the time of the surgery.

When laying out the legal issues, use words that will be familiar to your clients. They should be able to recognize the question they asked in their client interview when you restate it in the introductory paragraph in the form of an issue statement.

Example: Difficult to identify the clients' original question

To answer your question, I have researched whether Jonah's mental disability will toll the statute of limitations.

Example: Easy to identify the clients' original question

As you requested, I have conducted some research to determine whether you will be able to bring a lawsuit against the hospital.

Be sure to include your opinion and your reasons for that opinion at the end of the introductory paragraph. You do not want to keep your clients in suspense. Even if the news is bad, your clients will appreciate knowing what you have concluded and why, right away. To protect yourself, be absolutely clear that you are simply stating your *opinion* in the letter, not offering any guarantees. Speak in terms of probabilities, not absolutes. Say, "Jonah will probably be able to bring a lawsuit against the hospital"; not, "Jonah will definitely be able to bring a lawsuit against the hospital"; or even, "Jonah will be able to bring a lawsuit against the hospital."

Your introductory paragraph will be different depending on whether you decide to write to Jonah and James together or separately. Because you want to show the same level of respect to Jonah as to James, you should probably write the letter primarily to James while including Jonah in the salutation. If you decide to write to them together, your salutation and introductory paragraph might look like this:

Dear Jonah and James:

I enjoyed meeting with you both last week and look forward to working with you on this case. As you requested, I have conducted some research to find out whether you will be able to bring a lawsuit against the hospital. Normally, a person cannot sue a hospital for medical injuries after more than three years have passed, but you will probably still be able to sue because Jonah was mentally disabled at the time of the surgery. Also, it should not matter that you, James, were appointed as Jonah's guardian because that appointment did not take away the mental disability that prevented Jonah from protecting his legal rights.

Writing to both James and Jonah at the same time presents some challenges, particularly in deciding when to use their names or the pronoun "you" when addressing one or the other of them. In the introductory paragraph above, an attempt has been made to include Jonah, but the letter is obviously being written to James, the client who is more capable of understanding its contents.

For that reason, you might decide to write only to James, who is acting on Jonah's behalf, or to James and Jonah separately. If you were writing only to James, very few changes would be needed.

Dear James:

I enjoyed meeting you and Jonah last week and look forward to working with you both on this case. As you requested, I have conducted some research to determine whether Jonah will be able to bring a lawsuit against the hospital. Normally, a person cannot sue a hospital for medical injuries after more than three years have elapsed, but you will probably still be able to pursue a lawsuit because Jonah was mentally disabled at the time of the surgery. Also, it should not matter that you were appointed as Jonah's guardian because that appointment did not affect the mental disability that prevented him from protecting his legal rights.

If you were writing only to Jonah, you would need to make the introductory paragraph a bit simpler:

Dear Jonah:

I enjoyed meeting with you and James last week and look forward to working with you. You and James asked me to find out whether you could sue the hospital for doing such a bad job with your knee operation. I do think you will be able to do that. Usually, people cannot sue hospitals when more than three years have gone by since their operations, but you should be able to do it because you were not really capable of doing that on your own when you had your operation. Even though James later became your guardian, you are still not able to sue the hospital by yourself. Now you should be able to do it with James's help and mine.

5.1.2. Summary of the Facts

Although your clients already know the facts of their case, you need to include a summary of the facts in your opinion letter for three reasons.

First, you need to create an accurate narrative that includes the legally significant facts, necessary background facts, and any other facts that might be significant to the outcome of the case, including emotionally significant facts. Second, you want to give your clients the opportunity to review the facts as you understand them and inform you if you have misstated or omitted any facts that may be important. Reading the summary of the facts in your opinion letter might jog your clients' memory about something important they failed to tell you. You and your clients need to have the same understanding of the facts. Third, you want to protect yourself by communicating clearly that the opinion stated in your letter is dependent on the facts you have presented there. If the facts were to change in any significant way, your opinion might not be the same. Also, should potentially damaging facts surface in the future, you will have informed your clients that your opinion in this letter was based solely on the facts known at the time it was written.

Be careful not to include legal conclusions in your summary of the facts. Although legal conclusions may sometimes sound like facts, they go one step too far. Example of a fact: John killed his brother. Example of a legal conclusion: John murdered his brother. The fact that John killed his brother does not necessarily mean that he murdered him. That John "killed" his brother is a simple fact. That he "murdered" him is a legal conclusion that is dependent on a prosecutor's ability to establish all the elements of the crime of "murder" at trial. In Jonah's case, you cannot say, as a fact, that the hospital was negligent; you can say only that Jonah's knee had to be amputated following knee surgery.

The summary of the facts in the opinion letter should closely resemble the facts in your memo. Try to keep it as short as possible. Be careful not to stray into facts that might be legally significant later but are not legally significant when analyzing the issue at hand. For example, you need to focus on the facts that establish whether Jonah was mentally ill at the time of the operation in the letter, not whether the hospital was negligent. Thus, you need to include all the facts that establish his mental abilities and disabilities at that time. You also need to include the date of the operation, the date James was appointed guardian, and the fact that Jonah was mentally disabled from birth. How Jonah has changed since the surgery is not legally significant right now, but it does seem emotionally significant, especially to James and Jonah. Facts about what hospital personnel might have done wrong are not legally significant here and should be omitted.

If you were writing the letter primarily to James, your summary of facts might look like this:

My conclusions are based on the following information, which you and Jonah provided in our recent meeting. Jonah, who is now 30 years old, was born with a mental disability. Although he has never been able to read beyond a third-grade level; learn to drive a car; or perform complex intellectual tasks, like balancing a checkbook, he was able to care for his own basic needs before undergoing knee surgery at Maine General Hospital on February 4, 2009. He was able to prepare simple meals for himself and shower and dress himself. In fact, he was holding down a janitorial position he enjoyed at a daycare center and living semi-independently in a group home before the knee surgery. He was an outstanding athlete, who was happy with his life. After his leg was amputated following the surgery, Jonah fell into a deep depression. He is now living with you, after you became his legal guardian on March 15, 2009.

If you were writing a separate letter to Jonah, you might describe the facts in simpler terms, as follows:

I have reached my conclusions based on what you and James told me about your situation when we met last week. You were born 30 years ago with some learning problems that have kept you from being able to read as well as other adults, drive a car, or do difficult jobs that require a lot of thinking. Before your knee operation, though, you were a great athlete and could do lots of other things on your own like preparing meals for yourself, taking a shower, and getting dressed. You even had a job you liked, working as a janitor at the daycare center, and were able to live almost on your own at the group home. You were really happy until February 4, 2009, the day you had that knee operation. After that, especially when you lost your leg, you became very sad and had to move in with your brother James, who became your legal guardian on March 15, 2009.

5.1.3. Explanation of the Law and How It Applies

Your explanation of the law should be much shorter in your client letter than in your memo. You should not include the texts of statutes or make specific references to prior court cases. Instead, just explain the legal rules without citing to authority. Then show how those rules apply to your clients' situation. Explain what must be established, including any points that will not be in dispute. What your clients want is to be able to understand how the law will probably apply to their situation, what the outcome is likely to be, and how you came to your conclusions.

Often, using the facts from the present case is the best way to explain the legal rules. For example, you can explain the statute of limitations and the tolling provision by describing what they mean for Jonah in this letter primarily intended for James:

According to Maine law, Jonah would ordinarily have only three years to sue the hospital for injuries he may have suffered because of his knee operation. Jonah's operation took place on February 4, 2009, more than three years ago. However, an exception exists for people who had serious mental disabilities at the time the hospital may have caused their injuries. This exception effectively stops the clock from beginning to run until the person is no longer mentally disabled. It would allow Jonah to sue the hospital even though more than three years have passed if his mental disability was severe enough at the time of the operation.

For the exception to apply, Jonah's mental disability must have been present at the time of the operation and it must have been severe enough to prevent him from protecting his own legal rights. There can be no question that Jonah's mental disability—however severe it might have been—was present at the time of the operation because Jonah was born with it. All that needs to be shown, then, is that his disability is severe enough to prevent him from protecting his own legal rights.

At the time of the operation, Jonah was able to care for his own basic needs, work as a janitor, and live semi-independently in a group home. However, he could not read very well or handle complex intellectual tasks. Understanding how to file a lawsuit is an intellectually challenging task for anybody, regardless of how intelligent and well educated they are. Especially knowing what the deadline is for filing a suit, or even that such a deadline exists, is not something that should be expected of a person who reads at a third-grade level. Learning to prepare simple meals, take a shower, get dressed, and perform janitorial duties does not prepare someone for the complexities of the legal system. The fact that Jonah was not able to live independently points up his inability to protect his legal rights on his own.

Thus, the exception to the three-year time limit should apply to Jonah unless your appointment as his guardian makes a difference. Someone might say that Jonah's disability no longer mattered when you took responsibility for him on March 15, 2009, long before the three-year time limit for filing a lawsuit had expired. However, virtually every time this question has come up, the answer has been the same: If the person was mentally disabled enough to stop the clock from running at the time the injuries occurred, it does not matter that a guardian was later appointed. Thus, it should not matter in Jonah's case either.

Below is an explanation of the law and how it applies that would be appropriate to send to Jonah:

In Maine, people usually have to sue a hospital for injuries that happened during an operation before three years have passed since their operation. If you have to follow this rule, you will not be able to sue Maine General Hospital because your operation happened more than three years ago. However, people who had big enough learning problems at the time of the operation do not have to sue within three years. Those people will not have to meet the three-year deadline because they were not really able to protect their legal rights on their own at the time they were injured.

You were probably one of those people at the time of your operation. The learning problems you had that day were the same ones you have had since the day you were born. Even though you were good at many things, like cooking, getting dressed, and taking a shower, you did not read well enough to understand how to sue a hospital all by yourself. Just as you got the day-to-day help you needed in the group home, you would have needed quite a bit of help to sue the hospital. It does not even matter that James became your guardian a few months after the operation. The three-year deadline should still not apply to you and you should be able to sue the hospital.

5.1.4. Concluding Paragraph

In your concluding paragraph, you should reaffirm your relationship with your clients and explain what the next step will be. Be honest in your assessment of the situation. If your clients are not likely to achieve the outcome they are seeking, say so, but in a positive way. As a lawyer, you should always be able to offer some kind of assistance. In some situations, you will suggest a meeting with your clients to discuss ways of settling a case without going to court. Other times, you will describe any court filings you need to prepare or legal steps by the opposing party that might be anticipated. You should always end by reiterating your willingness to answer any questions and help in any way you can.

Your concluding paragraph to James and Jonah is an optimistic one. You are able to give them the good news that Jonah's lawsuit will probably be able to proceed. In other future correspondence regarding the strength of the case, you may not be able to be so positive. That is why it is important to establish a good relationship with your clients, one that will be strong enough to carry you and your clients through the ups and downs of litigation. Whether the case ultimately settles or goes to trial, your clients' trust in you is critical. Demonstrating your competency, respect, and empathy for their situation is the best way possible to cement that relationship of trust.

Below is a concluding paragraph for the letter primarily intended for James:

Based on my research and the information you have provided me, it is my opinion that Jonah will probably be able to go forward with a lawsuit against Maine General Hospital for the injuries he suffered after the knee surgery he underwent on February 4, 2009. He should not be held to the three-year deadline because of the severity of his mental disabilities at the time of the operation, even though you were appointed as his guardian on March 15, 2009. Thus, if you and Jonah are still interested in filing a lawsuit against the hospital, I can begin to research the applicable law to assess the strength of your case. I will want to meet with you and Jonah again to discuss the specifics of his knee injury, the operation, and Jonah's current condition. Once we have determined the nature of the claim, we can file a complaint with the court. In the meantime, please contact my office to set up an appointment for you and Jonah to meet with me. If you have any questions before we meet, please give me a call. I look forward to seeing you again and working with you to seek compensation for Jonah's injuries.

Sincerely,
[Your Signature]
[Your typed name]

Below is a concluding paragraph for the letter primarily intended for Jonah:

Based on what I know about the law and your situation, you should be able to sue Maine General Hospital for the injuries you suffered after your knee surgery on February 4, 2009. The three-year deadline should not apply to you because of your learning problems at the time of the operation, even though James became your guardian shortly after the operation. If it looks like you have a good chance of winning, we will let the court know in writing that you are suing the hospital. James will be calling my office to set up a time for us to meet again. If you have any questions before our meeting, please call me. I am looking forward to seeing you again and helping you in any way I can.

Sincerely,
[Your Signature]
[Your typed name]

SAMPLE ANNOTATED CLIENT LETTERS: Showing sections corresponding to objective memorandum

LETTER INTENDED PRIMARILY FOR JAMES

Dear James and Jonah: ◄——— *HEADING*

I enjoyed meeting you both last week and look forward to working with you on this case. As you requested, I have conducted some research to determine whether you will be able QP to bring a lawsuit against the hospital. *QP* Normally, a person cannot sue a hospital for medical injuries after more than three years have elapsed, but you will probably still be able to pursue a lawsuit because Jonah was mentally disabled at the time of the surgery. Also, it should not matter that you were appointed as Jonah's guardian because that appointment did not affect the mental disability that prevented him from protecting his legal rights. *BA*

My conclusions are based on the following information, which you and Jonah provided in our recent meeting. Jonah, who is now thirty years old, was born with a mental disability. Although he has never been able to read beyond a third-grade level; learn to drive a car; or *FACTS* perform complex intellectual tasks, like balancing a checkbook, he was able to care for his own basic needs before undergoing knee surgery at Maine General Hospital on February 4, 2009. He was able to prepare simple meals for himself and shower and dress himself. In fact, he was holding down a janitorial position he enjoyed at a daycare center and living semi-independently in a group home before the knee surgery. He was an outstanding athlete, who was happy with his life. After his leg was amputated following the surgery, Jonah fell into a deep depression. He is now living with you, after you became his legal guardian on March 15, 2009.

According to Maine law, Jonah would ordinarily have only three years to sue the hospital for injuries he may have suffered because of his knee operation. Jonah's operation took place on February 4, 2009, more than three years ago. However, an exception exists for people who had serious mental disabilities at the time the hospital may have caused their injuries. This exception effectively stops the clock from beginning to run until the person is no longer mentally disabled. It would allow Jonah to sue the hospital even though more than three years have passed if his mental disability was severe enough at the time of *DISCUSSION* the operation.

For the exception to apply, Jonah's mental disability must have been present at the time of the operation and it must have been severe enough to prevent him from protecting his own legal rights. There can be no question that Jonah's mental disability—however severe it might have been—was present at the time of the operation because Jonah was born with it. All that needs to be shown, then, is that his disability is severe enough to prevent him from protecting his own legal rights.

At the time of the operation, Jonah was able to care for his own basic needs, work as a janitor, and live semi-independently in a group home. However, he could not read very well or handle complex intellectual tasks. Understanding how to file a lawsuit is an intellectually challenging task for anybody, regardless of how intelligent and well educated they are. Especially knowing what the deadline is for filing a suit, or even that such a deadline exists, is not something that should be expected of a person who reads at a third-grade level. Learning to prepare simple meals, take a shower, get dressed, and perform janitorial duties does not prepare someone for the complexities of the legal system. The fact that Jonah was not able to live independently points up his inability to protect his legal rights on his own.

Thus, the exception to the three-year time limit should apply to Jonah unless your appointment as James's guardian makes a difference. Someone might say that Jonah's disability no longer mattered when you took responsibility for him on March 15, 2009, long before the three-year time limit for filing a lawsuit had expired. However, virtually every time this question has come up, the answer has been the same: If the person was mentally disabled enough to stop the clock from running at the time the injuries occurred, it does not matter that a guardian was later appointed. Thus, it should not matter in Jonah's case either.

Based on my research and the information you have provided me, it is my opinion that Jonah will probably be able to go forward with a lawsuit against Maine General Hospital for the injuries he suffered after the knee surgery he underwent on February 4, 2009. He should not be held to the three-year deadline because of the severity of his mental disabilities at the time of the operation, even though you were appointed as his guardian on March 15, 2009.   Thus, if you and Jonah are still interested in filing a lawsuit against the hospital, I can begin to research the applicable law to assess the strength of your case. I will want to meet with you and Jonah again to discuss the specifics of his knee injury, the operation, and Jonah's current condition. Once we have determined the nature of the claim, we can file a complaint with the court. In the meantime, please contact my office to set up an appointment for you and Jonah to meet with me. If you have any questions before we meet, please give me a call. I look forward to seeing you again and working with you to seek compensation for Jonah's injuries.

Sincerely,

[Your Signature]

[Your Typed name]

CONCLUSION

LETTER INTENDED PRIMARILY FOR JONAH

Dear Jonah: ◄———   **HEADING**

I enjoyed meeting with you and James last week and look forward to working with you. You and James asked me to find out whether you could sue the hospital for doing such a bad job with your knee operation. I do think you will be able to do that. Usually, people cannot sue hospitals when more than three years have gone by since their operations, but you should be able to do it because you were not really capable of doing that on your own when you had your operation. Even though James later became your guardian, you are still not able to sue the hospital by yourself. Now you should be able to do it with James's help and mine.

I have reached my conclusions based on what you and James told me about your situation when we met last week. You were born 30 years ago with some learning problems that have kept you from being able to read as well as other adults, drive a car, or do difficult jobs that require a lot of thinking. Before your knee operation, though, you were a great athlete and could do lots of other things on your own like preparing meals for yourself, taking a shower, and getting dressed. You even had a job you liked, working as a janitor at the daycare center, and were able to live almost on your own at the group home. You were really happy until February 4, 2009, the day you had that knee operation. After that, especially when you lost your leg, you became very sad and had to move in with your brother James, who became your legal guardian on March 15, 2009.

In Maine, people usually have to sue a hospital for injuries that happened during an operation before three years have passed since their operation. If you have to follow this rule, you will not be able to sue Maine General Hospital because your operation happened more than three years ago. However, people who had big enough learning problems at the time of the operation do not have to sue within three years. Those people will not have to meet the three-year deadline because they were not really able to protect their legal rights on their own at the time they were injured.

DISCUSSION

You were probably one of those people at the time of your operation. The learning problems you had that day were the same ones you have had since the day you were born. Even though you were good at many things, like cooking, getting dressed, and taking a shower, you did not read well enough to understand how to sue a hospital all by yourself. Just as you got the day-to-day help you needed in the group home, you would have needed quite a bit of help to sue the hospital. It does not even matter that James became your guardian a few months after the operation. The three-year deadline should still not apply to you and you should be able to sue the hospital.

Based on what I know about the law and your situation, you should be able to sue Maine General Hospital for the injuries you suffered after your knee surgery on February 4, 2009. The three-year deadline should not apply to you because of your learning problems at the time of the operation, even though James became your guardian shortly after the operation. If you and James still want to sue the hospital, I would like you to come to my office to talk some more about your operation and what later happened to your leg. If it looks like you have a good chance of winning, we will let the court know in writing that you are suing the hospital. James will be calling my office to set up a time for us to meet again. If you have any questions before our meeting, please call me. I am looking forward to seeing you again and helping you in any way I can.

Sincerely,

[Your Signature]

[Your Typed name]

CONCLUSION

5.2. General Correspondence and E-mails

5.2.1. General Correspondence with Clients

Although lawyers often write opinion letters to communicate with clients, they also correspond with clients when simply delivering information, making requests, or responding to them. When the information being delivered is neutral and benign, the letter need only contain a brief explanation. When the information involves bad news, more context and sensitivity are needed. When the letter makes a request or responds to one, its length will depend on the complexity of the request.

Whatever the nature of the letter, however, you must always maintain a high level of professionalism. If the letter is going to be delivered in hard copy, it should be a formal business letter, typed on firm stationery. The letter should be as well organized as an opinion letter and contain no errors in spelling, punctuation, or grammar. It should convey the same level of respect as any other correspondence that comes from your office. Even if the letter merely indicates that something like a will or a copy of a complaint is enclosed, the letter should communicate the same respect and empathy for the client as the opinion letter. If the letter is informing the client that the court has denied an important motion or dismissed your client's case, it needs to communicate even more empathy. Maintaining high standards in all your correspondence is a hallmark of a quality lawyer.

Even when you know the client well, that client deserves the respect that can only be communicated by a literate, polished letter, typed flawlessly on firm stationery or sent electronically through e-mail. The same applies to all letters sent to opposing attorneys and other colleagues.

5.2.2. Using E-mail Effectively[1]

Ten or fifteen years ago, lawyers almost always wrote letters on lovely, cream-colored stationery with a letterhead engraved at the top. Such letters usually contained carefully written and proofread messages that opened with a salutation and closed with a hand-written signature. These days, clients, opposing attorneys, and other colleagues are just as likely to hear from lawyers by e-mail, a form of communication that combines the convenience of a phone call with the accountability of a written document. Although e-mails lack the graciousness of a letter typed on vellum, if used properly, they can be just as effective. Writing an e-mail usually takes less time and effort, both to compose and to deliver a message, so attorneys can keep their clients up-to-date on any new developments with ease. E-mails can also be sent to more than one recipient at a time, eliminating the additional work involved in producing copies for all interested parties.

These efficiencies, however, come with some dangers and drawbacks. The consequences of sending an e-mail to the wrong recipient, or attaching the wrong document to an e-mail message, can be far-reaching and even devastating. Furthermore, e-mail messages that are not composed carefully may communicate the wrong tone, leading to misunderstandings and disgruntled clients or opposing attorneys. E-mails can have unintended legal consequences as well, such as the formation of a contract or the creation of liability. Carelessness involving e-mails may even lead to disciplinary action or, in an extreme case, a finding of malpractice.

Rules have always existed for professional written communication. Some of these rules are unspoken but understood. Letters to clients, opposing attorneys, and colleagues have always needed to be polite, polished, concise, and correct. Such rules are at least as important with regard to e-mails because such electronic communication is virtually instantaneous, as is the potential damage a poorly written or inappropriate e-mail may inflict. Because you can write or respond to someone else's e-mail so quickly, you might find yourself dashing off a message and sending it without taking the time to consider your response carefully. When writing

---

1. Much of the material appearing in this section was originally published in the following article: Nancy A. Wanderer, *E-mail for Lawyers: Cause for Celebration and Concern*, 21 Me. B. J. 196 (Fall 2006).

a letter, you have many opportunities to reconsider your words: when you proof-read the letter, fold it, put it in an envelope, attach a stamp, and deliver it to a mail box. With an e-mail, however, the process moves more quickly, providing little time for reflection. All you need to do is type your message and hit the "send" button. Once you have hit that button, you will probably not be able to retrieve your message.

Sometimes, people respond hastily to upsetting and poorly written e-mails while they are still in an emotional state, perpetuating a problem that might never have occurred if the original e-mail had been written more carefully. Because people tend to communicate through e-mail as if they were talking to someone else, not writing to them, they sometimes become too informal or aggressive. Unlike a conversation in person, where people can judge others' intentions by the tone of their voice or their gestures, e-mail does not provide nonverbal cues and so lends itself to misunderstanding and hurt or angry feelings.

The next section contains rules of e-mail communication, which provide some guidelines to help you convey a professional image within and outside your employment setting, communicate what you are intending to say, and avoid misunderstandings.

5.2.3. Rules of E-mail Communication

Rule 1. Always remember that you are communicating with another human being, not a faceless computer screen.

When composing an e-mail message, consider what your reaction would be if you were on the receiving end of that message. When you are talking with people in person, it is easy to remember that they are human beings with feelings and sensitivities. For some reason, people seem to forget that when communicating by e-mail. Just as some people lose their inhibitions and start shouting at someone on television while inside the privacy of their living room, some ordinarily polite people do the same thing when composing a message on a computer screen. Those angry television viewers, like the rude e-mail writers, would probably never talk that way to another person face to face. Somehow, though, they forget their manners when separated from the other person by a television or computer screen.

Under this first rule of e-mail communication, such behavior is unacceptable. People need to maintain the same standards of civility in cyberspace that they would adopt in all other areas of life. In fact, it may be even more important to remain civil in e-mails because they are stored in other people's computers where the sender has no control over how they might be used in the future.

Rule 2. Maintain a professional appearance through your e-mail correspondence.

Although you cannot be judged by your personal appearance online, you will be judged by the quality of your writing. Contrary to many people's beliefs, spelling, grammar, and punctuation do count in cyberspace. After writing an e-mail, you should always proofread it carefully and check for spelling errors. You should also pay close attention to the content of your writing. Make sure that everything you say is accurate and complete. Even if you do not care what the immediate recipient of your e-mail message thinks about you, anything you write can be passed on indefinitely and might eventually reach someone you do care about. It may even be discoverable in litigation. Use discretion about what you say and how you say it. Always try to keep your message concise and polite.

Rule 3. Use extreme care when addressing e-mails and attaching documents.

Much harm can come from sending an e-mail to the wrong address, accidentally replying to all senders, or forwarding others' e-mail messages to the wrong recipients. Sometimes the consequences are disastrous. For example, you could accidentally send information your client gave you in confidence to opposing counsel, destroying attorney-client privilege.

To avoid such embarrassing and potentially disastrous situations, you should pay close attention to the address fields: The addresses on the "To" line are for the people you are directly addressing. The addresses on the "cc" line are for people you are indirectly addressing. The addresses on the "bcc" line are for people who are receiving the e-mail in secret. The abbreviation "bcc" means "blind carbon copy" because the people on the "To" line and the "cc" line will not be able to see the people addressed in the "bcc" line and so will not know that the e-mail was sent to them—they are "blind" to that fact. For that reason, use of the "bcc" line may be unethical and should probably only be used for recipients who want to keep their e-mail addresses private. The "Reply to All" button sends your e-mail to everyone whose e-mail address is listed at the top of the e-mail you have received. Hitting the "Reply to All" button often generates many unnecessary e-mails and should only be done when everyone listed above needs to read your reply.

You should not copy or forward a message or attachment without the author's permission. Asking for such permission conveys respect for the privacy of others and demonstrates integrity and professionalism.

When attaching a document, you should give it a title that makes it easy for recipients to find it once they download it to their computer. You should also mention any attached documents in your e-mail to make sure your recipients know they are there. If you are sending an attachment, make sure it is actually attached before hitting the "Send" button. Otherwise, you will end up having to send a second e-mail with the subject "Oops," explaining your mistake and taking up everyone's time.

ETHICS ALERT: Carelessness Involving E-mails

One Harvard Law School student paid a big price for not paying closer attention to his address field. While working as a summer associate at Skadden Arps (a major New York law firm), Jonas Blank sent an e-mail message to a friend, stating, "I'm busy doing jack sh*t. Went to a nice 2hr sushi lunch today at Sushi Zen. Nice place. Spent the rest of the day typing e-mails and bullsh*tting with people." Unfortunately, he accidentally sent the e-mail to the firm's entire underwriting group. Although Mr. Blank quickly wrote an apology to the forty attorneys who had already opened the e-mail, the damage was done. Within moments, Mr. Blank's tale spread around the world on the Internet. He will probably never be able to live it down.

The Talk of the Town, *The Bar: Oops*, The New Yorker, http://www.newyorker.com/archive/2003/06/30/030630ta_talk_mcgrath (posted June 6, 2003).

Rule 4. Use meaningful subject lines.[2]

The subject line should be an important part of your e-mail message. People can sort and prioritize their e-mail messages based on the subject lines. When writing your subject line, think of it as a brief summary of your e-mail message. Be specific. If an action is requested in the e-mail, indicate that in the subject line. For example, instead of using "Legal Memo" as your subject line, say, "First Draft of Malloy Memo Attached"; or instead of "Consent Form," write, "Consent Form Needed by March 5."

As the subjects of e-mails change, you should update the subject lines to give recipients a sense of the current subject. Try not to keep an e-mail exchange going back and forth with the original subject line if the topic of the exchange has shifted. Also, delete old e-mails piling up at the bottom of an e-mail exchange that no longer have any relevance to the subject of the current e-mail message.

---

2. Wayne Scheiss, *Better Legal Writing* 135 (Hein 2005) (emphasizing the need to update subject lines).

Rule 5. Use an effective format for your e-mails.

Generally, you should begin with a salutation, just as you would begin a letter. A salutation is a sign or expression of greeting that reflects the level of formality you want to convey. Identify the purpose of the e-mail in the first sentence, either by asking a question or stating the reason you are writing. If you are replying to an e-mail, indicate the question to which you are replying in the first line and quote relevant passages from the original e-mail rather than sending the entire original message back to the sender.

Use short, block-style paragraphs and double space between them.[3] Unless the e-mail is very brief, use more than one paragraph for readability. Be concise. If possible, keep e-mails to the length of one computer screen.

In a professional e-mail, do not use emoticons like smiley faces, e-acronyms like "IMHO" (in my humble opinion) and "LOL" (laughing out loud), multiple exclamation points (!!!), or question marks (???). They may convey an inappropriate level of informality. Also, using all CAPs in an e-mail is the equivalent of shouting in a spoken conversation and, thus, should never be done.

Just as you opened with a salutation, you should include a closing such as "Sincerely," "Best regards," or "Yours truly."[4] Be sure to sign your e-mail professionally with your full name and contact information. You can create an automatic signature line for this purpose. It is best to keep your automatic signature to a few lines of contact information, omitting inspirational quotations or other similar material at the end.

If you are using your professional e-mail account, include a confidentiality warning at the bottom of your e-mail. Such warnings caution recipients about confidentiality and tell them how to handle messages sent to the wrong recipient. You do not need to state that every e-mail is confidential.

Rule 6. Think. Pause. Proofread. Pause again. Send.[5]

Before sending an e-mail, think about whether it is the best form of communication to use in the circumstances. Often a real letter, with a professional letterhead and your actual signature, is preferable. No matter how formally and well written an e-mail is, it will not be able to communicate the seriousness and formality of an actual hard-copy letter. Sometimes a phone call would be better than an e-mail message. In a phone call, you and the person you are calling are able to exchange

---

3. *Id.* at 138.

4. *Id.* at 141.

5. Wayne Schiess, *Writing for the Legal Audience* 34 (Carolina Academic Press 2003) (coining the phrase "Think; pause; think again; send" and discussing when to use various forms of communication).

information and hear each other's tone of voice and inflections, reducing the change of misunderstanding. If serious matters need to be discussed or decisions need to be made, a personal meeting would probably be even better.

Some communications should rarely be conveyed by e-mail, such as messages of sympathy, congratulations, and thanks. Others, like disappointing court decisions, should never be sent by e-mail. Such messages should be conveyed with a warmer, more human touch.

Once you have decided that an e-mail is the appropriate form of communication to use, pause long enough to review your message and correct any writing errors. Take a moment to polish your writing and double-check that you have addressed it to the correct recipients and attached the intended documents. In addition, be sure you are not sending sensitive or confidential information that should not be sent at all. Check your tone to be sure you will not offend or anger your recipient unintentionally. Pausing for a moment before hitting "Send" can prevent the problems and embarrassment of making a mistake that could jeopardize your client's interest or your own job security.

During the pause, think again about the e-mail you have written, and ask yourself whether your tone is appropriate, whether you have written and proofread your e-mail as carefully as a letter, and whether the contents of the e-mail and any documents you are attaching are appropriate to send to this person and anybody else to whom this person might forward them.[6] Only when you feel satisfied with your answers to those questions should you hit the "send" button.

Rule 7. Be ethical.

Always maintain high ethical standards in cyberspace. That means applying all the rules of professional responsibility to your e-mail correspondence. Just as you should reply to phone calls promptly, you should try to respond to e-mails the same day they arrive. Also, it is unethical to address blind copies ("bcc") to individuals when you know that the primary recipients would not like copies to be sent to those individuals. Finally, it is unethical not to adhere to the instructions in a confidentiality warning if you happen to receive an e-mail in error. Even if no warning was affixed to the e-mail you receive in error, you must forward that e-mail to the correct recipient and notify the sender of the mistake.

---

6. *Id.* at 37-38.

ETHICS ALERT: Using Unethical Passwords

The American Bar Association (ABA) warns that lawyers must exercise care when choosing a password. Under the ABA's Model Rules for Professional Conduct, "the ethical requirements for adequate computer security are moving from general and exhortatory to specific and practical" because weak passwords may cause data breaches, destroying attorney-client privilege.

_____

ABA ETHICSearch, Ethics tip of the Month—February 2013, "How 'Ethical' is your Password?" http://www.americanbar.org/groups/professional_responsibility/services/ethicsearch/ ethicstipofthemonth.html.

Chapter 6

Using Your Legal Analysis in Other Contexts

6.1. Using the Legal Analysis from Your Memo in a Litigation Document

Based on the analysis in your objective memo and further conversations with James and Jonah, Ms. Walker filed a complaint against Maine General Hospital. The complaint alleged that the hospital was negligent in treating Jonah, resulting in the loss of his leg. The hospital filed an answer, in which it asserted the statute of limitations as an affirmative defense. At the same time, it filed a motion for judgment on the pleadings, arguing that the court should enter judgment in its favor because Jonah's claims are time barred by the statute of limitations. At this point, no discovery has taken place. Ms. Walker gives you a copy of the hospital's motion.

STATE OF MAINE	SUPERIOR COURT
CUMBERLAND, ss	CIVIL ACTION
	DOCKET NO. CV-13-202

JAMES MALLOY,	)	
EX REL. JONAH MALLOY,	)	
	)	
PLAINTIFF,	)	
	)	DEFENDANT'S MOTION
v.	)	FOR JUDGMENT ON THE
	)	PLEADINGS AND
MAINE GENERAL HOSPITAL,	)	INCORPORATED
	)	MEMORANDUM OF LAW
DEFENDANT.	)	

The Defendant, Maine General Hospital, by and through its counsel, moves this Court to enter judgment on the pleadings pursuant to Rule 12(c) of the Maine

Rules of Civil Procedure, on its affirmative defense that Jonah Malloy's claims against it are time barred by the applicable statute of limitations. In further support of this motion, the Hospital states the following:

INTRODUCTION

A motion for judgment on the pleadings based on noncompliance with the statute of limitations is the equivalent of, and is treated the same as, a motion to dismiss pursuant to M.R. Civ. P. 12(b)(6). *Chiapetta v. Clark Assoc.*, 521 A.2d 697, 700 (Me. 1987). "Such a motion is a facial challenge to the timeliness of plaintiff's complaint and . . . is adequately tested under the usual motion to dismiss." *Id.* The allegations in the complaint do not establish that Mr. Malloy is mentally ill for purposes of tolling the statute of limitations for his claim. Accordingly, his claims against the Hospital are time barred.

FACTS

Mr. Malloy is a thirty-year old man. He had knee surgery at Maine General on February 4, 2009. Although he had a mental disability at the time of his surgery, he was an outstanding athlete who was able to hold down a job at a daycare center and live semi-independently. Although he struggles with complex intellectual tasks and cannot read at a high level, Mr. Malloy has always been able to care for his own basic needs. For example, he can prepare simple meals for himself and shower and dress himself.

Following Mr. Malloy's surgery, his leg had to be amputated below the knee. As a result of the amputation of his leg, Jonah now lives with his brother, James Malloy, who was declared Jonah's legal guardian on March 15, 2009.

ARGUMENT

Maine has a three-year statute of limitations for medical malpractice claims. 24 M.R.S. § 2902 (2013). The relevant statutory language requires that malpractice claims "be commenced within three years after the cause of action accrues," and asserts that "a cause of action accrues on the date of the act or omission giving rise to the injury." *Id.* A separate Maine statute provides that the statute of limitations may be tolled when a person entitled to bring an action under section 2902 "is mentally ill . . . when the cause of action accrues." 14 M.R.S. § 853 (2013). Because Mr. Malloy is not "mentally ill" within the meaning of the tolling provision, his claims against the Hospital were time barred on February 4, 2012, three years from the date of his alleged injury. Further, even if Mr. Malloy is "mentally ill," the appointment of his brother as his legal guardian should trigger the running of the statute of limitations. Because James Malloy was appointed Mr. Malloy's guardian on March 15, 2009, the statute of limitations expired at the latest on March 15, 2012. Therefore, this Court should enter judgment on the pleadings for the Hospital.

1. The Complaint does not show that Mr. Malloy is "mentally ill" within the meaning of the tolling provision.

"Mental illness" is defined as an *overall inability* to function in society that prevents plaintiffs from protecting their legal rights." *McAfee v. Cole*, 637 A.2d 463, 466 (Me. 1994) (emphasis in original). Furthermore, the "legal standard of competency varies for different purposes." *Chasse v. Mazerolle*, 580 A.2d 155, 157 (Me. 1990).

For example, evidence that a mentally "retarded" woman had previously gotten married and divorced did not preclude her claim of mental illness for purposes of the tolling provision. *Id.* The Court concluded that such evidence did not indicate that she "possessed sufficient competence to comprehend and exercise her legal right" to withhold consent to a sterilization procedure arranged by her parents. *Id.* Similarly, a severely depressed woman with memory lapses was found to be mentally ill for purposes of the tolling provision even though she could drive and occasionally cooked for herself because she had difficulty performing those functions or even leaving her house. *Bowden v. Grindle*, 675 A.2d 968, 971-72 (Me. 1996). The woman had also had a long history or psychiatric problems, including depression, anxiety, and memory lapses, for which she had been hospitalized and medicated for decades, and evidence showed that her cognitive thinking was impaired. *Id.* Because of these limitations, the Court found that she did not possess an overall ability to function in society and, therefore, was not capable of making an "informed rational judgment" to convey her property. *Id.*

Mr. Malloy does not meet the requirement for mental illness in *McAfee* because the complaint does not allege that Mr. Malloy was unable to function in society at the time of his surgery. To the contrary, Mr. Malloy was able to function fairly well outside the home as evidenced by his work at the daycare center and his semi-independent living in a group home. Mr. Malloy is also able to read, albeit at a basic level, and take care of his basic needs. Unlike the plaintiff in *Bowden*, who suffered from severe depressions and memory lapses at the time the cause of action accrued, the complaint does not allege that Mr. Malloy suffered from any similar disabilities. Further, the plaintiff in *Bowden* had been hospitalized and medicated for decades; nothing in the complaint indicates that Mr. Malloy has been ever been hospitalized or medicated for his disability. Unlike the plaintiff in *Bowden*, Mr. Malloy's limitations do not preclude him from understanding and protecting his legal rights. For these reasons, Mr. Malloy is not mentally ill under the tolling provision; therefore, the statute of limitations expired on February 4, 2012, three years after the date of his injury.

2. James Malloy's appointment as Jonah's legal guardian removed Jonah's legal disability under the tolling provision and triggered the running of the statute of limitations.

The Maine Law Court has not considered whether the appointment of a guardian defeats the application of the tolling provision. Some courts have concluded that the appointment of a guardian has no effect on the tolling of the statute of limitations. *See Weaver v. Edwin Shaw Hosp.*, 819 N.E.2d 1079, 1083-85 (Ohio 2004) (citing opinions of several state courts adopting the majority rule). However, other states have concluded that the tolling provision is ineffective once a guardian is appointed. *See* Michele Meyer McCarthy, *Effect of Appointment of Legal Representative for Person Under Mental Disability on Running of State Statute of Limitations Against Such Person*, 111 A.L.R.5th 159 §§ 9-10 (2001 & Supp. 2013) (citing state courts adopting the minority rule: Hawaii, Kansas, New Hampshire, New York, North Carolina, Washington, and West Virginia). These courts have taken the view that the appointment of a guardian triggers the running of the statute of limitations when the guardian has the right or legal duty to pursue legal action on behalf of a ward. *Id. See e.g. Johnson v. Pilot Life Ins. Co.*, 7 S.E.2d 475, 477 (N.C. 1940) (reasoning that the "policy of repose which underlies statutes limiting the time in which actions may be brought would be imperfectly expressed if these statutes did not apply to all those who might bring such actions, and actions which might be brought in their behalf," like a guardian who has a duty "to bring suit, when necessary"). Further, in Colorado, the tolling provision expressly provides for the statute of limitations to run after a guardian is appointed. Colo. Rev. Stat. 13-81-103(1)(a); *but see Barton-Malow Co. v. Wilburn*, 556 N.E.2d 324, 325 (Ind. 1990) (holding that the appointment of a guardian does not remove a mentally incompetent adult's legal disability because the tolling provision did not state that the statute of limitations would begin to run upon such an appointment).

Some courts that have adopted the majority rule have reasoned that the claim belongs to "the person who suffered the legal wrong," not the legal guardian; therefore, the statute of limitations is tolled for as long as that person is under the legal disability of "unsound mind." *See e.g. Sullivan ex rel. Wrongful Death Beneficiaries of Sullivan v. Chattanooga Med. Investors, L.P.*, 221 S.W.3d 506, 511 (Tenn. 2007). Others have looked to the legislative intent to determine that the legislature did not intend for the statute of limitations to run. *See e.g. Sahf v. Havasu City Assn. for the Retarded and Handicapped*, 721 P.2d 1177, 1182 (Ariz. App. 1986).

This Court should adopt the position that the appointment of a legal guardian stops the tolling provision and triggers the running of the statute of limitations. A legal guardian has the right to bring an action on behalf of the ward. Because of this right and duty, the underlying purpose of the statute of limitations would be undermined by tolling the statute indefinitely. Further, Maine's statute is silent on the issue and no evidence exists to indicate that the legislature intended to indefinitely toll the statute of limitations when a legal guardian can bring an action on behalf of the ward. Thus, to the extent that Mr. Malloy is mentally ill for purposes of the tolling provision, that disability was removed the day that James Malloy was appointed as his guardian, and the statute of limitations started to run on that day. For that reason, the statute of limitations expired no later than March 15, 2012.

CONCLUSION

For the reasons set forth above, the Hospital is entitled to judgment on the pleadings on its dispositive affirmative defense that Mr. Malloy's claims are time barred by the applicable statute of limitations.
Dated at Portland, Maine this 20th day of June, 2013.

Jason Roberts, Esq.
Attorney for Maine General Hospital

NOTICE

Matter in opposition to this Motion must be filed not later than twenty-one (21) days after the filing of this Motion, unless another time is provided by the Maine Rules of Civil Procedure or set by the Court. Failure to file timely opposition will be deemed a waiver of all objections to the Motion, which may be granted without further notice or hearing.

Ms. Walker has asked you to respond by drafting an opposition to the motion for judgment on the pleadings with an incorporated memorandum of law. Because you are now writing a document that advocates on behalf of your client, you need to shift the tone of your writing from objective to persuasive. You should be able to tailor your analysis in the objective memo to a persuasive document with a few adjustments in style, organization, and format.

First, though, you need to do a little more research to determine the legal standard for the type of motion you are dealing with—here, a motion for judgment on the pleadings. Using your efficient research skills, you quickly find a few cases that set forth the standard. Based upon your research, you determine the standard and write the following:

A motion for judgment on the pleadings based on noncompliance with the statute of limitations is the equivalent of, and is treated the same as, a motion to dismiss pursuant to Rule 12(b)(6) of the Maine Rules of Civil Procedure. *Chiapetta v. Clark Assoc.*, 521 A.2d 697, 700 (Me. 1987). In reviewing a motion to dismiss, a court assumes that all factual allegations in the complaint are true, *Stevens v. Bouchard*, 532 A.2d 1028, 1030 (Me. 1987), and views the complaint in the light most favorable to the plaintiff to determine whether it alleges the elements of a cause of action or facts entitling the plaintiff to relief pursuant to some legal theory, *New Orleans Tanker Corp. v. Dep't of Transp.*, 1999 ME 67, ¶ 3, 728 A.2d 674. Dismissal is appropriate "only when it appears beyond doubt that a plaintiff is entitled to no relief under any set of facts that he might prove in support of his claim." *Id.*

You should put this standard at the beginning of your memo of law because it sets forth the standard that the court has to use when reviewing the complaint and deciding whether to grant the motion.

Next, use your memo as a basis for writing the rest of the memorandum of law. Start with the facts. In persuasive writing, you should use the Statement of Facts section as an opportunity to highlight the facts that are helpful to you and minimize those that are not. The adjustment may be subtle and you should not exaggerate or misstate any of the facts.

After the facts, you will move into the Argument section, which correlates to the Discussion section in your objective memo. Note that you are skipping the Questions Presented and Brief Answers in your objective memo. You do not need them in the memorandum of law to support the opposition to this motion. There may be instances, though, when you would need to include equivalent sections in a persuasive document, such as when you are writing an appellate brief. Then, you need to include the Questions Presented to the court as well as a Summary of the Argument before you get into the Argument itself. If you were writing a long memorandum of law to go with the opposition to the motion, you might consider including a Summary of the Argument as well in order to give the judge the big picture of your argument.

You can start the Argument section the same way you started your objective memo—by including an orienting section to give the reader the broad rules and a roadmap of where your argument is going. After the orienting section, keep the overall structure the same as in the objective memo, but change your issue statements from questions to assertions. This shift will mean that you will present your legal analysis for each issue in CRAAC (Conclusion, Rules, Analogous Cases, Application, Conclusion) form, instead of IRAAC. Your Rules and Analogous Cases sections for the first issue can remain largely the same, though you may want to look for ways to shape the rules and language in your favor. When you get to the Application section, you should focus only on Jonah's arguments. Let the hospital make its arguments in its own memorandum of law. Be assertive in the Application section; start with a sentence that states the main point that you are making. Everything that follows should be the reasoning that supports that point. Finally, end your argument for each issue with a conclusion in which you urge the court to rule in your client's favor. This conclusion should match the contention you stated for this issue. Thus, the "C" at the end of the CRAAC should be equivalent to the "C" at the beginning of the CRAAC. After you have written the arguments for both issues, you should include an overall conclusion that summarizes what you want the court to do and why.

When you are finished writing the memorandum of law, include it with the opposition to the motion for judgment on the pleadings. The opposition is a court pleading; as such, it should include a caption with information about the court, the docket number, and parties' names; it should also identify the type of pleading. After the caption, many jurisdictions traditionally include a paragraph explaining who is submitting the motion or opposition. Use plain English in this paragraph. You may see language like "Now Comes the Defendant" used in previously filed motions, but such language really is not necessary.

Example:

STATE OF MAINE   SUPERIOR COURT
CUMBERLAND, ss   CIVIL ACTION
                                                      DOCKET NO. CV-13-202

JAMES MALLOY,   )
EX REL. JONAH MALLOY,   )
)
              PLAINTIFF,   )
         v.   )   PLAINTIFF'S OPPOSITION
)   TO DEFENDANT'S MOTION
)   FOR JUDGMENT ON THE
MAINE GENERAL HOSPITAL,   )   PLEADINGS
)
         DEFENDANT.   )

The Plaintiff, Jonah Malloy, through his guardian James Malloy, and by his counsel, submits this Memorandum in Opposition to the Motion for Judgment on the Pleadings filed by the Defendant Maine General Hospital. For the reasons set forth below, this Court should deny the Motion for Judgment on the Pleadings.

INTRODUCTION

A motion for judgment on the pleadings based on noncompliance with the statute of limitations is the equivalent of, and is treated the same as, a motion to dismiss pursuant to M.R. Civ. P. 12(b)(6). *Chiapetta v. Clark Assoc.*, 521 A.2d 697,

700 (Me. 1987). In reviewing a motion to dismiss, the court assumes that all factual allegations in the complaint are true, *Stevens v. Bouchard*, 532 A.2d 1028, 1030 (Me. 1987), and views the complaint in the light most favorable to the plaintiff to determine whether it alleges the elements of a cause of action or facts entitling the Plaintiff to relief pursuant to some legal theory, *New Orleans Tanker Corp. v. Dep't of Transp.*, 1999 ME 67, ¶ 3, 728 A.2d 674. Dismissal is appropriate "only when it appears beyond doubt that a plaintiff is entitled to no relief under any set of facts that he might prove in support of his claim." *Id.*

STATEMENT OF FACTS

Jonah Malloy, a thirty-year-old man, was born with a mental disability. On February 4, 2009, Jonah had knee surgery at Maine General Hospital that resulted in the amputation of his leg below the knee. At the time of the surgery, Jonah could take care of his own basic needs, such as preparing simple meals and dressing himself, but he could not read beyond a third-grade level or perform any complex intellectual tasks, like balancing a checkbook. Jonah has never been able to learn to drive a car. Prior to the surgery, Jonah was able to hold down a job he loved performing janitorial services at a daycare center, and he was an outstanding athlete. He was unable, however, to live independently. Since the surgery, Jonah has fallen into a deep depression. He now lives with his brother, James Malloy, who was declared Jonah's legal guardian on March 15, 2009.

ARGUMENT

Maine has a three-year statute of limitations for medical malpractice claims. 24 M.R.S. § 2902 (2013). The relevant statutory language requires that malpractice claims "be commenced within three years after the cause of action accrues," and asserts that "a cause of action accrues on the date of the act or omission giving rise to the injury." *Id.* A separate Maine statute, however, provides that the statute of limitations may be tolled when a person entitled to bring an action under section 2902 "is mentally ill . . . when the cause of action accrues." 14 M.R.S. § 853 (2013). There can be no dispute that the onset of Jonah's mental disability meets the timing requirement of the tolling provision because he was mentally disabled from birth. Because his mental disability qualifies him as "mentally ill" within the meaning of the tolling provision, the statute of limitations for his claim has been tolled. Further, the tolling provision continues to apply even though James was appointed as Jonah's legal guardian.

1. Jonah was "mentally ill" within the meaning of the tolling provision because he had an overall inability to function in society at the time of his surgery.

"Mental illness" is defined as an "*overall inability* to function in society that prevents plaintiffs from protecting their legal rights." *McAfee v. Cole*, 637 A.2d 463,

466 (Me. 1994) (emphasis in original). Furthermore, the "legal standard of competency varies for different purposes." *Chasse v. Mazerolle*, 580 A.2d 155, 157 (Me. 1990).

For example, evidence that a mentally "retarded" woman had previously gotten married and divorced did not preclude her claim of mental illness for purposes of the tolling provision. *Id.* The Court concluded that such evidence did not indicate that she "possessed sufficient competence to comprehend and exercise her legal right" to withhold consent to a sterilization procedure arranged by her parents. *Id.* Similarly, a severely depressed woman with memory lapses was found to be mentally ill for purposes of the tolling provision even though she could drive and occasionally cooked for herself because she had difficulty performing those functions or even leaving her house. *Bowden v. Grindle*, 675 A.2d 968, 971-72 (Me. 1996). Because of these limitations, the Court found that she did not possess an overall ability to function in society and, therefore, was not capable of making an "informed rational judgment" to convey her property. *Id.*

Jonah meets the definition of mental illness articulated in *McAfee* because his severely limited abilities at the time of the operation show that he did not possess an overall ability to function in society. Jonah's limitations—not being able to live independently; learn to drive; read beyond a third-grade level; or perform complex intellectual tasks, like balancing a checkbook—are like the limitations of the plaintiff in *Bowden*, who could perform ordinary functions with difficulty, yet did not have the capacity to convey her property. Jonah is also like the mentally disabled plaintiff in *Chasse*, whose previous marriage and divorce had no bearing on whether she could protect her legal rights: The fact that Jonah was competent in some respects, such as his ability to perform the basic tasks of living and hold a janitorial position at the time of the operation, does not establish that he was competent to pursue a lawsuit. Because Jonah was incapable of protecting his legal rights without significant assistance, his condition meets the definition of mental illness laid out in *McAfee*: possessing an "overall inability to function in society that prevents plaintiffs from protecting their legal rights." Therefore, the statute of limitations for Jonah's claim has been tolled.

2. James's appointment as Jonah's legal guardian does not affect the tolling provision.

Although the Maine Law Court has not considered whether the appointment defeats the application of the tolling provision, an "overwhelming majority of courts . . . have concluded that the appointment of a guardian has no effect on the tolling of the statute of limitations." *Weaver v. Edwin Shaw Hosp.*, 819 N.E.2d 1079, 1083-85 (Ohio 2004) (citing opinions of state courts adopting the majority rule from Alabama, Arizona, California, Massachusetts, Michigan, New York, Nebraska, and Washington, and federal courts adopting the majority opinion applying Michigan, Missouri, New Mexico, and Nevada state law). *See also* Michele Meyer McCarthy, *Effect of Appointment of Legal Representative for Person Under Mental Disability on Running of State Statute of Limitations Against Such Person*, 111 A.L.R.5th 159 §§ 4-7 (2001 & Supp. 2013) (adding state courts adopting the majority rule from Arkansas, Florida, Georgia Illinois, Indiana, Kentucky, Maryland, Minnesota, Mississippi, New Jersey, Oklahoma, and Rhode Island and federal courts adopting the majority rule applying Illinois and Oklahoma state law). In Colorado, however, the tolling provision expressly provides for the statute of limitations to run after a guardian is appointed. Colo. Rev. Stat. 13-81-103(1)(a).

Some courts have held that the appointment of a guardian does not remove a mentally incompetent adult's legal disability because the tolling provision did not state that the statute of limitations would begin to run upon such an appointment. *See Barton-Malow Co. v. Wilburn*, 556 N.E.2d 324, 325 (Ind. 1990). In *Barton-Malow*, the Supreme Court of Indiana interpreted a tolling provision that provides: "Any person being [of unsound mind] when the cause of action accrues may bring his action within two years after the disability is removed." *Id.* (quoting Ind. Code § 34-1-2-5). Concluding that "the statutory language is clear and unambiguous [and the] appointment of a guardian does not alter the fact of mental unsoundness," it does not terminate the legal disability." *Id.* Declining to consider the parties' contentions regarding statutory construction, the court added, "We do not construe a statute that is unambiguous." *Id. Accord Weaver*, 819 N.E.2d at 1082 (concluding that the appointment of a guardian has no effect on the tolling provision because "the statute does not mention the effect of a guardian's appointment").

Other courts have reached the same conclusion, but for a different reason, concluding that because the claim belongs to "the person who suffered the legal wrong," not the legal guardian, the statute of limitations is tolled for as long as that person is under the legal disability of "unsound mind." *See e.g. Sullivan ex rel. Wrongful Death Beneficiaries of Sullivan v. Chattanooga Med. Investors, L.P.*, 221 S.W.3d 506, 511 (Tenn. 2007).

Adopting yet another rationale, the Court of Appeals of Arizona, Division 1, Department D, held that a mentally incompetent person's disability was not removed when a guardian was appointed based on legislative intent, asserting that the legislature considered not only a mentally disabled person's inability to sue when enacting the tolling statute, but also the disabled person's difficulties in testifying and providing information to a court. *Sahf v. Havasu City Assn. for the Retarded and Handicapped*, 721 P.2d 1177, 1182 (Ariz. App. 1986).

Some courts, however, have taken the view that the appointment of a guardian triggers the running of the statute of limitations when the guardian has the right or legal duty to pursue legal action on behalf of a ward. McCarthy, 111 A.L.R.5th at §§ 9-10 (citing state courts applying the minority rule: Hawaii, Kansas, New Hampshire, New York, North Carolina, Washington, and West Virginia). *See e.g. Johnson v. Pilot Life Ins. Co.*, 7 S.E.2d 475, 477 (N.C. 1940) (reasoning that the "policy of repose which underlies statutes limiting the time in which actions may be brought would be imperfectly expressed if these statutes did not apply to all those who might bring such actions, and actions which might be brought in their behalf," like a guardian who has a duty "to bring suit, when necessary").

This Court should follow the majority rule for the three reasons set out above: The Maine tolling provision does not provide for an exception if a guardian is appointed; the claim belongs to Jonah and not to his guardian; and the purpose of the tolling provision relates not only to his difficulty in bringing suit, which could potentially be remedied by the appointment of a guardian, but also his difficulty in testifying and providing information to a trial court. Jonah was, and continues to be, disabled even after James's appointment as guardian for the purposes of the tolling provision. Therefore, the tolling provision should continue to apply even though James was appointed Jonah's legal guardian.

CONCLUSION

Because Jonah is mentally ill for purposes of the tolling provision, and because James's appointment did not affect the tolling provision, this Court should conclude that Jonah's claims against the Hospital are not time barred by the statute of limitations. Therefore, the Hospital's Motion for Judgment on the Pleadings should be denied.

Ellen Walker, Esq. Bar # 10017
Attorney for Jonah Malloy

Before submitting the motion to the court, you should proofread it carefully, looking for and correcting any spelling, punctuation, and citation errors, and making sure the document is complete. The quickest way to lose credibility with a court is to submit a filing that has a page missing or numerous typographical errors. Attempting to justify the mistakes by pointing to problems with spell checking software or your firm's printing technology will just make matters worse.

ETHICS ALERT: Blaming "Today's Technology" for Errors

The Court of Appeals of Wisconsin declined to consider a lawyer's justification for inadvertently omitting several pages from a filing. The court refused to address the lawyer's "suggestion that today's technology requires" the court "to develop a definition of 'mistake' that takes into consideration 'technologically based mistakes,' such as computer printing errors." Although the court declined to detail other errors the attorney had made, it stated that "we are left shaking our heads! Frankly, we are at a loss to understand what is clearly [the attorney's] intentional disregard of the rules and the details, including his failure to proofread." In a footnote, the court helpfully provided that "[t]ips for proofreading can be found online at The University of Wisconsin-Madison's "the Writing Center." *See* http://writing.wisc.edu/Handbook/Proofreading.html (last visited Mar. 13, 2009).

Johnson v. Roma II-Waterford, LLC, 2009 Wisc. App. LEXIS 258 **1, 7, 10 n.8 (Wis. App. Dist. 2 April 8, 2009).

6.2. Transactional Documents

Creating transactional documents, such as contracts or planning documents, may seem like a completely different type of legal writing, and to a certain extent it is. However, when you are drafting transactional documents, you can apply many of the same principles that you already know about what constitutes good legal writing.

First, use clear, plain English. This is not to say that you cannot use sophisticated terminology or reference terms used in a particular trade. Nevertheless, many transactional documents are cluttered with unnecessary and confusing language simply because associates rely on previous documents as templates when drafting contracts and other transactional documents. Thus, the unnecessary and confusing language just gets passed from one agreement to the next. By all means, use a template to get an idea of what you need to address in the agreement, but think about what each section means and whether you can make the meaning clearer by using plain English. For example, one section of most contracts contains "recitals," which are statements that provide the background information for the agreement. Recitals are often introduced with "WHEREAS," even though this is an unnecessary introduction and is not required in the document. Go ahead and take it out. Do not be afraid to improve the clarity of the template you are using.

Second, know your audience. This is true for any legal document you draft, whether it is an objective memo, a client letter, a motion to the court, or an agreement. If you know your audience, you can adjust the level of sophistication in the language and terminology that you use in drafting the agreement.

Likewise, know the purpose of the document. What are your client's needs and what are you trying to achieve with the transactional document? You need to understand your client's needs in order to ensure that all of the language included in the document best reflects and serves your client's needs. When you are working with a template or with language in a proposed document sent to you by an opposing attorney, you must carefully evaluate the language and tailor it to ensure that your client's needs are addressed and advanced by the document.

For example, imagine you are the attorney for Henry Miller, who has come to your firm because he wants to allow his neighbor, Susan Brown, to construct a driveway over his property, allowing her and her guests to go back and forth to her home. Henry tells you that he and his wife have several young children and, thus, do not want too many cars using the driveway. Susan's attorney has drawn up the following easement deed. Before signing it, Henry has brought it to you for your advice. You read it carefully, keeping in mind Henry's objectives in granting the easement.

EASEMENT DEED

KNOW ALL BY THESE PRESENTS THAT, **HENRY MILLER**, of the Town of Falmouth, County of Cumberland, State of Maine ("Grantor"), for good and valuable consideration, the receipt and sufficiency of which is hereby acknowledged, hereby grant to **SUSAN BROWN**, of the Town of Falmouth, County of Cumberland, State of Maine, and their successors and assigns (collectively "Grantee"), a right-of-way road easement, over Grantor's land located at 101 Stone Mountain Road in the Town of Falmouth, County of Cumberland, and State of Maine, for which the Grantee and her guests, may use as a driveway for ingress and egress by pedestrians or vehicles to access the residence on land owned by Brown. Said Easement is further described as follows:

. . . .

You immediately notice a few things you might like to change, including the language specifying that Susan and her guests may use the driveway "for ingress and egress by pedestrians or vehicles to access the residence" on Susan's land. You are not sure whether everyone would understand those words to mean that Susan can only use the driveway for residential purposes, not for anything bordering on a commercial venture. You realize that most people would probably read the language to exclude commercial purposes. Yet you know how important this limitation is to Henry, especially because the increased traffic a commercial venture would probably entail. So, to remove any doubt, you revise the language as follows to state more clearly the restriction that Henry wants to put on the use of the easement: "the Grantee and her guests may use the easement as a driveway to access Brown's property for residential purposes only, not for sales of any kind." If you did not have a good understanding of Henry's priorities, you might not have noticed that the language included by the other attorney was not as clear as it needed to be. In addition, you decide to omit the unnecessarily formal language at the beginning ("KNOW ALL BY THESE PRESENTS THAT") and replace the legalese expression "said easement" with the plain English words "this easement" at the end of the sentence. By making these changes, you have ensured that your client's objectives have been met and communicated in language both parties can understand.

Finally, know the expected format for the document. Use previous documents of the same kind as templates for the one you are drafting, keeping in mind that you can improve upon the clarity of the language.

Although transactional documents come in various forms, most contain the same basic parts. First, the document should have a title, and if the document is long, a table of contents. Next, many documents contain some sort of introduction to convey information such as the parties to be bound by the document and the date. Next comes the recitals section; however, many lawyers label this section as "Background" or "Findings" because that is exactly the type of information contained in the recitals section. The recitals section sets forth the important facts that were already in existence before the agreement was executed.

After the recitals, the body of the document makes up the bulk of the agreement. This is where the document explains what the parties have agreed to do (or not do). As with any legal document, the body of the agreement should be broken up into subsections with headings to help the reader navigate through the material in the document. When you are writing the body of an agreement, put the most important aspects of the agreement at the front. Your audience does not want to wade through pages and pages of legalese in order to get to the most important aspects of the agreement. Exactly what goes into the body of the document and the types of things you need to consider and address in the document largely depend upon what type of document you are drafting. Finally, every document should end with a date and signatory line.

The term "transactional documents" covers a vast array of documents, including wills, settlement agreements, business contracts, purchase and sale agreements, liability waivers, noncompetition agreements, employment contracts, security agreements, deeds, and easement deeds. Each has its own unique set of considerations that you must take into account while drafting that document, but regardless of what type of transactional document you are drafting, remember to use the principles of good writing.

Chapter 7

Effective Legal Writing

7.1. Quoting and Paraphrasing

7.1.1. Importance of Accuracy

As a new attorney, you may feel uncomfortable explaining a court's rule, holding, or rationale in your own words, believing that you can only be certain you are accurately reporting what the court stated if you use the court's exact words. You are absolutely right to be concerned about representing accurately what the court has stated. Too often, lawyers misrepresent the law they are citing. Usually this happens because they have misread or misunderstood the law; sometimes, however, they state something as they wish the court had stated it, changing what the court has stated to support the point they are trying to make. Regardless of how it happens, misstating the law is a serious matter. Attorneys very quickly lose credibility with law partners and courts when they are found to be misstating the law or shading it to support their contentions. Once that credibility is lost, it may never be recovered.

Keeping in mind the imperative of stating the court's words accurately, you should always begin by reading the court's words thoroughly, making sure you understand exactly what the court is saying. Then, you must decide how best to explain those words to your reader. You should not assume, however, that the best way to do that is to quote those words verbatim. Because the legal proposition you want to explain will appear within the context of your own writing, just as the court's words originally appeared within the context of the opinion, you will probably need to change at least some of the court's words in order to weave the proposition smoothly into your writing. The words that worked perfectly within the context of the opinion may end up sounding awkward and out of place in what you are writing if presented as a direct quote. Learning when to use a direct quote and when to paraphrase takes some practice. Deciding what to do depends, in part, on the nature of the words you want to include.

ETHICS ALERT: Inaccurate and Misleading Quotations

The United States Court of Appeals for the Federal Circuit affirmed a reprimand of an attorney who attempted to mislead the United States Court of International Trade by omitting limiting language in a quotation from a case dealing with the definition of "forthwith" and failing to include the words "emphasis added" after her citation when quoting from a dissent by United States Supreme Court Justice Clarence Thomas. The court held that the attorney should be sanctioned "for misquoting and failing to quote fully from two judicial opinions in a motion for reconsideration she signed and filed."

Precision Special Metals v. United States, 315 F.3d 1346, 1347-48 (Fed. Cir. 2003).

7.1.2. Using a Direct Quotation

If a particular passage is perfectly suited to your needs, just as the court has stated it, you will probably want to use a direct quotation. For example, when researching the meaning of "mental illness," you located the following passage in *McAfee v. Cole*: "Mental illness under the tolling statute refers to an *overall inability* to function in society that prevents plaintiffs from protecting their legal rights." You confirmed that this definition continued to be used in subsequent cases and, thus, it seems to be exactly what you need to begin laying out the rules that govern the issue in your memo. For this reason, you decide to use a direct quotation for the actual definition, although you may decide to alter the introductory words a bit. In your memo, you decide to introduce the definition as follows, citing to the source immediately afterwards: "Mental illness" is defined as an "*overall inability* to function in society that prevents plaintiffs from protecting their legal rights." *McAfee v. Cole*, 637 A.2d 463, 466 (Me. 1994) (emphasis in original). Note that you have included a pin cite (466) to tell the reader exactly where the quote appears in the case and also the words "emphasis in original" in parentheses to let the reader know that the court emphasized those words, not you.

Using a direct quote for that definition was the right decision. If you had tried to paraphrase it, you might have altered the court's meaning. Also, a paraphrase would probably have been much wordier than the direct quote, like the paraphrase that follows:

> The definition of "mental illness" is when a person is generally unable to do every day things in society and, thus, is not able to safeguard their rights under the law.

No one would think that paraphrase was an improvement over the original. Furthermore, the court itself has consistently quoted the exact words from *McAfee* in later cases dealing with the definition of mental illness under the tolling provision.

7.1.3. Quoting Only Key Words

Sometimes, you may wish to quote only a key word, a term of art, or a special phrase that you would like to use throughout your document. For example, when you were researching the law of easements for another client, Susan Brown, you found the following passage in a case from 1910, explaining how an easement deed may be interpreted: "And the interpretation of it may be aided, in case of doubt, by the practical construction which the parties placed upon it by their conduct, by acts done by one party and acquiesced in by the other, especially when such conduct is proven to have continued for a long time." The key phrase you would like to take from this passage is "acquiesced in." You plan to analyze whether Susan's neighbor "acquiesced in" Susan's use of her driveway for weekly summer yard sales. You do not really need to include a direct quote including all the words in the passage, although you should probably include the part that says the acquiescence needs to have "continued for a long time."

Thus, you decide to include the following sentence in your memo:

> The parties' conduct, including whether one party has "acquiesced in" acts done by the other party, can be evidence of intent for a particular purpose, especially if that conduct has "continued for a long time." *Drummond v. Foster*, 107 Me 401, 404, 78 A. 470, 471-72 (1910).

Note that you have cited to a Maine case that requires a parallel citation, providing pin cites for both the Maine and the Atlantic reporters. Because you plan to use the term "acquiesced in" or some derivative of it throughout your memo, you need to cite to the case in which you found the term and enclose it in quotation marks the first time you use it. However, you do not need to provide a citation or enclose it in quotation marks when you refer to it later in your memo. The same is true of the phrase "continued for a long time." For example, you might include the following sentence in the Application section of your memo:

Susan would argue that Henry Miller, like the landowner in *Drummond v. Foster* who acquiesced in an expanded use of a right-of-way, did acquiesce in her use of the driveway for weekly summer plant sales by allowing the sales to continue for five years, which is a long time. *Drummond v. Foster*, 107 Me 401, 404, 78 A. 470, 471-72 (1910).

Quoting just the key words of a passage is an effective way to draw your reader's attention to them. Of course, you must be careful not to change the meaning of the passage, but you can show your reader what is important by quoting only those key words. You can also draw the reader's attention to the key words in a block quote or longer quoted passage by using italics or underlining to show emphasis. Then, even if readers skim over the rest of the quotation, they will notice the part you think is most important. Below is an example showing how key words can be emphasized:

Although the Maine Supreme Judicial Court has not considered whether the appointment defeats the application of the tolling provision, an "overwhelming majority of courts" have found that to be the case.

Here is another example showing the use of emphasis to focus readers' attention:

Although the Maine Supreme Judicial Court has not considered whether the appointment defeats the application of the tolling provision, an *"overwhelming majority of courts"* . . . have concluded that the appointment of a guardian has no effect on the tolling of the statute of limitations." *Weaver v. Edwin Shaw Hosp.*, 819 N.E.2d 1079, 1083-85 (Ohio) (emphasis added).

You may also wish to use quotation marks around a word that you want to include, but that may have a negative connotation in today's society. For example, the court referred to the plaintiff in the 1990 case of *Chasse v. Maserolle* as a "mentally retarded woman." The term "retarded" is no longer held in high regard in today's society. Yet, you want to include that term because it is the term that would have been used to describe Jonah back in 1990 as well, and you want to show the similarities between the facts in that case and Jonah's situation. One way to do that is to include the term "retarded" in quotation marks, indicating that it was the court that described her that way, not you, but letting the reader know exactly what her disability was. Your sentence would look like this:

For example, evidence that a mentally "retarded" woman had previously gotten married and divorced did not preclude her claim of mental illness for purposes of the tolling provision.

By enclosing "retarded" in quotation marks, you have achieved your goal of showing the similarity between the plaintiff in *Chasse* and Jonah without offending anyone's sensibilities.

7.1.4. Altering a Direct Quote

If a passage is well suited to your needs but must be altered to fit your text, you may omit part of the passage, change the tense of a verb, condense the passage by replacing a phrase with a word, or modify the passage in some other minor way. You should keep the quotation marks around the passage, but alter it by using square brackets ("[ ]") to show additions or substitutions of letters or words or ellipses (. . .) (three periods with spaces on either side) to show the omission of one or more words. For example, using the same passage from *Drummond v. Foster*, you could alter it as follows.

Original passage:

"And the interpretation of it may be aided, in case of doubt, by the practical construction which the parties placed upon it by their conduct, by acts done by one party and acquiesced in by the other, especially when such conduct is proven to have continued for a long time."

Altered passage:

"[T]he interpretation of [a deed] may be aided . . . by the practical construction . . . placed upon it by [the parties'] conduct, by acts done by one party and acquiesced in by the other, especially when such conduct [has been] proven to have continued for a long time."

7.1.5. Paraphrasing

If you want to include the content of a passage that needs to be rewritten substantially to fit into your own text, you should paraphrase the passage. That will be true when the passage goes into more depth than you need, the style is difficult to read, or the style does not fit well with your own style of writing. In general, it is better to paraphrase than to use a direct quote unless you have a good reason for quoting a passage, like those discussed above. Even though you may not be including a direct quote in your writing, you still need to provide a proper citation, including a pin cite, to the source of the passage you are paraphrasing.

For example, you may decide to paraphrase the statute of limitations for health care providers and practitioners in your memo because it is the language of the tolling provision, not the statute of limitation, that is really at issue. You just want to let the reader know how long a plaintiff ordinarily has to bring a claim against a hospital. Here is the text of the statute: "Actions for professional negligence shall be commenced within 3 years after the cause of action accrues. For the purposes of this section, a cause of action accrues on the date of the act or omission giving rise to the injury." 24 M.R.S.A. § 2902. You might decide to simplify your presentation of the statute of limitations as follows:

Under the statute of limitations, an action for professional negligence against a hospital must be filed within three years following the act or omission that allegedly caused an injury. 24 M.R.S.A. § 2902.

Note that you must cite to the statute, even though you have paraphrased it and not included any quoted language at all. You might wonder whether you should put quotation marks around "act or omission," but it is probably not necessary to do so because those words are commonly used and are not special enough in this context to warrant quotation marks to set them apart. The same is true of other language like "action for professional negligence" and "allegedly caused an injury."

7.1.6. Using Quotations Sparingly

Many legal writers, even experienced ones, sometimes end up filling their writing with long block quotes and sentences pieced together with a series of shorter direct quotes, in patchwork fashion. Although block quotes, even lengthy ones, are occasionally the best way to communicate complex legal concepts, and it is not wrong to include a series of short direct quotes within a sentence, those approaches are usually unnecessary and ineffective.

The truth is, direct quotes are difficult to weave seamlessly into text, and most people tend to avoid reading block quotes, especially long ones. Quotations that contain at least fifty words, or four lines of text, are called "block quotes" because they must be reformatted into a single-spaced block of text, with the left and right sides indented. Usually, documents are expected to be double-spaced, with one-inch margins, making them fairly easy to read. A long quote, squeezed into a smaller, single-spaced block, is not really something a reader welcomes. In fact, only the most dedicated readers actually read block quotes as carefully as they read the double-spaced text. Many readers just skip right over them. Because you have presumably included a quotation—word for word as it appeared in the legal source—because you thought it was so well written and important, it is unfortunate when your reader decides not to read it. By putting the quotation into a block quote, you have probably ensured that the material you thought was so essential will never be read carefully, if it is read at all.

Consider the following example: You want to describe the facts in *Bowden v. Grindle*, a good analogous case showing what it means to be mentally ill under the tolling statute. Because you think all the facts are so important, and you like the way the court described a woman's mental condition, you decide to use a block quote. This is how that block quote would appear to the reader, who has presumably been enjoying your double-spaced text up to this point:

> Bowden had been treated for chronic depression her entire life, had been prescribed medications for anxiety and depression, and was hospitalized for depression for parts of December 1982 and January 1983. After she was released, she received psychiatric treatment and medication as an out-patient. In September 1983, [her husband] died. The medical testimony revealed that after her husband's death, Bowden's condition became acute and suicidal. Bowden's friends testified that her depression grew worse and she could not think, remember, or understand what was going on. She does not remember much of what happened during the year following her husband's death. She took medications and was hospitalized "off and on."

Bowden v. Grindle, 675 A.2d 968, 971-72 (Me. 1996).

If your reader is like most, her heart probably sank when she saw that block quote approaching and either forced herself to plow through it, skimmed it, or skipped it all together. To make matters worse, the block quote did not even include all the relevant facts. Thus, right after the long block quote, you will need to add another quote, explaining that "the medical testimony confirmed that there were times when Bowden had difficulty cooking her own meals, leaving the house, and driving." *Id.* at 972. By now, the reader may have lost her train of thought entirely, wondering what all this quoted material adds up to.

Later, when you realize that your memo has gotten too long, you decide to shorten it by jettisoning the quotations altogether and summing up the facts as follows:

Similarly, a severely depressed woman with memory lapses was found to be mentally ill for purposes of the tolling provision, even though she could drive and occasionally cooked for herself, because she had difficulty performing those functions or even leaving her house. *Bowden v. Grindle*, 675 A.2d 968, 971-72 (Me. 1996).

Although your reason for omitting the quotations was to save space, you have succeeded in accomplishing several other important objectives at the same time. You have removed a long block quote that many people would have skipped over and replaced it with a brief sentence identifying the important fact that a woman was suffering from severe depression and memory lapses. In that same brief sentence, you have also described her occasional difficulties with driving, cooking, and leaving her home. You were even able to insert some analysis into your brief sentence by introducing the sentence with a transitional word—"Similarly"—preparing the reader for what is to come and informing her that the mental problems experienced by this woman made her mentally ill for the purposes of the tolling provision. In 42 words of highly readable text, you were able to state the holding of the case and explain the legally significant facts, something you were not able to accomplish in the 141 words of quotations in the earlier draft. Furthermore, you can probably rest assured that your reader will read and understand what you have written. Finally, by not using direct quotes, you were better able to weave the necessary material into your own text, meshing it smoothly with the previous sentence by using a transitional word, something that is often difficult to do with direct quotes and especially block quotes.

QUOTE VERSUS PARAPHRASE?

"The choice to paraphrase or to quote is more art than science. What matters is the readability and effectiveness of the result, not enslavement to some seemingly arbitrary rule ('What am I supposed to do here?'). In any particular instance, when in doubt, try it one way, then try it the other, and see which you think works better. Getting good at using outside material in your own writing is less a function of mastering rules than it is a matter of intelligent trial and error, of time on task over the course of your legal education, both as a student and even more as a lawyer."[1]

What is plagiarism?	A passage of another's thoughts or words presented as your own. Quoting direct language without quotation marks or without citing your source. Paraphrasing without citing your source. Note: Legal writing does not recognize the "rule" that information found in more than three sources is "general" and thus needs no citation. To the contrary, a passage whose source goes uncited in legal writing bears no authoritative weight whatsoever.

(continued)

When do I *not* need to cite?	When you are stating the Question Presented or Issue (pink section of the IRAAC); summarizing your opinion in the Brief Answer (in an objective memorandum) or your argument in the Summary of the Argument (in a brief); explaining how a general legal standard might apply to novel facts (green section of the IRAAC); or predicting how a court would rule (in an objective memorandum) or concluding your argument (in a brief) (blue section of the IRAAC).

1. LWI listserv participant [author unknown], summer 2003.

7.2. Purpose and Proper Use of Citation

Our legal system relies almost entirely on the holdings in prior cases. Whether legal analysis or opinions are based on enacted law or common law, readers must be able to find all the sources of law to determine their accuracy and persuasiveness. Citations are the shorthand you will use to show readers that the sources you cite are sound and authoritative. They are a kind of language you and your reader share with which you can communicate where to find an authority, the weight of that authority, and how that authority supports your proposition. The *ALWD Guide to Legal Citation*, *The Bluebook*, and state-specific citation manuals, such as *Uniform Maine Citations*, are like grammar books, providing the rules for communicating in the language of legal citation. These citation manuals establish a uniform method of citation and outline acceptable citation practices. The *ALWD Citation Manual* and *The Bluebook* are equally authoritative, although *The Bluebook* is primarily geared for scholarly writing while the *ALWD Guide to Legal Citation* focuses more on the writing of lawyers and courts. State-specific citation manuals, like *Uniform Maine Citations*, lay out the local citation rules and conventions for that particular jurisdiction, which should be followed when practicing there.

7.2.1. Purposes of Citation

Legal citations serve several purposes. First and foremost, they tell readers where to find the cited source in order to verify what the source says, to learn more about that source, or to find additional sources cited within it. Thus, the citation must contain all the information needed to locate both the source and the particular reference within that source.

Your use of citation also shows that you have thoroughly researched the law and found relevant authorities to support your discussion of the relevant legal principles and how they apply to the case at hand. Even more importantly, citations give proper credit to the courts and other authorities who originally expressed the words, ideas, and principles you are including in your own work. Giving proper attribution to the work of others is a core principle of legal writing.

Here are some examples of citations to particular references in sources you have found:

- Bryan A. Garner, *A Dictionary of Modern Legal Usage* 516 (2d ed., Oxford University Press 1995) (the entry for "legalese" in a legal dictionary)
- 51 Am. Jur. 2d *Limitation of Actions* § 209 (2003) (a legal encyclopedia topic)
- Michele Meyer McCarthy, *When is Person, Other than One Claiming Posttraumatic Stress Syndrome or Memory Repression, Within Coverage of Statutory Provision Tolling Running of Limitations Period on Basis of Mental Disability*, 23 ALR6th 697, 698 (2007 & Supp. 2013) (an ALR annotation)
- *Bowden v. Grindle*, 675 A.2d 968, 970 (Me. 1996) (a state case)
- *Douglas v. York County*, 433 F.3d 143, 145 (1st Cir. 2005) (a United States Court of Appeals case)
- *Priestman v. Canadian Pacific Ltd.*, 782 F. Supp. 681, 683 (D. Me. 1992) (a United States District Court case)
- William M. Schrier, *The Guardian or the Ward: For Whom Does the Statute Toll?* B.U. L. Rev. 575, 575 (1991) (a law review article)

You also found several statutes in Maine Revised Statutes Annotated, including Maine's tolling provision. Statutes can be cited using two different formats: the standard format appearing in the *ALWD Citation Manual* and *The Bluebook*, and the format required by local rule. The tolling provision would be cited as follows according to the standard format: Me. Rev. Stat. Ann. Tit. 14, § 853 (West 2003). According to Maine local rules, however, the statute would be cited as follows: 14 M.R.S.A. § 853 (2003). When citing to Maine Revised Statutes Annotated, the date in parentheses is the copyright date, found on the back of the title page. In Maine, you may also cite to Maine Revised Statutes, a statutory collection that does not include annotations, found online and softbound in many libraries: 14 M.R.S. § 853 (2013). When citing to Maine Revised Statutes, the date in parentheses is the year the softbound volume was published. Because you are practicing in Maine, you should use the local rules and cite to either 14 M.R.S.A. § 853 (2003) or 14 M.R.S. § 853 (2013). If you were practicing in another jurisdiction, like New York, and you wanted to cite to Maine's tolling provision, you would use the standard format: Me. Rev. Stat. Ann. Tit. 14, § 853 (West 2003).

Another purpose of citation is to give the reader some information about the weight and persuasiveness of that source. For example, from looking at a citation, a reader can determine whether that source is mandatory authority, how old the authority is, what level of court decided a case, and whether an article was written by a respected authority or appears in a reputable source. For example, this citation to a Maine case—*Bowden v. Grindle*, 675 A.2d 968, 970 (Me. 1996)—tells the reader that the case is mandatory authority in Maine courts because it was decided by the Maine Supreme Judicial Court (the abbreviation "Me." in parentheses stands for the Maine Supreme Judicial Court), and that it is fairly recent. On the other hand, a reader will know that *Douglas v. York County*, 433 F.3d 143, 145 (1st Cir. 2005) is not mandatory authority in Maine courts because the name of the reporter (Federal Reporter, Third) and the court-date parenthetical indicate that the case was decided by the United States Circuit Court for the First Circuit. It may be persuasive authority because the First Circuit applied Maine law in its opinion, but it cannot be mandatory authority if it was not decided by Maine's highest court. A case decided by the United States Supreme Court like *Brown v. Board of Education*, 347 U.S. 483 (1953), however, is always mandatory authority in every jurisdiction as long as it is still good law. The reader can recognize that *Brown v. Board of Education* was decided by the United States Supreme Court because the reporter in the citation is abbreviated "U.S.," which stands for United States Reporter.

Citation is also used to convey the type and degree of support the legal authority provides for a particular proposition through the use, or non-use, of introductory signals.[1] Introductory signals are words that appear before the citation, such as "*See*," "*See also*," and "*Accord*," that convey a message to the reader about the type and degree of support provided by the cited authority. Signals can indicate that a cited authority provides implicit or explicit support. They can also draw a comparison between two cited authorities, or indicate that a cited authority provides contradiction, background material, or an example.

For example, "*See*" is used when the cited authority supports the proposition implicitly or supports the proposition only in dicta. No signal would precede the citation if the cited authority supported the proposition explicitly. "*Accord*" is used after one authority has been cited to introduce some additional authorities that support the same proposition as that first

---

1. *See generally* Coleen M. Barger, *ALWD Guide to Legal Citation* 312-14 (5th ed., Wolters Kluwer Law & Business 2014); *The Bluebook: A Uniform System of Citation* 54-56 (Columbia Law Review Assn. et al., eds., 2010) (explaining the use of signals).

authority. "*See also*" serves much the same purpose, but this signal is not as strong as "*Accord*." "*Cf.*" is used when the cited authority supports a stated proposition, but only by analogy. "*Compare . . . with*" is used to draw a comparison between two or more cited authorities. "*Contra*," "*But see*," and "*But cf.*," indicate that a cited authority contradicts the stated proposition. "*See generally*" indicates that the cited authority contains useful background material, and "*E.g.*" indicates that the cited authority provides an example of many authorities that support the stated proposition.

When you use a signal, it is helpful to add an explanatory parenthetical after the cited authority to show why you have used that signal. For example, when discussing whether the appointment of a guardian terminates the legal disability of mental illness for purposes of the tolling provision, you quote the Supreme Court of Indiana stating, "We do not construe a statute that is unambiguous." After that, you cite to *Barton-Malow Co. v. Wilburn*, 556 N.E.2d 324, 325 (Ind. 1990). Then, because you want to show that the Supreme Court of Ohio came to the same conclusion, you add a cite to *Weaver v. Edwin Shaw Hospital*, 819 N.E.2d 1079, 1082 (Ohio 2004), preceded by the signal "*Accord*" and followed by an explanatory parenthetical. If this was the first time you were citing to those two cases, the legal proposition and full citations would look like this:

"We do not construe a statute that is unambiguous." *Barton-Malow Co. v. Wilburn*, 556 N.E.2d 324, 325 (Ind. 1990). *Accord Weaver v. Edwin Shaw Hosp.*, 819 N.E.2d 1079, 1082 (Ohio 2004) (concluding that the appointment of a guardian has no effect on the tolling provision because "the statute does not mention the effect of a guardian's appointment").

7.2.2. Proper Use of Citation

You may be wondering when you need to use citation and when you do not. Especially when writing a memo for an experienced attorney or a brief for a court, it might seem like some ideas and legal principles have become so well established that they need no citation. Especially if you have seen the same principle stated over and over in case after case, you may think it has become general knowledge. However, that is not the case.

In legal writing, you must cite to your sources whenever you state a proposition that is not your own. If the words or ideas are entirely your own, however, you do not need to cite to authority, even when you are interpreting legal principles you introduced earlier and for which you already provided citations. In an objective memo, for example, you do not need to cite to a source for your statement of the issues, your application of the legal rules to the facts in your case, or your conclusions because those ideas are your own. On the other hand, you do need to cite to authority for any legal rules you explain as well as your descriptions of the facts, holdings, and rationales of the analogous cases you present. Even a reference to something as familiar as the Free Speech Clause of the United States Constitution requires a citation, as follows:

"Congress shall make no law . . . abridging the freedom of speech. . . ." U.S. Const. amend. I.

You must cite to authority whether you are quoting the actual words or paraphrasing those words, like this:

The First Amendment guarantees a right to freedom of speech. U.S. Const. amend. I.

If the authority supports your contention implicitly, you will need to introduce the citation with the signal "*See*," as follows:

The Founders recognized the importance of citizens speaking freely. *See* U.S. Const. amend I ("guarantee[ing] a right to freedom of speech").

When in doubt, always err on the side of providing a citation.

All the citation rules you will ever need are available in the *ALWD Guide to Legal Citation*, *The Bluebook*, and a state-specific citation manual, if one is available for your jurisdiction. It is not necessary to memorize citation rules, although you are bound to become familiar with the most commonly used citation rules for citing cases, statutes, treatises, and law review articles. The most important thing you can do is to study the organizational scheme of the manuals you plan to use and figure out how to look up various citation rules. It is actually a good idea to keep both the *ALWD Citation Manual* and *The Bluebook* on your desk, along with your state-specific citation manual. The rules are fairly consistent in the *ALWD Citation Manual* and *The Bluebook*, but sometimes one manual or the other may explain a rule more clearly or provide a better set of examples.

Use the table of contents, index, and other quick reference aids to find the rules you need. Do not let the size of the manuals intimidate you. Many of the rules presented will not be important to you on a daily basis. In fact, some of them you may never need. The manuals are long and complicated because they contain rules for just about any situation you can imagine.

You will be glad those rules exist if and when you need them, but many of them you will rarely ever use. Just concentrate on getting familiar with the common rules and how to find the more obscure ones using the reference aids.

In legal memos, briefs, and opinions, citations are usually placed within the text of the document, either after a sentence as a "citation sentence" or within a sentence as a "citation clause." Most of the time, it is better to use citation sentences because citation clauses break up the flow of a sentence. Here is an example of a citation sentence:

"Mental illness" is defined as an "overall inability to function in society that prevents plaintiffs from protecting their legal rights." *McAfee v. Cole*, 637 A.2d 463, 466 (Me. 1994).

The following is an example of a citation clause:

In *McAfee v. Cole*, 637 A.2d 463, 466 (Me. 1994), the court defined "mental illness" as an "overall inability to function in society that prevents plaintiffs from protecting their legal rights."

You can see that it is better to wait until the end of the sentence for the citation.

Sometimes, however, you may need to insert one or more citation clauses into a sentence. Usually this occurs when you want to include legal material from more than one authority in the same sentence. For example:

The legal standard for mental illness, which is defined as an "overall inability to function in society that prevents plaintiffs from protecting their legal rights," *McAfee v. Cole*, 637 A.2d 463, 466 (Me. 1994), varies for different purposes, *Chasse v. Mazerolle*, 580 A.2d 155, 157 (Me. 1990).

Each citation clause refers to the material that comes directly before it. The citation to *McAfee* has to do with the definition of "mental illness"; the citation to *Chasse* establishes that the legal standard for mental illness varies for different purposes. Because it is so much harder to read sentences loaded with legal citation, you should try to avoid using citation clauses unless it is absolutely necessary. It is virtually never necessary to introduce a sentence with a citation and, thus, that common practice should especially be avoided.

Some jurisdictions and all law reviews require legal citation to be in footnotes. When practicing in such a jurisdiction, you might want to rely on *The Bluebook*, which is geared for scholarly writing and focuses on the use of footnotes in legal documents.

ETHICS ALERT: Citation Errors

A United States District Court in Washington pointed out that many of the cases upon which the plaintiff relied "most heavily contain[ed] citation errors." After pointing out several faulty citations in the plaintiff's brief, the court reminded the plaintiff's attorney "that it is of paramount importance to cite cases accurately."

Hathaway v. U.S., 1993 WL207532 at *4 n.2 (W.D. Wash. Mar. 16, 1993).

7.2.3. Avoiding Plagiarism

A. *Recognizing Plagiarism*

Plagiarism is the act of presenting someone else's words or ideas as your own. Plagiarism occurs when an author fails to acknowledge the proper source of ideas or fails to use quotation marks to indicate that the words themselves came from another source. Plagiarism may be intentional or unintentional. Either way, it is cheating and must be guarded against.

In a legal setting, plagiarism may seem like a confusing concept, especially because *stare decisis* requires that the words and ideas from earlier cases be passed down to present cases, and law firms rely on form files and memo and brief banks in which documents prepared by one lawyer can be used by other lawyers to prepare new documents.[2] In addition, law clerks write opinions signed by judges, in which sections of attorneys' briefs are often incorporated without attribution.[3] Associate attorneys routinely write briefs and other court filings that are signed by senior partners.[4] Nevertheless, as an officer of the court and a member of your state's bar,

---

2. Linda H. Edwards, *Legal Writing: Process, Analysis, and Organization* 10 (2d ed. Aspen Publishers 2006).

3. *Id.*

4. *Id.*

you are obligated to give proper attribution to the ideas and words that appear in your documents. You are not obligated, however, to cite to another attorney's memo or brief if you are merely using it as a way to find the law and determine how best to apply it to your particular set of facts. In that case, you are only required to cite to the legal authority from that brief, not the other attorney's brief itself. Similarly, if you are using a document from a form file as the basis of a deed or other transactional document, you do not need to cite to that document. As for judges and senior partners taking credit for the work of law clerks and associates, the practice is so widespread and accepted, no one considers it plagiarism although technically, of course, it is.

B. Avoiding Plagiarism Through the Proper Use of Quotation Marks

Quotation marks are used to indicate that you have included someone else's exact words in the document you are writing. Using quotation marks ensures that the correct person gets the credit for speaking those words and lets readers know that they are reading that person's exact words, not your paraphrase or interpretation of what was said. Thus, you should not use quotation marks when you paraphrase because that would send the wrong signal to your reader.

If you include an entire sentence or paragraph of exact words, you will, of course, put quotation marks around the entire thing. It is more difficult to determine when you need quotation marks if you paraphrase someone else's words but have included some words from the original text in your paraphrase. To decide when to use quotation marks, you need to consider how many words in a row are the same as the original text, how much of the sentence contains words from the original text, whether your sentence structure mirrors that of the original text, and whether you have used any distinctive language used in the original text.

If you have used seven or more words of original text in a row, you should enclose those words in quotation marks.[5] For example, the following paraphrase contains more than seven words of original text in a row, and those words have been enclosed in quotation marks:

The relevant statutory language requires that malpractice claims "be commenced within three years after the cause of action accrues." 24 M.R.S. § 2902 (2013).

---

5. *Id.* at 206.

The following paraphrase, however, would not require quotation marks:

The relevant statutory language requires that malpractice claims be filed no later than three years after the act or omission giving rise to the claim. 24 M.R.S. § 2902 (2013).

Although the meaning is the same, the second paraphrase does not use enough words from the original text to warrant quotation marks. Furthermore, the second paraphrase does not use any distinctive language from the original text such as "after the cause of action accrues." If that language had been used, it should have been enclosed in quotation marks.

You should not try to avoid plagiarism by changing every seventh word, however, especially if all the other words are the same as the original text and you use the same sentence structure.[6] You need to ask yourself whether objective readers would conclude that the words were your own if they were able to see the original text. If not, you need to either rewrite the passage completely or quote the passage in its entirety, enclosing it in quotation marks.

Even if a unit of text is not seven words long, you should enclose it in quotation marks if it contains distinctive wording or a memorable phrase.[7] Justice John Marshall Harlan used just such a phrase when taking exception to the Court's acceptance of "separate, but equal" treatment of African American passengers on railway cars in *Plessy v. Ferguson*, 163 U.S. 537, 552 (1896) (Harlan, J. dissenting). You would never want to even look like you were trying to take credit for a memorable phrase like that, even though it is only three words long. When courts announce standards like "the best interests of the child" or "the reasonable person standard," you should always enclose them in quotation marks the first time you discuss them. Later, you can apply them without using quotation marks.

Because credibility is so essential to your success as a lawyer, you do not want to do anything that places your integrity in doubt. Citing meticulously to authority for every proposition or statement that is not your own will enhance your reputation. Taking the time to cite correctly, using citation manuals to determine the proper form for your citations, and remembering to use a pin cite in every citation will inspire respect from your colleagues and the courts. Few attorneys are sufficiently attentive to the intricacies of citation; those who understand its importance and devote the time and energy to doing it right are held in high esteem.

---

6. *Id.*
7. *Id.* at 206-07.

QUOTING, PARAPHRASING, AND PLAGIARIZING*

As you read cases, law review articles, or even good journalism, pay attention to how competent authors use their sources. An author can respond in five ways to the need to incorporate the information from any one source: the direct quotation, the "phrase that pays," the altered quotation, the paraphrase, and—egads!—plagiarism. This chart is meant to help you decide how best to incorporate information from another source into your documents.

TYPE OF SOURCE	RESPONSE	HOW?
1. A passage perfectly suited to your needs	**Direct Quotation** (The source of the quotation **must** be cited.)	Quotation marks before and after quoted words. Terminal punctuation: commas and periods within, generally, all else outside quotation marks. See **ALWD Rule 47.4(d) (1). (2).** **Caveat:** Quotes distract. This is a good thing if you wish to emphasize. This is a bad thing, though, if used to excess because it distracts and becomes visual clutter. Use direct quotation judiciously. Your reader should be drawn to it, not repelled by it so that her eye leapfrogs lengthy or frequent quotations to get back to your analysis. Too many direct quotes suggest that the writer has not processed the material and is merely "cutting and pasting" information into the document.
2. A key word, term of art, or phrase you wish to use throughout your document	**The "phrase that pays"** (The source of the quoted phrase **must** be cited the first time, but need not be cited thereafter.)	Quote the phrase the first time, but assume the reader understands its importance thereafter. If much water has passed under the bridge before its next use, which could happen by the time the piece concludes, you may wish to revive the quotation marks. **[First reference] The court held that defendant's conduct was "privileged under the circumstances." [cite]** **[Later reference] In this case, defendant's conduct was not privileged under the circumstances because. . . .**

3. A passage *nearly* perfectly suited to your needs, but **requiring some adaptation to fit your text.**	**Altered Quote** (The source of the altered quotation **must** be cited.)
Why? You may wish to - omit part of the passage - change the tense of a word - condense the passage, as by replacing a phrase with a word - modify the passage in some other minor way	**Keep** the quotation marks, but … - **Bracket** [ ] additions or substitutions. Bracket, as well, a capital letter required by the grammar of the quoted phrase but absent in the original. See **ALWD Rule 48.** **ORIGINAL: "We all agreed that the Red Sox finally did it."** **ALTERATION: "[T]he Red Sox finally did it."** - Place an **ellipsis** (…) ([space] [dot] [space] [dot] [space] [dot] [space]) where one or more words are omitted (but not at the beginning of a sentence). See **ALWD Rule 49.** **ORIGINAL: "We all agreed that the Red Sox finally did it."** **ALTERATION: "[T]he Red Sox … did it."** Don't forget **periods.** If the source sentence ends where you want it to end, no ellipsis is needed—just the original period. If your whole sentence is in quotation marks, however, and your quote omits the end of the sentence, give the period after the ellipsis marks (spaces are indicated below with carats). (You should, however, generally avoid using a whole sentence quote.)

TYPE OF SOURCE	RESPONSE	HOW?
		ORIGINAL: "We were thrilled when the Red Sox beat the Yankees in the 2004 ALC playoffs. The Curse of the Bambino had been looming for too long, and it looks like we're now moving forward, at last." ALTERED, or REDACTED: "The Curse . . . had been looming for too long. . . ." More commonly, you will use a quoted phrase or clause in the text of your own sentence. If you do this, do not use an ellipsis at the beginning or the end of the quoted material.
		CLAUSE USED IN YOUR OWN SENTENCE: Red Sox fans were ecstatic about the team's 2004 ALC win because "[t]he Curse of the Bambino had been looming for too long."

4. A passage you wish to rewrite substantially so it will mesh more seamlessly into your style and document
 	
Why rewrite?
• Source has greater breadth and detail than is appropriate.
• Style is unreadable or a bad fit (jargon, complex, antiquated).
	Paraphrase:
	
	The rewriting conveys the ideas in the passage with your own words and more compatible with your style and the demands of your document.
	
	(The source of the paraphrase is **always** cited.)
		TIPS: In general, paraphrase rather than quote **unless** you are
		  (1) stating a rule or a "phrase that pays," or
		  (2) discussing specific language at issue.
		
		Observations on the pros and cons of paraphrasing:
		Pros: (1) most successfully integrates outside information into writer's own text
		      (2) creates shorter, smoother documents
		Cons: (1) requires writer to take more care to provide effective signals

Caveat: If you find yourself changing a word here and there simply because you want to avoid the appearance of a quotation, pause to reconsider: if the passage needs no substantial revision, then quote it, showing omissions or minor alterations.

If, on the other hand, you have good reason to tailor it to the needs of the document, recast it in your own words to meet that goal, retaining, however, the meaning of the passage.

---

(2) avoid when exact wording is in dispute

(3) can fail if indicators of who said what are too weak for reader to follow

(4) can confuse reader if more than one source is cited in a single sentence

EXAMPLE OF INEFFECTIVE QUOTING:[1]

In *Allridge v. Scott*, 41 F.3d 213, 222 (5th Cir. 1994), the court noted:

> We ... read *Simmons* [*v. South Carolina*] to mean that due process requires the state to inform a sentencing jury [in a capital trial] about a defendant's parole ineligibility when, *and only when*, (1) the state argues that a defendant represents a future danger to society and (2) the defendant is legally ineligible for parole.

Unlike South Carolina, "Texas did not statutorily provide for parole ineligibility at the time of Allridge's conviction," so the requirement in *Simmons* that the jury be informed as to the defendant's future dangerousness and ineligibility for parole did not apply in *Allridge*.

EXAMPLE OF EFFECTIVE PARAPHRASING (plus effective quoting):[2]

The ... Fifth Circuit read *Simmons* to require that a sentencing jury in a capital trial be informed of a defendant's ineligibility for parole "when and only when" he arguably "represents a future danger to society and ... he is legally ineligible for parole." *Allridge v. Scott*, 41 F.3d 213, 222 (5th Cir. 1994). Because at the time of Allridge's conviction, Texas statutes included no provision for parole ineligibility (or "life-without-parole"), *Simmons* did not apply.

ETHICS ALERT: Plagiarism

The Supreme Court of Illinois affirmed the censure of an attorney who plagiarized two published works in the thesis he submitted to Northwestern University to satisfy a requirement for a master's degree in law. In an attorney disciplinary proceeding, the Hearing Board concluded that the attorney's plagiarism "constituted 'conduct involving dishonesty, fraud, deceit, or misrepresentation' violating the Illinois Code of Professional Responsibility." The attorney received a six-month suspension for his unprofessional conduct.

_____

In re Lambris, 443 N.E.2d 549, 550-53 (Ill. 1982).

7.3. Grammar, Punctuation, and Style

Using correct grammar and punctuation is especially important in legal writing for several reasons. First, the law is a complex subject. Your job as a legal writer is to make it understandable. That objective can only be achieved through clear, concise writing that conforms to established rules of grammar and punctuation. Furthermore, your credibility depends in part on convincing your readers that you know what you are talking about. If your readers are distracted by frequent grammar and punctuation errors in your memos or briefs, they will lose faith in your ability to analyze the law. Regardless of how brilliant your legal analysis is, readers who are turned off by your improper use of personal pronouns or apostrophes are unlikely to be impressed by your logic.

Your writing style is equally important. To guide your readers through a maze of complex legal concepts or an argument that depends on a logical flow, you must know how to write clearly and concisely. To do this, you need to choose the right words and write effective sentences and paragraphs, employing signposts and transitions to lead your readers through your analysis.

7.3.1. Basic Grammar Review

You were probably taught about grammar long before you entered law school. Maybe it was so long ago that you have forgotten much of what you learned, or maybe you had an eighth grade teacher who made the rules of grammar so unforgettable that you rarely make a mistake. Either way, it is a good idea to refresh your memory, especially about some of the more confusing areas like pronoun/antecedent agreement, incomplete and run-on sentences, misplaced modifiers, the use of "which" and "that," parallelism, voice, and mood. If you have not already done so, you should buy a style manual like *The Elements of Style*, by William Strunk Jr. and E.B. White, or *A Writer's Reference*, by Diana Hacker, and keep it handy, right next to the citation manuals on your desk.

A. Subjects, Verbs, and Predicates

Everyone knows what a simple sentence looks like. It has a subject and a predicate:

The judge ruled.

"The judge" is the subject; "ruled" is the predicate. In a simple sentence, the predicate is simply the verb.

In some sentences, the subject acts upon an object directly through an action verb:

The judge delayed the trial.

"The judge" is still the subject, but now the predicate is made up of both the action verb ("delayed") and the direct object ("the trial"). Sometimes the object is indirect:

The jury gave the verdict to the judge.

In this sentence, "jury" is the subject, "gave" is the action verb, "verdict" is the direct object, and "judge" is the indirect object.

Sometimes the subject takes a linking verb, expressing a state of being, which requires a subject complement, that is, a noun, pronoun, or adjective to complete the sentence:

Attorneys are writers.
It is I!
The defendant was guilty.

"Attorneys," "It," and "defendant" are nouns and the subjects of the sentences. "Are," "is," and "was" are linking verbs, expressing states of being in the present ("are" and "is") and past ("were"). "Writers," "I," and "guilty" are subject complements. "Writers" is a noun linked with "Attorneys"; "I" is a pronoun linked with "It"; and "guilty" is an adjective, linked with and describing "defendant."

B. Subject/Verb Agreement

The subject of the sentence must agree in number with the verb. Thus, if your subject is plural, your verb must also be plural:

A defendant sometimes lies.
The facts never lie.

The subject "Defendant" is singular, so the verb, "lies," must also be singular. The subject "facts" is plural, so the verb, "lie," must also be plural.

Words that come between the subject and verb do not change the number of the verb:

The difficulty of standing trial—the uncertainty and anxiety of facing the jury each day—causes high blood pressure in some defendants.

The singular subject, "difficulty," takes a singular verb, "causes," even though the words "uncertainty" and "anxiety" intervene.

Do not make the mistake of changing the number of the verb when the words "one of" or a similar expression is the subject of the sentence. It is correct to say, "One of the jurors is making faces at the judge," not "One of the jurors are making faces at the judge." The subject of the singular subject of the sentence is "one," not the plural noun "jurors." Thus, it takes the singular verb "is making."

You should always use a singular verb after the words "each," "either," "everyone," "everybody," "neither," "nobody," and "someone":

Everybody thinks he will win at trial.

"Everybody" is singular, so the verb "thinks" is singular.

"None" can be used as a singular or a plural noun. When you mean "no one" or "not one," it is singular and takes a singular verb:

No one is going.

When "none" suggests more than one thing or person, it takes a plural verb:

None are so unhappy as those who are caught cheating.

Here, "none" is a plural subject because it refers to people caught cheating and, thus, takes the plural verb "are."

A compound subject, made up of two or more nouns joined by "and" always takes a plural verb:

The district attorney and the criminal defense lawyer are good friends outside of court.

Some compound subjects, however, are seen as a unit and, thus, take a singular verb:

Love and marriage is a time-honored tradition.

The same is true of plural subjects following the words "each" and "every":

Each of the law clerks goes home before dark.
Every witness, juror, and attorney is hungry.

A singular subject remains singular even when other nouns are added to it by "with," "as well as," "in addition to," "except," "together with," and "no less than":

The court clerk as well as the bailiff wants to go to law school someday.

Some nouns that appear to be plural because they end in "s" are really singular, like politics, headquarters, and chambers:

The judge's chambers is on the other side of the building.

C. Nominative and Objective Pronouns

Pronouns that can serve as the subject of a sentence, like "I," "he," "she," "we," and "they," are said to be nominative pronouns.

I am happy.
They are sad.

Pronouns that can serve as a direct or indirect object of an action verb, like "me," "him," "her," "us," and "them," are said to be objective pronouns:

The judge reprimanded him.
The judge read him the verdict.

A pronoun used as a subject complement of a linking verb should always be nominative:

The best oral advocates are Deborah Barker and I.

A pronoun in a comparison is nominative if it is the subject of a stated or understood verb:

My client is taller than I am.
The judge talks more quickly than she. ["Than she *talks*" is understood.]

Be careful to notice whether pronouns are being used as subjects, subject complements, direct objects, or indirect objects. Sometimes, people think it sounds better to say, "The Moot Court Team chose Samuel and I as Best Oralists," especially when two people are direct objects. Yet, no one would say, "The Moot Court Team chose I as Best Oralist." Taking out the first name is a good way to check yourself: "The Moot Court Team chose me as Best Oralist" sounds much better. Thus, it is correct to say, "The Moot Court Team chose Samuel and me as Best Oralists."

Similarly, you should not say, "My client and me went to court." You would never say, "Me went to court," so you should also not say, "My client and me went to court." The correct form of the sentence is "My client and I went to court."

The rules about objective pronouns also apply to the use of prepositions like "with," "of," "over," "under," and "through." Like action verbs, prepositions take objects. Some people are tempted to say, "Jennifer went to court with Harry and I," but that would be incorrect. The object of the preposition "with" must be the objective pronoun "me." Thus, the sentence should be, "Jennifer went to court with Harry and me."

The pronouns "it" and "you" do not have nominative or objective forms. They can be used as subjects or objects. When you use "who" and "whom" or "whoever" and "whomever," however, you must follow the rules laid out above. "Who" and "whoever" are nominative pronouns; "whom" and "whomever" are objective. Thus you would say, "Who is going to court?" and "The impersonator could be whoever you wanted him to be." In those sentences, "who" is the subject of the sentence and "whoever" is the subject complement of the linking verb "could be." However, you should use the objective form in the following sentences: "We called my brother, whom we hope to visit" and "Peter will attend the trial with whomever shows up." In those examples, the objective pronouns "whom" and "whomever" should be used because "whom" is the object of the verb "hope to visit" and "whomever" is the object of the preposition "with." You may be able to remember this rule by remembering the title of Ernest Hemingway's novel, *For Whom the Bell Tolls*. In that title, "whom" is the object of the preposition "for." It just does not sound right to say "*For Who the Bell Tolls.*"

D. Pronoun/Antecedent Agreement

Pronouns take the place of nouns. Thus, they often refer back to a noun that was introduced earlier; that noun, which is called the "antecedent" of the pronoun, would have been male or female and singular or plural. The pronoun should always agree with its antecedent in gender and number. A singular, male antecedent (like "boy") should be followed by a singular, male pronoun (like "he," "him," or "his"):

The *boy* ate *his* lunch.

Similarly, a singular, female antecedent (like "mother") should be followed by a singular, female pronoun ("she" or "her"):

The *mother* sang a lullaby while *she* rocked her baby to sleep.

Likewise, a plural antecedent should be followed by a plural pronoun (like "they," "them," or "their").

Jurors should make up *their* own minds.

Unlike singular pronouns, plural pronouns do not have a gender.

Deciding which pronoun to use presents a problem, however, when you do not know the gender of the antecedent. For example, if you wanted to talk about the effect of a defendant not testifying at trial on a hypothetical juror (the antecedent), you would not know whether to use a male or female pronoun. You could say, "A *juror* would have trouble making up *his* mind." For centuries, that is how the problem was solved. Writers simply used the masculine pronoun to represent both males and females. Fortunately, that practice is no longer acceptable. Some writers try to avoid the gender question by using pronoun "their":

A *juror* would have trouble making up *their* mind.

That solution is no better, however, because the pronoun "their," which is plural, does not match with its antecedent "juror," which is singular. A better solution would be to use both a male and a female pronoun:

A *juror* would have trouble making up *his or her* mind.

It is better than using "their," but it can get tiresome to read "his or her" or "his/her" numerous times in a document. The best solution is probably to rewrite the sentence, making "juror" plural, so it will match with the plural pronoun "their":

Jurors would have trouble making up *their* minds.

If the word "each" or "every" precedes one or more nouns in a plural antecedent, you should use the singular pronoun and verb:

Each pencil and pen *was* emblazoned with *its* team colors. *Every* man and woman *is* entitled to *her* voice.

When a pronoun refers to two or more antecedents joined by "or" or "nor," the pronoun and verb should agree with the closest antecedent:

Neither the girls nor the *boy sees his* future in tea leaves.
Either the killer or his *accomplices are* responsible for *their* capture.

With an indefinite pronoun like "all," "any," "each," "either," "everyone," "neither," "none," or "something" that does not refer to any specific person or thing, use a singular pronoun and verb:

All is well.
Nobody was home.
Somebody has dropped *his* or *her* wallet. [Incorrect: Somebody has dropped *their* wallet.]

Pronouns with the following endings are indefinite pronouns: "–one," "–body," and "–thing."

When the antecedent is a collective noun like "jury," "Supreme Court," "family," or "Congress," use a singular pronoun and verb if you are referring to the group as a unit:

Congress *is* taking *its* time debating the president's budget proposal.

7.3.2. Writing Effective Sentences

A. Sentence Fragments and Run-on Sentences

Including sentence fragments and run-on sentences in your writing leaves a bad impression on your reader. When judges and lawyers find errors like that in your writing, they immediately begin to doubt your credibility, an outcome you really want to avoid.

A sentence fragment is an incomplete sentence. Usually, a sentence is incomplete because it is missing a verb. For example, the following set of words is a sentence fragment because it has a subject, but lacks a verb:

The prosecutor jumping from his seat to object to the motion.

It looks like a sentence because it has a subject ("prosecutor") and two action words that resemble verbs ("jumping" and "to object"), but neither of those action words is operating as the verb in the sentence. To correct this sentence fragment, you would need to convert those verb-like words to the actual verbs in the sentence:

The prosecutor jumped from his seat and objected to the motion.

A sentence fragment may also occur when a phrase begins with a word that prevents it from being a complete sentence. Such words include "until," "although," "if," "when," and "because." They are used to introduce "dependent" clauses, which need to be attached to "independent clauses" to form complete sentences. The following is a dependent clause:

Because the defendant was not guilty.

You would need to attach it to an independent clause to form a complete sentence, as follows:

Because the defendant was not guilty, he was able to leave the courtroom immediately after the trial.

The independent clause can come before or after the dependent clause:

The defendant was able to leave the courtroom immediately after the trial because he was not guilty.

Run-on sentences occur when the writer joins two independent clauses together without using a coordinating conjunction, like "and," "but," "or," "nor," "for," "yet," and "so":

The lawyer talked the client listened.

Adding "and" makes this run-on sentence complete:

The lawyer talked, and the client listened.

You could also punctuate the sentence with a semicolon or a period:

The lawyer talked; the client listened.
The lawyer talked. The client listened.

If you join two independent clauses with a comma, you create a "comma splice," which is similar to a run-on sentence and just as bad:

The lawyer talked, the client listened.

You should correct a comma splice by substituting a coordinating conjunction, semicolon, or period for the comma, just as you corrected the run-on sentence above.

Run-on sentences and comma splices often occur because the writer mistakes conjunctive adverbs like "consequently," "furthermore," "therefore," "however," and "then" for coordinating conjunctions:

The company was at fault, however, the jury did not award compensation for the injury.

"However" is not a coordinating conjunction like "but"; thus, it is not strong enough to hold two short sentences together. To correct the sentence, you need to replace "however" with "but," divide it into two separate sentences, or use a semicolon:

The company was at fault, but the jury did not award compensation for the injury.
The company was at fault. However, the jury did not award compensation for the injury.
The company was at fault; however, the jury did not award compensation for the injury.

An even better idea would be to start the sentence with the word "although," which expresses the relationship between the two ideas:

Although the company was at fault, the jury did not award compensation for the injury.

B. Misplaced and Dangling Modifiers

Modifiers need to be near the word or words they modify. The misplacement of modifiers can change the meaning of a sentence or lead to humorous and even embarrassing results. For example, changing the placement of "only" changes the meaning of the following sentences:

Only his mother thought the boy was honest. ["Only" modifies "his mother," meaning that no one but his mother thought the boy was honest.]

His mother *only thought* the boy was honest. ["Only" modifies "thought," meaning that his mother merely thought he was honest, but was not certain.]

His mother thought *only that the boy was honest*. ["Only" modifies "that the boy was honest," meaning that his mother only thought that one thing, nothing more, nothing less.]

Phrases can be misplaced modifiers as well as single words like "only." Consider the following sentence:

Dreading another night in jail, the judge refused to grant bail for the accused murderer.

The modifier, "Dreading another night in jail," was mistakenly placed near "the judge" rather than "the accused murderer," whom it was intended to modify, leading the reader to believe it was the judge who was dreading another night in jail, not the accused murderer. To fix the sentence, the modifier needs to be placed next to the correct person:

The judge refused to grant bail for the accused murderer, who was dreading another night in jail.

If you added another thought into the sentence, you could say:

Dreading another night in jail, the accused murderer was disappointed that the judge refused to grant bail.

A dangling modifier does not have a noun in the sentence to modify, potentially causing ambiguity and confusion:

Before deciding how to rule, the motion was withdrawn.

The modifier, "Before deciding how to rule" does not have a noun in the sentence to modify. You can probably guess that the attorney withdrew the motion while the judge was still deciding how to rule on it, but that is not what the sentence says. Here is a better version of the sentence:

While the judge was still deciding how to rule, the attorney withdrew the motion.

C. Active and Passive Voice

Too many lawyers seem to love using the passive voice. Perhaps it sounds more formal or erudite to them, but it is not the most effective way to communicate most of the time. Unless you have a good reason to hide or downplay the actor in a sentence, or you do not know who or what the actor is, you should use the active voice.

The active voice is more direct and concise than the passive voice. The subject of the sentence is the actor:

The burglar ransacked the apartment.

Using the passive voice results in this less vivid, wordier sentence:

The apartment was ransacked by the burglar.

Sometimes, however, you may not have a specific noun to use as a subject and you must use the passive voice:

The Framers of the Constitution have always been held in high esteem.

You might also want to use the passive voice if you were representing a person who committed a heinous act. Rather than drawing attention to your client, the defendant, by saying, "The defendant killed the child," you might decide to say, "The child was killed by the defendant."

Sometimes people confuse the past tense with the passive voice because the words "past" and "passive" are similar. However, the passive voice has nothing to do with tense. You can use it with verbs that are in the past, present, and future tense.

Active voice:
The client called the lawyer. [past tense]
The client calls the lawyer. [present tense]
The client will call the lawyer. [future tense]

Passive voice:

The lawyer was called by the client. [past tense]
The lawyer is called by the client. [present tense]
The lawyer will be called by the client. [future tense]

ETHICS ALERT: Imprecision and Use of Passive Voice

A United States District Court in New Hampshire observed that "the imprecision, passive voice, and circumlocutions employed throughout the amended complaint [gave] the impression of drafters more intent on avoiding defamation liability than plainly and directly leveling factual allegations in support of legal claims."

S.E.C. v. Patel, 2009 WL 3151143 *3 (D. N.H. Sept. 30, 2009).

D. Parallel Structure

A good writer uses parallel structure to simplify sentence structure and help the reader focus on the content and meaning of a sentence. Parallel structure requires using the same grammatical structure for things that are logically parallel. It creates a framework that helps the reader navigate a series of words or ideas and must be used when creating lists and making comparisons.

For example, parallel structure should be used to list parallel qualities:

The robbery victim was bloody, confused, and frightened.

Without parallel structure, the sentence would be wordier and harder to follow:

The robbery victim was covered in blood, confused, and acted frightened.

Parallel structure should also be used to list parallel actions:

The attorney raced to the courthouse, ran up the steps, and filed the motion on time.

The same sequence of actions, presented without parallel structure, is less vivid and forceful:

The attorney was racing to the courthouse, ran up the steps, and then he filed the motion on time.

Parallel structure is particularly necessary in the facts section of an issue statement or question presented:

Under the tolling provision, can a 30-year-old man bring a medical malpractice claim after three years have passed when, at the time of the surgery, he was unable to read beyond a third grade level, drive a car, or perform complex intellectual tasks, but could live semi-independently in a group home, hold down a janitorial job, and prepare for his own basic needs at home?

Navigating a complex series of facts like that would be almost impossible without parallel structure.

Parallel structure is an effective way to draw comparisons and distinctions, especially when comparing an analogous case to your client's situation:

Like the mentally disabled plaintiff in *Chasse*, who was found to be *mentally ill, despite her ability to get married and divorced*, Jonah should be found to be *mentally ill even though he was able to hold a job as a janitor*.

The parallel structure of the sentence makes it easy to see the comparison between the plaintiff in Chasse, who was found to be mentally ill even though she was able to get married and divorced and Jonah, who should be found mentally ill even though he is able to hold down a job. Parallel structure can also be effective when distinguishing the facts from an analogous case:

Unlike the plaintiff in *Bowden*, who was declared mentally ill at the time she conveyed her property *because she was severely depressed and suicidal*, Jonah was not mentally ill at the time of the surgery *because he was not even mildly depressed or suicidal*.

In this sentence, parallel structure bolsters the hospital's argument that Jonah was not like the plaintiff in *Bowden* because she was severely depressed and suicidal while Jonah was not even mildly depressed or suicidal.

7.4. Punctuation

People can get very worked up about punctuation. Some people, who swear by the punctuation rules they learned in grade school, will go to the mat to defend those rules. Others say they never learned anything at all about punctuation in school. Those people just punctuate by "feel": If it feels right to throw in a comma or a semicolon, they do it and hope for the best. Generally, educated people manage to use correct punctuation most of the time, but they often do not know why their usage is correct. Regardless of your background or experience, you should know some basic principles about punctuation, especially because your use of punctuation affects both the meaning and clarity of your writing and your credibility as a legal writer and practicing attorney.

7.4.1. Commas

The comma is the most used—and least understood—punctuation mark in the English language. Understanding when to use a comma, and when not to, is essential. Here are the top ten rules of comma usage.[8]

Rule 1. Use a comma before a coordinating conjunction joining two independent clauses.

The jurors entered the courtroom, and the defendant stood to face them.

Rule 2. Use a comma to set off introductory words or phrases.

Following their closing arguments, the lawyers went to lunch.

Rule 3. Use a comma to set off nonrestrictive phrases and clauses.

The law clerk, acting as bailiff, announced the judge's arrival in the courtroom.

---

8. Anne Enquist & Laurel Oates, *Just Writing* 215-22 (4th ed. Wolters Kluwer Law & Business 2013) (providing an overview of comma rules).

Rule 4. Use a comma to avoid ambiguity and confusion.

The police officer called Sarah Fields, the victim's girlfriend.

(Without the comma, it would be difficult to tell whether the police officer called the victim's girlfriend, whose name is Sarah Fields, or the police officer referred to Sarah Fields as the victim's girlfriend, whether she was the victim's girlfriend or not.)

Rule 5. Use commas to set off transitional words and phrases.

The victim's testimony, however, contradicted the police report. Nevertheless, the jury found her to be a credible witness.

Rule 6. Always place a comma within quotation marks, unless the quotation marks come after words introducing a quote.

Three words came to mind: "yes," "no," and "maybe." Jan smiled and said, "I am so glad to be here."

Rule 7. Use a comma for items in a series.

She learned about how to use periods, commas, semicolons, and apostrophes.

Note that you should always put a comma before the conjunction ("and" or "or") coming before the last item in the series, despite anything you may have learned to the contrary.

Rule 8. Use a comma to set off words of contrast.

Torts, not Contracts, was my favorite class in law school.

Rule 9. Use a comma between two adjectives coming before a noun.

The judge drives a big, black Cadillac.

Rule 10. Place commas between and after cities and states, and also between and after dates and years.

On June 31, 1941, Marge and Ed moved to New Kensington, Pennsylvania, where they lived for more than 50 years together.

It is just as important to know when *not* to use a comma as it is to know when you should use one. Here are some rules and explanations about when a comma is unnecessary.

Rule 1. Do not use a comma to set off a restrictive clause that follows an independent clause.

Lawyers are reprimanded when they commit ethical violations.

When the restrictive clause comes first, you should use a comma.

When they commit ethical violations, lawyers are reprimanded.

Rule 2. Do not use a comma to separate the subject and verb or a verb and its object. The following sentence is correctly punctuated:

Attorneys who are writing motions and briefs on behalf of their clients may encounter various kinds of resistance from opposing attorneys.

You should omit the comma inserted before "may" in the following sentence:

Attorneys who are writing motions and briefs on behalf of their clients, may encounter various kinds of resistance from opposing attorneys.

That comma incorrectly separates the subject "Attorneys" from the verb "may encounter."

Rule 3. Do not use a comma before the word "because." The comma before "because" should have been omitted from the following sentence:

The trial lasted 93 days, because so many experts testified.

It causes an unwelcome break between the cause ("so many experts testified") and effect ("the trial lasted 93 days").

Rule 4. Do not use a comma with the word "that." No commas are needed in either of the following sentences:

The waitress testified that the defendant did not leave her a tip.
The fire that was later discovered in the wood shed was much more destructive than the earlier blaze that had begun in the kitchen.

7.4.2. Semicolons

The semicolon should only be used in one of three ways: (1) to join two independent clauses, (2) to separate items in a series if the items are long or contain any internal commas, and (3) to separate citations in a string cite. Any other use of the semicolon is incorrect.

Writers use semicolons to join two independent clauses when the ideas in those clauses are closely related or parallel:

The sky was blue; the clouds were puffy.

Sometimes, writers become enamored of semicolons and use them in practically every paragraph they write, but that is not a good idea. Semicolons should be reserved for special occasions when the writer wants to show a close relationship between two short sentences. Most of the time, sentences should stand on their own and not be joined to other sentences by semicolons.

Using semicolons to separate items in a series helps the reader to identify each separate item:

The prosecutor called several witnesses to testify, including the car salesman, who was to testify first; the manager of the dealership, who first noticed the Prius was missing; and the owner of the Prius, who had left the car to be serviced.

Sometimes, using semicolons in a series prevents confusion and ambiguity:

She invited a number of people to the party, including Dean, my brother, Susan, Dean's sister-in-law, and Edward.

Without semicolons, it is difficult to tell whether she invited five people or fewer than five. With semicolons, it is clear that she invited only three people (Dean, Susan, and Ed):

Dean, my brother; Susan, Dean's sister-in-law; and Edward.

In a string cite containing more than one citation to authority, you should separate the citations using semicolons:

Priestman v. Canadian Pacific Ltd., 782 F. Supp. 681, 682 (D. Me. 1992); *Chasse v. Mazerolle*, 580 A.2d 155, 157 (Me. 1990); *McCutchen v. Currier*, 94 Me. 362, 363, 47 A. 923, 924 (1900).

7.4.3. Colons

Colons are used to introduce quotations and lists and to set up explanations and elaborations. The function of the colon is to introduce what will follow. Most of the time, the introductory clause that precedes the colon should be a complete sentence. For example, the following is correct:

Jurors were told to refrain from the following activities during deliberations: reading the newspaper, watching television, and talking on the telephone.

It would be incorrect to write this:

Jurors were told to refrain from: reading the newspaper, watching television, and talking on the telephone.

The words "Jurors were told to refrain from" is an incomplete sentence. Occasionally, a writer might set up a list, as below, where each category or topic is introduced by a heading like "Introducing a quotation." In such a situation, it is permissible to precede the colon with an incomplete sentence, but such instances are rare in legal writing.

Introducing a quotation:
The Supreme Court of Tennessee reached the same conclusion, but for a different reason: "The claim belongs to the person who suffered the legal wrong, not the guardian."

Introducing a list:
The recipe required three main ingredients: eggs, butter, and flour.

Setting up explanations and elaborations:
The statute of limitations is short: just three years from the time the cause of action accrues.

7.4.4. Apostrophes

Apostrophes show possession—who belongs to what and what belongs to whom. The rules are fairly simple; yet, people sometimes get confused, especially when nouns end in the letter "s." Basically, two rules apply, with one refinement: to make a singular noun possessive, add "'s"; to make a plural noun ending in "s" possessive, simply add an apostrophe. If a plural noun does not end in "s," add "'s".

Below are some examples that illustrate the rules.

Singular nouns:
defendant's testimony
everyone's concern
James's brother [notice that you add "'s" even when the noun ends in "s"; it is not correct to say James' brother, although people commonly make this mistake, even newspaper editors]

Plural nouns ending in "s":
the Framers' intent
sixty days' notice
the Joneses' house [notice that you have to make the name "Jones" plural before adding the "s" to show possession]

Plural nouns not ending in "s":
the children's school
the women's department
the people's choice

Exceptions are sometimes made for certain expressions that include the word "sake" and end in "s," when the "s" sound is not pronounced:

for goodness' sake
for righteousness' sake

Exceptions have also been made for some other nouns that end in "s":

United States' promise
General Motors' employees

Usually, it is better to revise your sentence to avoid these awkward constructions:

---

the promise of the United States
the employees of General Motors

To show joint possession, use "'s" only after the last noun in the group:

James and Jonah's home
the Congress and president's dispute

To show individual possession of more than one member of a group, use "'s" after each of the nouns:

Mom's and Dad's home towns
the dog's and cat's water dishes

The possessive form of pronouns does not use an apostrophe: "my," "ours," "your," "yours," "her," "hers," "his," "their," "theirs, "whose," and "its." Be careful not to confuse "its," "their," "theirs" and "whose" (possessive forms) with "it's," "they're," "there's," and "who's" (contractions for "it is," "they are," "there is," and "who is").

Apostrophes are also used to indicate that one or more letters or numbers are missing:

---

it's = it is

---

they're = they are

Class of '69 = Class of 1969

7.4.5. Quotation Marks, Ellipses, and Brackets

Quotation marks are used to designate quoted material. If the words you are quoting clearly comprise a portion of the original quote, you should put quotation marks at the beginning and end of the quoted material. You do not need to use an ellipsis (. . .):

The court concluded that she "possessed sufficient competence to comprehend and exercise her legal right" to withhold consent to a sterilization procedure arranged by her parents.

However, if you omit a word or phrase within a sentence, use an ellipsis to indicate the omission. If the omission is in the middle of the quote, put a space before and after the ellipsis:

"Excessive bail shall not be required . . . nor cruel and unusual punishments inflicted."

Always put the period at the end of the sentence within the quotation marks ("."). If an omission is at the beginning of the sentence, you can indicate that by using brackets:

"[T]he right of the people to keep and bear Arms shall not be infringed."

If you are omitting the end of a complete sentence, put a space before the ellipsis and a space and period after the ellipsis and add a period to indicate the end of the sentence:

"The right of the people to be secure in their persons, houses, papers, and effects, against unreasonable searches and seizures, shall not be violated. . . ."

You do not need to use an ellipsis before or after fragments that are incorporated into your sentence structure:

Because "the statute does not mention the effect of a guardian's appointment," the language is not ambiguous.

Do not use quotation marks around a quotation that contains more than 50 words or takes up four lines of text. Rather, you should provide a lead-in, and then set it off as a block quote by single-spacing the quoted language, indenting the left and right margins, and separating the block quote from the text with an extra line above and below it. The citation would be placed outside the block quote, at the original left margin.

The Fourteenth Amendment establishes civil rights for all citizens:

> All persons born or naturalized in the United States and subject to the jurisdiction thereof, are citizens of the United Sates and of the State wherein they reside. No State shall make or enforce any law which shall abridge the privileges or immunities of citizens of the United States; nor shall any State deprive any person of life, liberty, or property, without due process of law; nor deny to any person within its jurisdiction the equal protection of the laws.

U.S. Const. amend XIV, § 1.

If you want to quote language that appears within another quotation, you should use single quotation marks for the internal quote and enclose the larger quote in regular, double quotation marks:

"The magistrate judge initially found . . . that she did not suffer from an '*overall inability* to function in society that prevents [her] from protecting [her] legal rights.'" *Douglas v. York Co.*, 433 F.3d 143, 147 (1st Cir. 2005) (quoting *McAfee v. Cole*, 637 A.2d 463, 466 (Me. 1994)) (emphasis in original).

Note that you must include a parenthetical explanation with your citation, indicating the source of the quote within the quote. The parenthetical explanation after the citation to *McAfee* informs the reader that the *McAfee* court italicized the words "overall inability," not you or the *Douglas* court.

You can also use quotation marks to indicate that words are being used in a special way:

"Mental illness" does not always refer to a diagnosed mental disorder like schizophrenia.

Commas, like periods, should always be placed within quotation marks, except for the comma that comes when introducing the quote:

The little girl said, "Good-bye, Mom" as her mother dropped her off at school.

On the other hand, semicolons and colons should always be outside quotation marks:

The professor surprised the class when he explained that the test was "just for practice"; the students heaved a sigh of relief.

The following verbs are called "linking verbs": is, am, was, and were.

Quotation marks may come before or after question marks or exclamation marks, depending on the context of the sentence:

The drowning man cried, "Help!"
I love "Law and Order"!

In the first example, the exclamation was part of the quotation and, thus, goes within the quotation marks; in the second, the exclamation goes with the sentence itself and, thus, belongs outside the quotation marks. The same principle applies to question marks. The following examples are correct:

She asked, "Did you see the moon last night?"
Why does he never feel "fit as a fiddle"?

Brackets are used to indicate changes made in a quote. You can use brackets to change a letter from upper case to lower case, to substitute words or letters, or to show that a word or letter has been removed:

The plaintiff "ask[ed] the court to toll the statute of limitations."
"[I]n contrast to the circumstances existing in the cited cases, [the] Legislature has clearly spoken."

You may use brackets around "sic" to indicate mistakes occurring in an original quote, but only if those mistakes are significant or may cause confusion:

"The court decline [sic] to grant bail."

7.4.6. Hyphens

Hyphens are used to combine words to form compound modifiers or nouns. If the modifiers do not precede the noun they modify, they should not be hyphenated:

The effects are far reaching.

If they do precede the noun they modify, they should be hyphenated:

The court wrote a well-reasoned opinion.

You should always hyphenate modifiers and nouns that begin with the prefixes "all," "ex," and "self":

---

all-purpose
ex-wife
self-defense

Other prefixes, including "anti," "co," "inter," "multi," "semi," and "re" do not usually take a hyphen, but you may need to consult a dictionary to be sure:

---

antitrust
coconspirator
interfaith
multinational
semiannual
redistribute

You should always use a hyphen to avoid confusion ("re-create") or prevent a double vowel ("re-enter"). Hyphens are also used to create compound numbers ("eighty-nine") and to join a number and a noun ("first-year associate"). Do not use a hyphen when the first word in a two-word modifier is an adverb that ends in "ly" ("newly minted money") or when the compound modifier contains a foreign phrase ("*de facto* rule"). When two or more compound modifiers share the same second element, use a hyphen after each first element ("large- and small-scale plans").

7.4.7. Dashes

In a sentence containing an explanatory phrase or a list, dashes can be used to signal the beginning and end of the inserted words:

The young man eating fast food—Wendy's hamburgers, McDonald's shakes, and Burger King's fish sandwiches—driving from one to the other all day long.
The prisoner's age—92 years—made him a good candidate for clemency.

You can create a dash by typing two hyphens together, directly before and after the inserted words.

ETHICS ALERT: Spelling, Grammar, and Punctuation Errors

The Supreme Court of Minnesota imposed a public reprimand on an attorney for his "repeated filing of documents rendered unintelligible by numerous spelling, grammatical, and typographical errors," which were so "serious that they amounted to incompetent representation." In addition to the public reprimand, the court ordered the attorney to attend "a program of at least 10 hours in legal writing."

In re Disciplinary Action Against Hawkins, 502 N.W.2d 770, 770-72 (Minn. 1993).

7.5. Style

Style refers to the choices you make in writing: the words you choose, the way you structure sentences and organize paragraphs, your use of transitional words and phrases, your tone, and the appearance of your final draft. In other kinds of writing, style may be a reflection of the writer's individuality and creativity. In legal writing, however, style is not a matter of personal preference; legal writers need to adopt a style that will communicate their ideas most clearly, concisely, and effectively to their readers. Legal writing is not all about the writer; it is all about the reader. Thus, legal writers should make all decisions about style with an eye toward clear communication, not artistic expression.

7.5.1. Choice of Words

In the past, lawyers often used words nobody else could understand, including Latin terms like "*arguendo*" and archaic legalisms like "aforesaid," "whereof," and "hereunto." Apparently, some lawyers thought clients might not be sufficiently impressed if they spoke and wrote in plain English. Even worse, they may have believed that people would quit hiring lawyers if the law became more transparent. Nevertheless, lawyers will always be needed to represent clients in transactions and in court, even when they speak and write in words their clients can actually understand.

Furthermore, most clients really do want to understand what their lawyers are saying and doing on their behalf and would never consider firing them just because those lawyers were able to communicate clearly in plain English. To the contrary, modern clients appreciate lawyers who can explain complicated legal principles effectively. These days, being able to communicate clearly and concisely is one of the most important skills a lawyer can possess. Clients, law partners, opposing attorneys, law clerks, and judges all appreciate clear, concise legal writing; lawyers who can communicate complex legal principles and arguments in simple terms are held in the highest regard.

Using plain English means choosing words that are easy to understand. You should not use archaic phrases, obscure abstractions, or big words just to impress your reader. Rather, you should choose the shorter, simpler word whenever possible. You do not want to force your reader to consult a dictionary if at all possible. For example, it is better to use "stop" than "cease," "after" than "subsequent," "start" than "originate," and "use" than "utilize." You never need to use the word "said" or "such" when referring to someone or something you have already discussed:

The inventor filed for a patent. *Said* patent was pending for five years.

Instead, just say:

The inventor filed for a patent. *That* patent was pending for five years.

Similarly, you do not need to introduce a motion with the words, "Now comes the plaintiff" or use any of the following foreign words and phrases: *arguendo, et al., inter alia, seriatim, sui generis,* or *viz.* Some Latin phrases have legal significance and must be used when relevant to the legal issues you are discussing, like *res judicata, res ipsa loquitur, caveat emptor, de novo, ex parte,* and *prima facie.* Some Latin phrases are familiar to most readers and may be used when appropriate, like *gratis, persona non grata, ad hoc, modus operandi, bona fide, quid pro* quo, and *per se.*

Furthermore, unlike other forms of writing that feature the creative use of synonyms, legal writing requires the consistent use of terms. If a statute includes several "factors," legal writers need to refer to them as "factors" throughout their writing, not randomly calling them "elements" or "principles," just to provide variety. In legal writing, unlike in poetry or essay writing, such "elegant variation" does not lead to eloquence, just ambiguity and confusion.

Using the correct word also promotes understanding. The words listed below often create problems for writers and readers alike. Knowing their precise meanings and how to use them properly will eliminate those difficulties.

Affect and effect: "Affect" is a verb meaning "to influence":

The temperature of the room affected the time of death.

"Effect" is a noun meaning "consequence."

The prosecutor noted the effect of the defendant's testimony on the jury.

Common law and case law: "Case law" encompasses both "common law" and other court opinions interpreting or applying enacted law.

Flout and flaunt: "Flout" means to treat with contemptuous disregard; "flaunt" means to display conspicuously.

She flouted the law when she flaunted her smoking by lighting a cigarette right in front of the desk clerk.

Fewer and less: Use "fewer" for objects that can be counted; use "less" when referring to an amount.

He gained fewer pounds as he ate less food.

Held, ruled, and stated: When a court applies a legal rule to the facts of a case, it "holds" something. A "holding" is the court's decision in a particular case. The court "rules" something when it announces a legal standard to be used in all cases, not just the case at hand. The court "states" something when it makes a comment that is not directly related to the current case or its holding. Such a statement is called a "dictum." Several statements are called "dicta," the plural of "dictum."

Lay and lie: "Lay" means to set down; it always takes a direct object.

The attorney lays down the transcript.

"Lie" means to recline or remain in place. It does not take a direct object.

The cat lies in the sun.

Oral and verbal: "Oral" means "spoken out loud."

We all listened to the oral argument.

"Verbal" means "in words." Something that is verbal may be written or spoken. It would be wrong to say that the judge explained the law "verbally" if you mean that he explained it out loud. If you want to say that the judge explained the law out loud and in writing, you would have to say exactly that the judge explained the law orally and in writing. To say that the judge explained the law verbally merely means that the judge used words in explaining the law. It does not explain whether the judge used written or spoken words to explain the law.

Since and because: Do not use "since" unless you are referring to a time period.

Since Wednesday, I have been ill.

Use "because" when you are saying "for the reason that."

The witness could not testify because she had laryngitis.

While and although: Use "while" only when you mean "during the time that."

While you were reading, I washed the dishes.

Use "although" when you mean "in spite of" or "even though."

Although Andrew was not yet two years old, he could read simple books.

Who, which, and that: Use "who" to refer to people and "that" or "which" to refer to things. To figure out whether a clause should start with "which" or "that," consider the following: If you can drop the clause and not lose the point of the sentence, use "which." If you cannot, use "that." A "which" clause, which is called a "non-restrictive clause," should be enclosed in commas. A "that" clause, which is called a "restrictive clause," takes no commas. Restrictive clauses restrict the noun they modify; non-restrictive clauses do not.

Non-restrictive clause:
David's orchid, which was pure white, won first prize.[9]

In this sentence, the orchid that won first prize was David's. The point of the sentence is that the orchid won first prize. The fact that the orchid was pure white is incidental and appears within commas as if it were an added parenthetical explanation, not essential to the main idea in the sentence. You could remove that information and the essence of the sentence would be in tact:

David's orchid won first prize.

Thus, the clause, "which was pure white," is non-restrictive. It does not restrict the orchid in the sentence, just gives more information about it.

Restrictive clause:
David's orchid that was pure white won the prize.

In this sentence, the information following "that" is essential. Here, the point of the sentence is not merely saying that David's orchid won first prize, but explaining *which* of David's orchids won first prize: the orchid that was pure white, not one of David's other orchids. If you remove the clause beginning with "that," you lose the main point of the sentence—that it was the orchid that was pure white that won the prize. The sentence would simply read, "David's orchid won first prize," omitting the crucial information identifying the orchid as the one that was pure white. Thus, the clause, "that was pure white," is restrictive; it restricts David's orchids to one particular orchid: the orchid that was pure white.

---

9. Patricia T. O'Conner, *Woe is I: The Grammaphobe's Guide to Better English in Plain English* 3-4 (G.P. Putnam's Sons 1996) (using the example of "Buster's bulldog" winning a prize, which is similar to the example provided above).

Some people think that using clauses beginning with "which" sounds more refined or elegant. Those people tend to use such clauses all the time. Nevertheless, using clauses beginning with "that" leads to clearer, more grammatical writing. Especially in legal writing, where unessential information should be omitted from sentences as much as possible, clauses beginning with "which" should rarely appear. You can root out those clauses by doing a "which" hunt, searching your document for the word "which," changing any "which" clauses you find to "that" clauses if they contain essential information, or omitting them altogether. It also might help to remember this little jingle called "Comma Sense":

Commas, *which* cut out the fat,
Go with *which*, never with *that*.[10]

7.5.2. Effective Sentences and Paragraphs

Effective sentences come in many varieties. All of them have a subject and a predicate. Some are short, simple sentences:

Education is important.

Others are compound sentences, composed of two or more independent clauses, joined together with a coordinating conjunction:

Lawyers appear before judges, and clients appreciate their efforts.

Still others are complex sentences, composed of an independent and a dependent clause:

Although the lawyer argued brilliantly, the appeals court did not vacate the judgment.

Regardless of sentence structure, a good sentence needs a strong subject/verb unit. Subjects that are real people and things make the strongest subjects. They are concrete, not abstract, and much easier for a reader to visualize. Similarly, verbs that show real action rather than a state of being make the strongest verbs. For example, you should avoid using nominalizations for verbs as subjects of sentences. Nominalizations are nouns

---

10. *Id.* at 4.

made from verbs, like "decision" (from the verb "to decide"), "argument" (from the verb "to argue"), and "requirement" (from the verb "to require"). For example (using the nominalization "decision"):

The decision of the judge was to grant the motion.

Better example (using the verb "decided"):

The judge decided to grant the motion.

Notice that using the nominalization "decision" triggered the use of a verb that indicated a state of being, the linking verb "was." Making "decided" the verb in the sentence, eliminated the use of the linking verb entirely, replacing it with an action verb and creating a much stronger subject/verb unit.

Sentences are also more effective when the subjects and verbs are placed close together. When too many words separate the subject and the verb, readers get lost in the sentence. For example (with subject and verb widely separated):

An explanation by the judges of the pros and cons of including sentencing guidelines in the printed material distributed to new attorneys will take place tomorrow.

Better example (with subject and verb close together):

Tomorrow, the judges will explain the pros and cons of including sentencing guidelines in the printed material distributed to new attorneys.

Both sentences are long, but the sentence that keeps the subject and verb close together is much easier to read. Also, the nominalization ("explanation") has been converted into an action verb ("will explain"), creating a stronger subject/verb unit ("judges will explain").

A good paragraph features a mix of sentence types. Writing only short, simple sentences may leave an impression that the writer lacks sophistication. Including too many compound sentences can make a paragraph repetitious and boring. Writing only long, complex sentences may result in a paragraph that is too dense and complicated. Inserting a short, simple sentence in the midst of longer compound and complex sentences adds emphasis and relief for the reader.

In legal writing, each paragraph should focus on one point, which is identified in a topic sentence that usually comes at the beginning of the paragraph. For this reason, one-sentence and one-page paragraphs are rare in legal writing. Having a topic sentence and some content takes at least two sentences; a paragraph that is the length of an entire page probably contains more than one point.

Good paragraphs also feature signposts and transitional words and phrases that lead the reader through the text. Signposts include headings ("Issue," "Question Presented," "Discussion," "Conclusion"), and numbers, letters, and words that help the reader understand the organization of the paragraph ("first," "second," "third"; "first," "next," "finally"). Sometimes, it is enough to simply identify how many points are being made ("The defendant is guilty for three reasons: He had the motive, he had the means, and he had the opportunity"). The following paragraph begins with a topic sentence and prepares the reader for three main points. It also provides transition from the preceding paragraph by referring to ideas developed there.

Jonah would argue that the majority rule should be adopted in Maine for the three reasons set out above: The Maine tolling provision does not provide for an exception if a guardian is appointed, the claim belongs to him and not to his guardian, and the purpose of the tolling provision relates not only to his difficulty in bringing suit, which could potentially be remedies by the appointment of a guardian, but also his difficulty in testifying and providing information to a trial court.

Like signposts, transitional words guide the reader through a paragraph and lead the reader from one paragraph to the next.[11] Transitional words and phrases can be used for contrast ("however"), comparison ("similarly"), to show cause and effect ("thus"), for addition ("also"), for example ("for instance"), for emphasis ("in fact"), for evaluation ("most importantly"), for restatement ("in other words"), for concession ("granted"), for resumption after a concession ("nevertheless"), for time ("meanwhile"), for place ("nearby"), for sequence ("next"), and for conclusion ("therefore"). Transitions serve many other purposes as well, such as the following: to create context ("during the 1960s"); refer to a time ("at 10:00 p.m."), date ("on January 18, 1948"), or case name ("In *McAfee v. Cole*"); give a historical perspective ("since Bill Clinton's presidency"); and suggest a case's importance ("in a widely criticized opinion").

---

11. Oates & Enquist, *supra* n. 8, at 55-72 (explaining the uses of transitions).

Substantive transitions are especially effective in legal writing. Rather than using the popular, but unimaginative transition, "In *Bowden v. Grindle*," you should find something more meaningful, especially when moving from one major section of a document to another:

Recognizing that the legal standard for mental illness varies for different purposes, the court held that a woman who was legally competent to marry and divorce did not possess the necessary competence to withhold consent to a sterilization procedure.

Another effective way to lead a reader from one paragraph to the next is to employ "dovetailing."[12] Just as a cabinetmaker is able to join two parts of a table tightly with a dovetail, a legal writer creates a tight fit between two consecutive sentences or paragraphs by using similar words or concepts at the end of one sentence and the beginning of the next:

The severely depressed woman was declared mentally ill even though she was able to *prepare her own meals* at times. Likewise, although he too could *prepare his own meals*, Jonah should be considered mentally ill.

7.5.3. Conciseness

Conciseness is essential to good legal writing. Judges and lawyers are often compelled to read hundreds and even thousands of pages every day. They appreciate memos and briefs that are concise and clearly written. Also, in court filings, lawyers must adhere to strict page limits. Learning to write concisely is essential.

The first rule of concise writing is to omit unnecessary words that are sometimes called "throat-clearing expressions" like "It is important to note that," "It is conceivable that," and "It is significant that."[13] Many of these throat-clearing expressions can be condensed from four or five words to one word: "it seems likely that" is just a wordy way to say "probably." Sometimes lawyers use wordy expressions that say the same thing twice; for example, they say "cease and desist" when all they need to say is "stop," or they say "past experience," which means the same thing as "experience."

The secret to concise writing is understanding the point you want to make and including as few words as possible to make that point. Sentences

---

12. *Id.* at 62-66.
13. *Id.* at 118-19.

are made up of two kinds of words: "working words," which carry the meaning of the sentence, and "glue words," which are all the others.[14] In the sentence, "Jonah competed successfully in the Special Olympics," the working words are "Jonah," "competed," "successfully," "Special," and "Olympics"; the glue words are "in," and "the." The sentence would not be grammatical without the glue words, but if the proportion of them is too great, the sentence is wordy and ineffective.[15] Your goal as a legal writer is to make your sentences concise by keeping the glue words to a minimum.

To minimize the number of glue words, you should focus on the actor, the action, and the object. One way to remedy a wordy sentence is to ask yourself: "Who is doing what to whom in this sentence?" Then rewrite the sentence to focus on those three key elements. First, state the actor. Then state the action, using the strongest verb that will fit. Finally, state the object of the action if there is one. If your sentence begins with the word "it" or "there," followed by a linking verb, you are probably wasting words. For example, the following sentence takes ten words to complete the thought:

It has been nine weeks since we completed the report.

This revised, seven-word sentence expresses the same idea more concisely:

We completed the report nine weeks ago.

The revised sentence also features a stronger subject-verb unit after the linking verb "has been" was replaced by the action verb "completed."

Writing in the active voice also results in clearer, more concise sentences. When you use the active voice for the following sentence, you use only five words:

The lawyer prepared the will.

The same sentence, written in passive voice, requires seven words and buries the actor at the end of the sentence:

The will was prepared by the lawyer.

---

14. Richard Wydick, *Plain English for Lawyers* 7 (5th ed., Carolina Academic Press 2005).
15. *Id.*

Furthermore, the passive voice can create ambiguity. When using the active voice, you can tell who is doing the acting; in the passive voice, you may not be able to tell.

The will was prepared.

Index

Illustrations and tables are indicated by "i" and "t" following the page numbers.